WHISPERS IN THE PEWS

# Whispers in the Pews

*Evangelical Uniformity in a Divided America*

Amy D. McDowell

New York University Press

New York

NEW YORK UNIVERSITY PRESS
New York
www.nyupress.org



Library of Congress Cataloging-in-Publication Data
Names: McDowell, Amy D. author
Title: Whispers in the pews : Evangelical uniformity in a divided America / Amy D. McDowell.
Description: New York : New York University Press, [2026] | Includes appendices. | Includes bibliographical references and index.
Identifiers: LCCN 2025021691 (print) | LCCN 2025021692 (ebook) | ISBN 9781479827619 hardback | ISBN 9781479827633 paperback | ISBN 9781479827640 ebook | ISBN 9781479827657 ebook other
Subjects: LCSH: Multiethnic churches—United States | Social interaction—United States | Interpersonal relations—Religious aspects—Christianity | Evangelicalism—United States
Classification: LCC BV600.3 .M33 2026 (print) | LCC BV600.3 (ebook)
LC record available at https://lccn.loc.gov/2025021691
LC ebook record available at https://lccn.loc.gov/2025021692

This book is printed on acid-free paper, and its binding materials are chosen for strength and durability. We strive to use environmentally responsible suppliers and materials to the greatest extent possible in publishing our books.

The manufacturer's authorized representative in the EU for product safety is Mare Nostrum Group B.V., Mauritskade 21D, 1091 GC Amsterdam, The Netherlands. Email: gpsr@mare-nostrum.co.uk.

Manufactured in the United States of America

10 9 8 7 6 5 4 3 2 1

Also available as an ebook

*Linky!*

CONTENTS

# LIST OF FIGURES

# PREFACE

My path to Welcome Church began at a crisis pregnancy center, an extension of the pro-life movement that seeks to convince women and girls to carry their pregnancies to term. The first time I visited that center, I was with my historian friend Jessie Wilkerson. We were both teaching courses on feminism and gender at the University of Mississippi in Oxford, Mississippi, and were dismayed by the absence of family planning facilities in a college town famous for its wild fraternity parties.[1] As soon as we stepped inside the center, a neatly dressed woman with a fresh haircut and tasteful diamond earrings stood up from behind a tall wooden desk, greeted us briskly, and asked how she could assist us. Jessie and I nervously relayed a watered-down version of the classes we teach and told her we were there to learn about the resources the center provides. Diane, another volunteer with tightly permed curls and blue jeans, overheard our spiel and offered to show us around.

Our tour of the center involved a stop at the sonogram machine, a peek at the walk-in closet where baby supplies are stored, and concluded in a living room-like setting where "abortion-minded women" are counseled about their "options," to use Diane's words. The mission of the center is to "save the unborn," Diane said before rattling off the names of local Catholic and Protestant congregations that support their cause.[2] One of the newest additions to that circle of support was Welcome, a church that, according to Diane, is unlike any other church in town. "It's 'different,'" she beamed, "It's a church for everybody—they don't even meet in a regular church building!"

Diane's enthusiasm for Welcome stood out to me. The emphasis she placed on it being a church without walls reminded me of the Christian punk scene I had studied in the past, a subculture of bands, show promoters, and ministry groups that make space for born-again Christianity in hard-hitting music. Welcome Church and Christian punk appear nothing alike, but their attitudes about ministry overlap considerably.

Both place emphasis on taking church to unchurched spaces, and both claim to love and accept people regardless of who they are, how they dress, or how "broken" they are.[3] Diane appeared convinced that I should give Welcome a try, and I wanted to find out why.

I started attending Welcome in the late summer of 2016, not as a Christian in search of a new church home, but as a sociologist curious about how evangelicals form their political outlooks at church. At the time, a growing body of scholarship was emerging on the uptick in Christian nationalism, or the political ideology and movement that seeks to take America back to God.[4] Research on how everyday conservative Christians establish beliefs and opinions that accommodate or promote such an ideology, however, was hard to find. I decided that if I wanted to understand how evangelicals latch on to the right side of politics, I needed to listen to what they talk—and don't talk—about at church. Welcome was the place to do that listening. It was a church that had embraced a mantra of multiracial inclusivity in a historically conservative college town that, according to Mississippi Republican Senator Chris McDaniel, was being overtaken by "low-life" liberals.[5]

I studied Welcome for almost three years. To do that, I had to routinely break away from my own liberal bubble, and at a time in which the rise of the "alt right" was weighing heavily on my mind. According to a massive Pew Research Center study, political polarization is intensifying across the United States in part because liberals and conservatives are picking their friends by their political views and are electing to live in areas where their neighbors see the world as they do—choices that shrink the middle and pull the left and right political poles further apart.[6] Americans, in other words, are settling into *echo chambers*—social worlds in which their opinions or beliefs get reinforced through repeated interactions with peers or sources that have the same or similar worldviews.[7] And studies show that those furthest to the political right are most entrenched in their echo chambers.[8] For example, the Pew Research Center's "Political Polarization" data shows that conservatives are more likely to express antipathy toward the other side and toward the value of compromise than are liberals.

For me, being at Welcome involved scaling an "empathy wall" on a weekly basis. Sociologist Arlie Hochschild coined the term "empathy wall" to describe an obstacle that keeps us from seeing reality through the eyes of those who hold opposing beliefs or feel differently about the world than we do.[9] In her timely book about Tea Party supporters in politically red Louisiana, Hochschild depicts her empathy climb as an exhilarating challenge that entailed traveling to that part of the country, far removed from the liberal enclave where she resides in Berkeley, California.

In some respects, I live in a liberal enclave like the one that Hochschild describes. My friends have opinions similar to mine on a range of social and political matters. I spend most of my free time with other academics who think like me.[10] I live in a mixed-income neighborhood that has a reputation for being on the liberal side of the fence. I frequent coffee shops, restaurants, and markets where I am least likely to see the University of Mississippi's retired "Ole Miss" Colonel rebel mascot and MAGA hats.[11]

Yet unlike Hochschild, I had to climb an empathy wall that is professionally, psychologically, and physically close to me. It is at the university where I teach sociology to students from conservative religious backgrounds. It is in the hearts and minds of my extended family members. It is at the church I studied, which was merely a long walk or short drive away from my home. The close proximity of the wall is what made me feel exhausted by it. After a solid two years at Welcome, I journaled:

> I find this empathy climb frustrating. Maybe this is because I can and do identify with the church on some level. Many of the people who I've met here remind me of my cousins, aunts, and uncles who work in nursing homes, furniture factories, packing plants, and drive trucks in North Mississippi. They remind me of who and what I come from. I find myself wanting to confront them on the way the church votes, the way it ignores or downplays injustice. I have to remind myself that I am here as a social scientist, not as a disgruntled member of the community.

I entered Welcome as an estranged child of Mississippi who, as my extended family would say, finally made it "back home" for a job at its iconic flagship university. Upon my return, I was shaken by how strange I felt in the place where my accent took shape—the place where I grew up playing in the creek and loving an army of cats. I had lived elsewhere for over twenty years and was no longer a true Southerner, a feeling that my cousin Bubba made apparent when he called me a "foreigner" for favoring wheat crackers over plain white saltines. We were eating chili in my rental house in Oxford to celebrate my big university job, and crackers quickly evolved into a topic of conversation. Talk about college, or about my classes that center intersectional and queer feminist perspectives, was out of the question. I laughed off Bubba's comment. My other cousins, his brothers, laughed too. Before long, they were all teasing me for being "weird." The fun-loving exchange clung to me. I was not the same and we all knew it.

I am an "outsider" to Welcome to a certain degree. I am not an evangelical Christian, and I feel uneasy in conservative social circles. I do, however, have personal relationships with the White imagery and communities that form around born-again Christianity.[12] When I was in kindergarten, my parents team-taught "children's church" at a low-budget nondenominational charismatic congregation in Tupelo, the closest city to the red dirt road that I grew up on in Mississippi. My parents were serious about Jesus, and I was too. I used to drag our framed copy of Warner Sallman's painting, "The Head of Christ," around the house like a baby doll. I adored that painting of the light-eyed, light-haired Jesus.[13] He looked as soft and beautiful as a princess.

As I grew into adolescence, I was taught about the scarier side of the faith—the rapture, heaven and hell—at the old-time Southern Baptist church that my grandmother raised her kids in. At the age of twelve, her church invited me to be baptized in its lukewarm bathtub at the back of the altar, an act of faith that I did to prove that I was born again. After that, I was convinced that I was going to heaven when I died and that my uncle, who had not been baptized, was going to burn in hell. I remember begging him to come to church with me. I was desperate to save him.

Later, when my dad acquired a decent-paying job in Orangeburg, South Carolina, we transferred to a modernized Southern Baptist church that was mainly made up of the White middle class, a stark contrast to the public middle school I attended during the week in the majority Black city. That church's youth group program taught me that Michael Jackson was writing satanic music and that the heavy metal bands that my brother listened to were working for the devil. Its youth group also imparted that heterosexual marriage was very important, so much so that us middle schoolers were charged with creating a song and dance routine for "Do Wah Diddy," Manfred Mann's 1964 hit about first love and marriage. For our performance on the church main stage, we all wore salmon-colored T-shirts about the importance of "saving ourselves" for marriage. "I'm Not Doing It" was emblazoned on the front in bold black font. "Until marriage" was printed on the back in white lettering. Our youth group leaders never addressed the implications of our performance, or what "It" referred to on our T-shirts. I never asked either. I didn't know what to ask.

In my freshman year of high school, we relocated to the Gulf Coast of Florida and stopped going to church. I wasn't mad at Christianity. My parents weren't either. They had simply drifted away from church, and I drifted into the Pensacola punk scene, a vibrant ragtag community of self-taught zine makers, artists, and musicians who were calling out injustices that I had never thought of, much less heard about, at church.[14] Later, in my twenties, I ended up in Colorado Springs, Colorado, studying sociology and women's and ethnic studies during the George W. Bush years. Colorado Springs, home of Ted Haggard's New Life Church and James Dobson's Focus on the Family, is where I started dabbling in evangelicalism again.[15] But this time not as an impressionable kid fascinated by the endless love of Jesus, but rather as a college student learning ethnographic methods in a city where White Christian conservatives have tremendous political power.[16]

I share these things about myself—my political orientation, class background, relationship to Mississippi, to Whiteness and Christianity—to be up front: the empathy wall, and how ethnographers climb it, is shaped by where we stand in relation to our research. This book is based on data I collected at Welcome through my own filter, and I take ownership of that and draw attention to it where appropriate. The churchgoers I got to know are part of my filter, too. We created the data for this book together, as participants in the same church community, living in the same college town. To get along and keep the peace, we did what White people do when in mixed company: we lingered on small talk. We kept our differences to ourselves. We avoided delicate subjects such as anti-Black police profiling, border walls, LGBTQ+ church inclusion, and Trumpism. We showed up to church acting the same, and in the process accelerated the dangerous idea that deviation from the prerogatives of White cisgender heterosexual families and values, of any kind, is divisive and therefore un-Christian, and un-American.

# Introduction

Almost any book about American evangelicalism acknowledges, usually in the introduction, that churchgoers steer clear of talk about issues that they regard as too controversial, too political, or too personal.[1] But none grapple sufficiently with how such talk is avoided, or how its absence alongside the big talk at church shapes the political trajectory of evangelical Christianity. This is where my book comes in. It shows that small talk is just as consequential as bold statements from authority figures of the religious and political Right.

Small talk not only brings people together at church, it also absorbs thoughtful dialogue that could expose or generate progressive stances on hot-button issues. I came to this realization—that small talk does substantial political work—while getting to know Bird and the church he pastors in Oxford, Mississippi, a small historic college town with a big reputation for its fancy tailgating parties, Greek life, Confederate heritage, and a failed battle to keep James Meredith out of its all-White university in 1962. When I started visiting Bird's church, which I call Welcome, White evangelical Christians were prominent in the news for backing Donald Trump's 2016 bid for the presidency, and the college town that Welcome calls home was mirroring the country's mounting political divides. Yet even within this context, churchgoers carefully managed conversations about issues that could, in their words, tear them apart. Rather than engage in spirited discussion, they stuck closely to *small talk*, which I define as putative prosocial interactions that limit and prescribe what cannot be asked and what cannot be talked about. Small talk helped churchgoers establish and protect common ground, but it also drove out differences and open dialogue.

Bird and I met on a late summer day, less than two years after his church opened. He noticed me from across the parking lot of the town's Recreation Center, the church's temporary location, after Sunday service let out, then sprinted up a small grassy hill to introduce himself.

Wearing a faded pastel polo shirt and blue jeans, Bird smiled, shook my hand, and said he hadn't seen me at church before. The fine lines around his eyes, flecks of gray hair, and pink round face reminded me of a good friend. He had a down-to-earth vibe about him, too, one that made me feel like I wasn't wrong for being at church, no matter the reason I had come.

In the first five minutes of our conversation, I learned that Bird is a former youth pastor who was "called," not trained, to be a preacher, and goes by his nickname, Bird, not by "pastor" or by his last name, Lindsay. He learned that I am from a rural Mississippi community an hour down the road, am not a believer, and am a sociologist who specializes in religion. Without pause, Bird raised his voice to a persuasive pitch and told me that I should study Welcome. My study would be a good opportunity for him to see what the church needs to work on, he said, a comment that his wife Anne reiterated when I discussed the possibility with her. Bird said he trusted that I was not like "those atheists" who try to "dig up dirt" on a church without the church knowing about it. The fact that I was telling him about myself relieved any misgivings he had about that.

Bird was patently confident about creating a church where *all are welcome*, regardless of what they have, what they look like, or where they come from. I was jarred by his proclamation. Mississippi had recently passed a harmful anti-LGBTQ+ religious liberty bill, and the Unitarian Universalist Congregation of Oxford responded to it by publicly proclaiming that "All are Welcome." I had a hunch that Bird was not using that phrase in the same way that other, liberal congregations across the United States were using it to make explicit that they are an LGBTQ+-affirming congregation. He did, however, repeatedly touch on race and class divisions and was quick to call out other churches for being inhospitable.

I distinctly recall Bird telling me in a loud, upbeat tone that Jesus died on the cross for everybody, "Not just for people that look like me and you!" To drive home that point, Bird placed his hand on my shoulder and leaned in gently, "You know Amy, MLK said that Sunday is the most segregated hour of the week. The church has to do better than that."[2] Then, as if suddenly realizing the gravity of his mission, Bird shouted, "We believe the church is charged to take the Word to all nations!" He glanced over at the crowd spilling out of the Recreation Center's glass panel doors and announced proudly, "Blue-collar workers, white-collar workers, homeschool moms, students are all part of our community!" Welcome is not like other churches in town, Bird professed: "We're multiethnical [*sic*]! We welcome African Americans, Hispanics, 'mixed' couples—churches around here don't think too much about mixed families. We do."[3]

I accepted Bird's invitation and stayed at Welcome over the span of thirty-one months, starting in August 2016 and ending in February 2019. I attended Welcome's Sunday services, community outreach events like Whole Family Day, Spring is Here, and Trunk or Treat on Halloween, and conducted over 40 in-depth qualitative interviews with church leaders, affiliates, and congregants. I also spent a lot of time in church "small groups," intimate settings for open discussion and community building.

Despite the church's best intentions, I discovered that rather than promote diversity, as Bird indicated when we first met, Welcome encouraged an ethos of sameness that politely limited what churchgoers could say, think, or believe. These limits were evident in how the church participated in what sociologist Eviatar Zerubavel terms a "conspiracy of silence" that outwardly ignored the reproduction of power and privilege within their own congregation.[4] They tacitly agreed to abide by a rule that Lynn, a founding member of Welcome, remarked on in her private interview: "You don't talk about things that people hold close to their heart. That's why you don't talk about religion and you don't talk about politics."

Divisive issues, Lynn and others explained, have no place in church. Church is supposed to be a place where everyone feels comfortable, feels unified, in the eyes of God. Talk about disagreeable subjects like border control and the Confederate flag could expose differences of opinion, even opposition to the church's assumed stance, and was therefore off-limits.

Drawing on symbolic interactionist theories of impression management and denial, this book shows how small talk and its associated practices (i.e., silence, neglect, and avoidance) temper opposing points of view in evangelical communities, advancing the idea that spirited debate and deliberation are inherently disunifying. It argues that small talk at church expedites Christian nationalism, an ideology and political movement that seeks to remake America for White Christians who stand against religious, cultural, and political pluralism.[5]

## The Welcome Plant

My first official research visit inspired the pseudonym Welcome Church. I had dressed in dark slacks and a crisp navy-blue T-shirt covered in red sparkle dots. The pants felt like me. Sparkles are not my thing. I scanned the big pickup trucks and SUVs in the Recreation Center parking lot for "Make America Great Again" stickers. Based on news coverage of the evangelical support for Trump, I expected to find a few. I did not count one.

A lanky man in a bright, traffic control vest waved me across the paved pathway to the 32,000 square foot Recreation Center facility, as he cheerfully shouted, "Good morning!" The churchgoers behind me yelled the same in return. They looked glad to be there. A married couple with big toothy smiles used their bodies to prop open the double doors for us, greeting me and the others with "Welcome" and "How are you?" When I reached the other side of the bold WELCOME banner that hung above the entryway, a thin teenager with a goatee and silver glasses walked over and gave me a hug. It was the kind of hug that friends share after spending years apart. Startled at first, I shrugged it off and headed across the basketball court over to the "Connect" table where a young woman with heavy blue eyeliner shot a nervous smile in my direction, said hi, asked if it was my first time at Welcome, and then handed me an electronic visitor form that quizzed me about my parental and marital statuses, age, and gender.

By the time I finished the visitor form, the worship band was on a pop-up stage near the front entrance to the gym and had reached high volume, which was a cue for churchgoers to find a seat for service. I took a seat in a row of folding chairs serving as a makeshift pew at the back corner of the gym floor where I was able to watch small families, older couples, and a smattering of college students file into the building. A majority of them were White, but Black and Latino congregants were in attendance too. Some churchgoers dressed in their Sunday best. Button-up polo shirts and chinos for men. Ankle boots and sundresses for women. Others were dressed casually in sweatshirts, blouses, and stretchy pants. A few White men donned faded T-shirts and blue jeans. I felt unnoticeable in my informal attire, which put me at ease.

At 11:00 a.m. on the dot, the band paused and asked us to bow our heads in prayer. The building fell silent. When we raised our heads again, Bird was on stage ready to preach. "I'm so glad you're here this morning!" Bird shouted. "Thank you for coming! You have many choices in Oxford, and you chose to be here with us!" The Recreation Center was filled to the brim. Every single one of its three hundred steel folding chairs was taken, and more than a dozen people were left standing, including two White police officers in uniform. Bird continued with a message that went something like this—a message that was repeated on Sunday mornings:

> Everybody is welcome here! We're a church of all nations! No matter your race, your gender! No matter how broken you are! Even if you don't believe in Jesus—we want you to be here! Amen (crowd calls back amen). Come as you are! Blue jeans, sweatpants. We don't care!

Bird embodies the church's mission to be a community where all are welcome. He preaches in blue jeans and an untucked polo shirt. Sometimes paired with scuffed up cowboy boots. Sometimes sneakers. The church adores Bird—a self-made man from the Mississippi Delta who insists that everyone call him Bird, not Pastor Bird or Preacher. They like that he doesn't think he's better than others. That he is, in his own words, "jacked up" like everybody else.[6] The church finds Bird funny, too. They laugh when he pokes fun at his receding hairline or mispronounces a "big word" in the Bible. They smile when he speaks broken Spanish for those whom he calls his "Hispanic brothers and sisters" in the church. He makes the church laugh before scolding them for "running their mouth" on social media, or for sending text messages in the middle of a sermon.

Bird jokes around a lot, but according to churchgoers, he is serious about The Word, a phrase that evangelicals use to signal their belief that the Bible is from God and their interpretation of it factually correct. He invoked the phrase "The Word" from the church stage, and churchgoers treasured that he dedicates his life to sharing it with others around the world on global mission trips. Yet Bird was against outsiders calling him and Welcome "evangelical." That term, he explained to me, has become synonymous with racist.[7] He and others at Welcome preferred to be called "believers" or "Bible-believing."

Regardless of Bird's objection to the term evangelical, Welcome aligns itself with conservative White evangelicalism in critical ways. First, church leadership takes a literalist approach to the Bible (e.g., reads the creation story in Genesis as a historical account of how the world began), meaning they believe the Bible contains the literal words of God and is therefore an infallible resource that humans can consult for all of life's biggest questions and mysteries.[8] Second, the church believes in born-again salvation, which is achieved when one renounces their sinfulness and acknowledges Jesus as their personal savior.[9] Third, Welcome stresses the Great Commission, which refers to a passage in the Gospel of Matthew where Jesus urges his followers to "make disciples of all nations, baptizing them in the name of the Father and of the Son and of the Holy Spirit" (Matthew 28:19). Fourth, Welcome is associated with the Southern Baptist Convention (SBC), a national network of conservative evangelical churches that, since the 1970s, have sought to insert seemingly race-neutral "family values" into political, cultural, and legal affairs. And finally, Welcome was friendly to the Calvinist revival in the SBC; formal and informal leaders emphasized that happiness can only be acquired through worship, and that God is an all-knowing God that controls the human story.[10]

Welcome was especially committed to converting nonbelievers, or what Bird describes as "running after people," which he literally did to get to know me, a newcomer to the church. He opened Welcome after reading a 2010 Census report that said 70 percent of Lafayette County residents (the county seat of Oxford) are not evangelical and that over 40 percent have no desire to attend church. When he read those numbers, he was a youth pastor at a longer-standing Baptist church and pitched the idea of creating a church that could reach a wider range of people, especially students and the working class. The church where he was employed liked the idea of building a "come as you are" kind of church and helped Bird and Anne plant Welcome. Its leaders believed that Bird's team could change Oxford for the better, which in their minds involves making more people the same as them.

At our earliest meetings in his disheveled office, which is located in a brick-and-mortar office building a few miles out from the center of town, Bird handed me a laminated booklet titled, "Why Church Plant in Oxford?" "Church plant" is a term widely used in Protestant circles to refer to localized gatherings of Christians that have the support of an established "parent" church in their early years.[11] Church plants try to reflect the communities they want to reach.[12] They might make hip-hop music, old-fashioned Gospel hymnals, or Christian rock melodies part of their service, or encourage churchgoers, as well as church leaders, to have tattoos, wear suits and ties, or blue jeans and T-shirts. According to church plant leaders, the styles of church can and should change. Where people worship and what they look like when they do is a minor issue. Biblical truth and abiding by it, however, is nonnegotiable.

The motive that drives the church plant movement in the Southern Baptist tradition is to insert the same type of evangelical Christianity into diverse communities around the world. To do this, church plants often change the structure of how their faith is conveyed. Rather than emphasize God's wrath and judgment, as Southern Baptists have done in the past, church plants more typically place a mantra of "Love God, love each other, and love the world" at the forefront of their worship services and mission.[13]

Welcome, the booklet read, can be a "catalyst for the Gospel to expand to the nations through the discipleship of the men and women who will be sent out from this plant." Young people are turned off by church, Bird explained, and the church has to get better at "running after them." Welcome is doing that running, he insisted, and without "watering down the Bible," a phrase he and others used to criticize churches that teach what evangelicals consider a lenient version of the Bible that makes people feel good about themselves or justifies liberal stances on abortion, the ordination of women, and homosexuality. The church has to be like an aircraft carrier, Bird touted. "It needs to be ready to send people out for war!" Evangelical churches are losing too many people, he continued, especially in college towns where viewpoints and lifestyles that run counter to God are becoming the norm. He wants to entice people to church but without becoming what he and others call a "seeker-friendly" congregation that plugs all its energy and resources into making sure that people are not put off by the Word of God.[14]

Welcome refuses to become a church where people decide what faith means on their own, Bird told me. He believes in preaching "truth" from the Bible, even if the truth causes discomfort. He is upfront with the church that abortion is wrong, adultery is wrong, and heaven and hell are real, he said. While telling me this, Bird rose from his office chair and studied the untidy bookshelves of papers, folders, and sports memorabilia that encircled the room. He found what he was looking for: *Gaining by Losing: Why the Future Belongs to Churches that Send* by J. D. Greear, the former president of the Southern Baptist Convention (2018–2021) and pastor of the multisite Summit Church in Durham, North Carolina.[15] "You can keep the book," Bird told me. "I have plenty of copies."

After handing me the book, Bird remarked that *Gaining by Losing* explains the Welcome mission. Greear, the pastor of Summit Church, which has branch campuses near prestigious universities in the Research Triangle, is among the church plant movement's biggest stars. Before becoming president of the SBC in 2018, Greear avowed that the SBC has to put a stop to the alarming statistical drop in Southern Baptists. It has to invest in church planting. His book proposes that a franchise approach to church is the best way to reach that goal.[16] To build the franchise, Greear argues that churches need to train leaders in the gospel and then send those leaders out to plant more churches.[17] At first, sending might hurt the church's bottom line, Greear admits. It costs more money to train and send new leaders, he writes, than to build a bigger and better church. But, according to Greear, these initial costs merit the sacrifice. Churches that invest in a sending culture, he argues, gain more churches. More churches produce more Christians, which in turn improves their chances of turning the nation back to God.

Within two years of its opening, Welcome was on par with two other popular church plants in town. It had reached five hundred attendees and increased from one to two Sunday morning services. In response to the church's growth, Bird, Anne, and their team of elders strategized about how to create an intimate experience where congregants can, in their words, "do life together." Their solution was a small groups program, a potpourri of weekly gatherings that church members organize and lead in their homes or at the church office.[18] Each small group leader would be responsible for determining the theme (e.g., biblical parenting) and for recruiting participants via email or in person after Sunday morning service.

The small groups were a hit. When Ryan, one of my youngest interviewees, reflected on the group he joined, he said: "We are living life together, literally. We have a tight knit group that is working towards the same goal—multiply into more small groups with the same literal interpretation of the scripture." As he sees it, small groups are a vehicle for transforming America, group by group, step by step, into a church where all are the same kind of Christian. Have the same values, believe in the same God, and carry out their lives in the same way.

This book takes a close look at the interactional work that goes into building sameness in American evangelicalism. It focuses on the discussions that transpired in small group settings at Welcome and shows how churchgoers search out, perform, and uplift the idea that they all believe the same things and do life in the same way. Small talk is a major part of that sameness work in that it weakens differences of opinion, progressive perspectives, and alternative takes on biblical truth. It enables churchgoers to achieve what I term *biblical sameness*, a concept that builds on the convention of attaching "biblical" to a belief or cause that evangelicals think puts them on the right side of the moral lines they draw (biblical parenting, biblical manhood, biblical eldership, etc.). I use the phrase *biblical sameness* throughout the book because it allows me to underline that while there are internal differences within evangelicalism—which churchgoers have to work at containing!—the evangelical church is able to fortify that work by stressing the belief that theological and ideological homogeneity is a Godly cause.

## *The Place of Welcome*

Welcome's home state, Mississippi, is the most churchgoing state in the country, and the vast majority of its residents are Protestant evangelicals who believe in God with absolute certainty.[19] Southern Baptism, a denomination that prioritizes conservative traditional family values, leads the state religiously and politically.[20] In 2016, for example, state legislators who are Southern Baptist successfully championed a religious liberty law (HB 1523) in Mississippi that protects the "sincerely held religious belief" that biology determines sex and gender at birth and that sexual relationships and marriage should be restricted to heterosexuals. That law, "Protecting Freedom of Conscience from Government Discrimination Act," attempts to quash the LGBTQ+ fight for freedom, a fight that motivated the Supreme Court to legalize same-sex marriage nationwide in 2015 and encouraged President Barack Obama to expand Title IX protections to transgender kids in public schools one year later. Under Mississippi's HB 1523, Christian-owned businesses, organizations, and individuals can reject those and other basic LGBTQ+ rights. They can opt to only provide goods and services to people who meet their standards for sex, gender, and heterosexual marriage.

The power of conservative Christianity is palpable in Mississippi. But Mississippi also has a history of radical activism against racist structures and in recent years has become a hopeful site of southern LGBTQ+ Pride and protest. Sameness, in other words, has always been contested in Mississippi. And the stakes for achieving sameness in a red state that is far to the Right are enormous for all Americans, regardless of what state they call home.[21]

Oxford was becoming a little less hot for Republicans when I started at Welcome, a difference that locals were attributing to the University of Mississippi's incremental progressive-leaning makeup. In 2012, its Lafayette County favored Mitt Romney over Barack Obama by 15.5 percentage points, and in 2016 chose Donald Trump over Hillary Rodham Clinton by 14.7 percentage points. By 2020, Oxford's county seat was fading to a lighter shade of pink. The Republican Party won in Lafayette again, but it was the lowest it had been for the past three presidential elections (Trump beat Joe Biden by 12 percentage points). In 2024, after I had terminated my research, there was a shift back to a much darker shade of pink: Trump defeated Kamala Harris by 22 percentage points.

The fluctuation in votes for the Republican Party tell a bigger story about Oxford's squabbles over what the town, Mississippi, and America are and should be. For some living in or loving this college town, Oxford has turned too blue, even radically left. "Newcomers" from the university, they charge, are turning it into a "liberal bubble" and destroying their most cherished traditions: Confederate mascots, Dixie songs, and Christian prayer at Ole Miss football games.[22] For others, Oxford still exudes racism and conservativism and needs serious change, which is why Bird's emphasis on being a diverse and inclusive church for *everybody* captivated me.

### *The Talk of Welcome*

The church spoke explicitly about men's authority over women, about church unity, as well as the notion that the church has a divine right to express itself in public institutions such as schools. It was the kind of talk that evangelicals commonly use to strengthen their sense of moral superiority and distinction from religious and non-religious others.[23] But making clear that the evangelical church is distinct from others was not enough. To protect sameness from within, the church had to refrain from conversations that could cause tension, debate, and disagreement. They were quiet about the conflicts over racial profiling that were occurring across the nation. They ignored the protests that were breaking out over Confederate monuments in their own hometown. They evaded the tricky subject of LGBTQ+ rights and church membership. And they neglected to engage in hard conversations about how men's power over women in marriage impacts their families, relationships, and children.

Churchgoer's propensity to avoid touchy subjects is what prompted me to pay closer attention to small talk and how it functions in the evangelical church. Small talk is credited as light-hearted or casual banter that brings people together. A mechanism of sociality that amplifies, exaggerates, and extends shared attitudes, values, and feelings. Self-help authors praise small talk for paving the way to a life rich in friendships, love, and career opportunities.[24] Religious leaders and conflict resolution experts suggest small talk is the first step to healing broken bonds in a deeply polarized society.[25] Small talk has vocal detractors too. Novelist and cultural critic Karan Mahajan charges in *The New Yorker* that small talk is primarily empty, American talk.[26] It allows people to reassure one another that they like each other but "won't violate one another's privacies." Some Americans will know each other for years, he writes, before moving on to substantive conversations.

Small talk plays a profound role in bonding and belonging, yet surprisingly few sociologists take small talk seriously. This is in part because, as feminist sociolinguists point out, small talk is associated with femininity and therefore shrugged off as inconsequential and unimportant.[27] Before doing research at Welcome, I dismissed the significance of small talk too. I thought that it was pointless, space-filling talk that has no real bearing on what people think, what they do, much less on their faith or their politics. I assumed this book would solely be about what sociolinguists term "big talk," the influential talk that is linked to masculinity and understood as frank, factual talk that gets stuff done.[28] Big talk transpires at social movement meetings, on Christian radio programs, from the pulpit, and on the debate stage. A focus on big talk falls in line with scholarly conventions, especially the research on Christian nationalism. A focus on small talk and what it accomplishes does not.[29]

My perception of small talk changed at Welcome. Over and over again, I heard congregants talk at length about rudimentary aspects of life—things like junk emails, school lunches, and football games—and rarely broach subjects or raise questions that could stir or expose disagreements. I noticed that small talk, or what some churchgoers referred to as "surface talk," brought people together, but it also made it difficult for churchgoers to open up or explore opinions that deviated from White conservative dogmas.[30]

Small talk permitted churchgoers to pretend as if they were all on the same page, especially when the stakes were high. This is because small talk hinders what sociologist Paul Lichterman describes as "reflective talk," or talk that encourages members of a group to ponder who they are and how they relate to others in the wider social world.[31] Small talk stands in for and supplements the stuff that is complicated and uncomfortable to talk about.

A short exchange at Recharge, a monthly potluck of food and fellowship for women, illustrates how small talk sorts out the potential for discussion and disagreement. It happened on a Monday night under the fluorescent lights of the church kitchen, which is up the stairs from Bird's office. About ten White women, counting me, ranging from millennials and Gen Xers to baby boomers, were there. The chatter around the table moved from recipes to annoying emails, from managing Facebook to the rising cost of electric bills, but never to Shane Claiborne, a Christian activist who was in Oxford the night before to speak on the death penalty, homelessness, and poverty.

Eager to know what the women of Recharge thought about Claiborne's talk, I intervened and asked if anyone had attended the event, which a member of Welcome's worship team helped organize. Marsha, a happy-go-lucky youth group minister, grinned, "It was great!" Curious if I could push the conversation further, I told the group that I had seen

Claiborne when George W. Bush was president, and that Claiborne had taken a firm stance against the war in Iraq. Then I probed, "What did he talk about last night?" Marsha spoke up again, "He met Mother Teresa!" Mrs. Betsy, a senior and respected member of the group, leaned forward, "Wow, really?" Marsha did not elaborate, and Mrs. Betsy did not ask her to. Instead, Marsha began running her hands down her thighs and saying that his pants "were different" with lots of colorful patches on the front. "All the guys were like 'Wow, those pants are really cool! I want a pair like that!,'" she exclaimed. Several others at the table nodded agreeably, and one added, "Yeah, they were cool!" The conversation ended there. The substance of Claiborne's critique of the death penalty remained untouched.

When, in private interviews, I raised the subject of what kind of talk is prohibited, churchgoers were quick to declare that they can "talk about anything" at Welcome. Yet, ironically, those same individuals admitted to confining what they implicitly deemed contentious discussions to private spaces: at home with a spouse, at lunch with a coworker, or on the back porch with only their best friends. In church settings, they said, the norm is to let silence on social and political matters prevail. Churchgoers were proficient with this norm, especially if the matters in question might lay their differences of opinions on race, gender, and sexuality bare.[32]

Churchgoers did what volunteers in sociologist Nina Eliasoph's study on political apathy did: they avoided spirited conversations out of "fear that talk itself" could lead to political fallout.[33] Situations were deemed political, even un-Christian, if and when they could expose differences of opinion within the church. This did not mean, as I noted earlier, that politics were completely off the table. In small group conversations and on the church stage, churchgoers raised issues that social scientists consider political, issues that touch on the "reproduction or negotiation of relations of power and privilege."[34] They remarked on their belief in the inherent differences between men and women, on their belief that abortion is immoral, and on their belief that the government is wrong to block Christian prayer in school, on the football field, or at the hospital. These beliefs were addressed out in the open because these beliefs drew the line between "us" and "them." Talk about racial profiling, Trump, anti-LGBTQ+ religious freedom laws, or diverse experiences and identities, on the other hand, could get morally messy and was therefore vigilantly carved out of church. Small talk was the tool they used to do that carving.

Small talk came in handy for me too. I used it to evade topics of conversation that might alienate me from the many small groups I attended. I never shared my stance on marriage, gender, or reproductive rights, nor did I ever feel like I had to. I never shared that I was in a long-term relationship and living with my partner out of wedlock ("living in sin"). No one asked. Not one person in the three years of my study at a church that is adjacent to Southern Baptism, a denomination that is notorious for forcefully endorsing monogamous heterosexual marriage. Further, with the exception of one interviewee who cautiously inquired if I am lesbian at the end of her interview, none of the regular churchgoers asked about my sexuality or if I have kids. If they had asked about these aspects of my life, they would have had to engage with answers that conflict with the work they were putting into being the same. It was strategic to not know.[35] Knowing about difference was an inconvenience and inefficient.

It was also unclear if, or how many, congregants assumed that I was Christian. I was only asked about my faith on four occasions. Bird asked the first day we met. Two congregants asked at the end of one-on-one interviews. And Carol, an older woman who grew up Southern Baptist, asked point blank: "Are you a believer?" one night from across the room at the Women's Book Club. I kept my answer simple: "No, I am not." Before Carol could follow up, another participant interjected to tell me about *The Case for Christ*. "It's a movie about an atheist journalist who finds Jesus. . . . I think you would like it," she said encouragingly. I thanked her for the recommendation and promised to check it out. No one from book club raised the issue again. Instead, we stuck to the things that exaggerated our similarities: our cravings for fried okra, the parts of Mississippi that we know and visit, and our dismay at housing prices in Oxford. Minimizing our differences was the polite, Christian thing to do.[36]

Indeed, my own experiences at Welcome influenced my conceptualization of small talk and the sameness it achieves.[37] Throughout my research, churchgoers inquired, "Do you feel welcome here?" My answer was almost always some version of a courteous, "Yes, thank you, everyone is so nice here," which is true. Welcome churchgoers are a friendly, loving bunch. When my dad unexpectedly died, I was crushed. We were extremely close and losing him was a heart-wrenching shock. The Be the Bridge (BTB) group that I was participating in at the time prepared home-cooked meals for my family and sent sympathy cards and messages. Then later, when I bought a house, several members of BTB volunteered to help me move, insisting that this is what friends do for each other. They believed in helping others out in their community and they never hesitated to offer that help to me. Yet despite the warmth I felt at Welcome, no one there ever really got to know me. And until we sat down for interviews, I never really got to know them. The small talk made it appear like we were all in compliance with White religious conservatism, and keeping up that appearance thwarted our ability to bring up how our social and political behavior was directly impacting each other's lives.

*Studying Welcome*

This book is based on 111 field site visits that yielded 648 pages of single-spaced ethnographic field notes. Collectively, my research assistants and I logged in 247 hours of fieldwork between August 2016 and February 2019. Each field visit lasted an average of two and a half hours; some visits were only an hour and a half, while others were as long as five. My total time and page count for the field observations and notes, however, excludes the books I read for book club, the newsletters I read from church, the meals I prepared for potlucks, and the 43 transcribed interviews that lasted over an hour each. In Appendix A, I describe my reasons for naming Oxford and the challenges I faced doing an ethnography where I live and work. Appendices B and C catalog the small groups, sermons, outreach events, and conferences studied.

I attended church services, outreach events, and affiliate ministry conferences, but most of my time at Welcome was spent in small groups that ranged from five to twenty-five participants. I acquired permission to study these groups by contacting the group leader about my interest and reasons for joining. Then, upon my initial visit, I announced myself and my interest in learning how the group was "doing church" before the meeting got underway. If Bird or Anne were present, they introduced me and told churchgoers that I was studying how they build a welcoming community. I informed participants that they had every right to opt out of the study and could do so by contacting me or the small group leader without any hard feelings. Every group that I asked to sit in on gave me permission to do so, and with little hesitation. The only group to request that I wait a few weeks before joining was Be the Bridge (the racial reconciliation group). They were brand new and wanted to use their first few sessions to build rapport with one another before launching into the difficult subject of race.

I have ethnographic data on eight different small groups: 1) Be the Bridge; 2) Sunday Group; 3) New Families; 4) Reasoned Defense; 5) Women's Book Club; 6) Recharge for women; 7) The Rock for men; and 8) Back to Basics.[38] The first four in this list fit the church's definition of a "Welcome group," which the church announced before service began on Sundays at the beginning of the fall and spring semesters (most of Oxford is organized around the university's academic calendar). Churchgoers were told that they could learn the menu of options for Welcome groups by staying around after service and asking to see the Welcome groups sign-up sheet. The average Welcome group consisted of ten to fifteen people who met in a churchgoer's home or at the church office once a week. These types of small groups were the most time-consuming events at Welcome, as these were the spaces where churchgoers socialized and learned what it means to be a believer in intimate settings that purportedly encouraged open discussion. Group meetings lasted about three hours, starting with a potluck dinner or appetizers, and then ending with more time for socializing after the official part of the discussion had ended.

The first four groups listed above were part of Welcome's small groups ministry. Be the Bridge (BTB) was started by a White college student who was upset by the evangelical support for Trump. When she left Oxford, a Black congregant who had participated in that first semester of meetings took over the group and led it for two additional semesters. The name for the group, Be the Bridge, was inspired by Latasha Morrison's work. Morrison, a nationally acclaimed "bridge-builder," published the BTB discussion guide and book *Be the Bridge: Pursuing God's Heart for Racial Reconciliation* that the group loosely followed to facilitate its discussions of race and the Bible. Sunday Group focused on evangelism and putting God first. Its leader was an influential member of the church who met Bird in a ministries program called Downline, an evangelical institute in Memphis, Tennessee, that focuses on spreading the gospel to "all nations." The New Families group was an informal Bible study for young parents with small children that involved a meal and plenty of time for chitchat. Reasoned Defense was for self-described evangelical apologists who wanted to learn how to defend themselves and their beliefs in secular settings.

The last four groups listed (Women's Book club and on) were offered in addition to the small groups that met weekly. These groups also tended to be small in scale and were formed to either give men and women time to make friends in gender-homogenous spaces, or to teach gendered compliance in a heterosexual marriage. The gender-segregated ministry meetings, Recharge and The Rock, convened once a month or less during the school year, while the Women's Book Club met less frequently. Back to Basics was a short-term ministry.

Most of my field research happened on Sundays, which meant my Monday morning hours were spent turning voice-recorded field notes into written descriptions of what I had witnessed. When I attended events on another day of the week, I scrambled to find enough time to write up rich accounts of what I saw, heard, and experienced. In other words, those notes from other days of the week were usually not as good. Realizing this, I gravitated to groups that met on Sundays and only attended Recharge (which met on Mondays) occasionally. My approach mirrored sociologist Annette Lareau's advice in *Listening to People*. I selected what to study based on my availability to write descriptive notes within twenty-four hours of exiting the field.[39] Luckily, several small groups met on Sunday evenings, or could be attended by my graduate research assistant, who had a different schedule than me.

I was a meticulous notetaker at the small group meetings. I used journals for shorthand jottings and then, immediately after leaving the field site, I made voice memos on my cell phone to recount the context and trajectory of a conversation, as well as gestures and sounds like headshakes and moans. Once in front of a computer, I utilized a comprehensive method of notetaking.[40] I listened to my audio recording and described the sequence of events from beginning to end, noting changes over time. I tracked who spoke, when, and about what; when and how discussions shifted from one topic to the next; what topics incited lively engagement; what topics were avoided; and what topics either fell flat or disappeared quickly. In many ways, my note taking reflects the approach that sociologist Kathleen Blee took in her study of new activist groups for *Democracy in the Making: How Activist Groups Form.*[41] I simultaneously recorded what was happening or being talked about alongside what was not happening or being talked about. In doing this, I captured what is absent and what is silenced and how those absences and silences form the politics of evangelical Christianity.

I traced the "intricacies of talk and interactions" for three main reasons.[42] First, church is the place where evangelical Christians spend extraordinary amounts of their free time; a place where their identities, relationships, and political leanings are forged.[43] Second, evangelicals who frequent church often are among the most likely to hold ultraconservative positions that promote Christian nationalism, yet how they arrive to those positions in their everyday efforts to bond and belong at church is rarely considered.[44] Finally, ordinary conversation matters—it structures what social phenomenologist Alfred Schütz coined the "zone of primary relevance"; it orders what knowledge is worthwhile, as well as who or what is off the table for discussion.[45]

My careful notetaking also provided peace of mind. Unlike the qualitative study I did on Christian and Muslim punk rock music, I knew I would be unable to leave the field site when the study was over.[46] Welcome Church was close to home, literally. What if someone from Welcome read this book and accused me of misrepresenting them when our paths crossed at the grocery store? Or at the dentist's office? Or when I needed to have my driver's license renewed? Fears of backlash drove me to obsess about methodological precision—a precision that enabled me to write this book about how small, seemingly innocuous talk keeps progressive attitudes, opinions, and people out of church.

In addition to data collected on small groups and broader church life, 43 tape-recorded semi-structured interviews were conducted with Welcome leaders, churchgoers, and founding affiliates. I performed 41 of the 43 interviews. My sociology graduate research assistant, Pace Ward, conducted two with members of Reasoned Defense. Interviews lasted about one and a half hours and covered topics that were avoided at church, such as how interviewees feel about racial diversity in the church, what they thought about the Trump presidency, and their opinions on LGBTQ+ membership. Before turning to these politically sensitive prompts, I learned about each person's religious biography and about what drew them to Welcome (see Appendix D). Most interviews were one-on-one; however, a few men opted to be interviewed with their wives. They likely worried that sitting alone with a woman for a coffee could jeopardize their standing as decent men of faith.[47] There were also two women who arrived to the interview with their husbands, unannounced, which meant I had to try to gather their perspective on men's headship under the watchful eye of their husbands.

Once the interview was over, I emailed or texted participants an anonymous survey link that they filled out in private. The survey asked about their race, gender, and sexual identity, relationship and employment status, income and educational levels, and about their frequency of church attendance, past and present denominational affiliation, and how they categorized themselves on a seven-point political index scale that ranges from extremely liberal (on the left) to extremely conservative (on the right).

The interview sample is indicative of the people who participate in the church most by either joining one of its small groups, being part of the worship or leadership team, and/or volunteering for the church in some capacity. The majority of my interviewees were White (88 percent), heterosexual (100 percent) women (60 percent), between the ages of thirty-five and fifty-four years of age (54 percent) and had attained a bachelor's degree or higher (63 percent). There was also a good share of interviewees who never attended or finished college (37 percent) and who were between the ages of eighteen to thirty-four (23 percent) or fifty-five years and older (23 percent). The total household income of interviewees was fairly mixed, a finding that reflected Bird and Anne's emphasis on creating a church for people across the economic spectrum. For example, whereas most interviewees fell within the $50,000 to $74,999 income range (32 percent), there were also participants who reported incomes of $49,999 or less (27 percent), or, to the contrary, $75,000 or more (also 27 percent); the remaining 14 percent marked "prefer not to say" on the question about income.

Politically speaking, the congregation leans conservative: 75 percent of respondents identified as conservative or moderately conservative (none identified as extremely conservative); however, a sizable portion (25 percent) were moderates, the category at the center of the seven-point index. A few interviewees commented that they enjoyed the interview but found it "controversial" or "political." When I pressed them to say more about that, their responses went something like this: 1) they think about these topics often (such as whether a gay couple should be allowed membership in the church); 2) they appreciated that the interview gave them space to work through some dilemmas; or 3) they shy away from "touchy subjects" at church and therefore were unsure if an answer made sense or if it was the right, Christian position to take. What interviewees shared in our private conversations verified what I detected during participant observations: churchgoers abstain from talking about the very disputes that preserve the church's seat on the right of the political spectrum. The interview had pushed them into a space of contemplation, and participants found that space both unsettling and fun.

## Chapter Outline

This book offers a journey through Welcome. It shows how the church sees itself and its mission, how churchgoers relate to each other, and how the church institutes the idea that being the same is the right, Christian thing to do for the church and the nation.

Chapter 1, The Welcome Plant, sets the stage for understanding who Welcome was started for and how Welcome positions itself in an evangelical church plant movement that seeks to build new, updated versions of Southern Baptism. With close attention to one of its small groups, the chapter shows how a mixed-income church for "everybody" protected the ideological roots of White evangelical conservativism, as well as inspired its members to organize ministries that strengthen and spread the seeds of biblical sameness in their community.

Chapter 2, We Don't Build Walls, We Build Longer Tables, underscores how the church envisions its inclusive mission in a college town split along racial, class, and political lines. It shows that rather than "build longer tables" that embrace difference, churchgoers rely on what I call "welcome talk," a counterpart to small talk, to exaggerate their attainment of racial diversity and inclusivity without having to confront racial inequalities.

Chapter 3, America Is Divided (But the Church Cannot Be), examines how Welcome avoided talking about subjects that could rouse discussion and disagreement. It shows how churchgoers sidestepped talk about politically charged issues such as the Trump presidency, Confederate monuments, and high-profile cases of racialized police violence, even when members of its very own community felt under fire. It makes the case that the lack in substantive dialogue normalized a White ultraconservative position as the default position, and therefore the one that unified the church.

Chapter 4, Back to Basics, shows that when it came to gender, church leadership pivoted away from its standard of avoidance and silence to preach that God made men the bosses of women and that men and women need to get back to this basic gender arrangement. The chapter also reveals that proponents of the basics, who were primarily men in leadership, felt emboldened to make their stance explicit and, in their words, "offensive," while opponents of it, namely women, were nudged into silence. The chapter also points out that the church was overt in its support of gender hierarchies because those hierarchies stand in for other social hierarchies that the church was reluctant to name or openly condone.

Chapter 5, Don't Ask, Don't Tell, expands on chapter 4 to show how the church naturalized the basics of gender by unseeing and silencing LGBTQ+ people. At the time of my study, evangelical campaigns for religious freedom were targeting LGBTQ+ individuals and rights, but churchgoers actively avoided "that stuff" (i.e., religious liberty laws, LGBTQ+ church inclusion) when they convened at church. For many, the problem isn't that people are gay. The problem is that people are *openly* gay. Churchgoers push their disagreements to the side, and they resented openly LGBTQ+ people who they say force Christians to choose sides. Evangelicals work hard to appear the same, and they felt it was only reasonable for LGBTQ+ people to make their jobs easier.

Chapter 6, Take Down the Red Tape, is the last substantive chapter of the book and is the one that emphasizes how evangelicals assert themselves in the wider community. It shows how the church takes down the red tape, a phrase that describes the people, policies, and practices that try to limit the extent to which Christians dominate other religious and nonreligious people in public life. With a focus on how the church thinks about and relates to Oxford, a college town where a small but growing contingent of left-leaning professors live and teach, the chapter shows how the church plays its part in a conservative movement that champions religious and cultural uniformity.

The Conclusion argues that small talk is just as powerful as the big talk by the loudest voices of the religious right. It underlines how small talk, avoidance, and silence drive differences and debate out of American evangelicalism, and consequently amplifies an unspoken assumption that the vocal proponents of Christian nationalism are right about God. The book concludes by addressing the myth that small talk is restricted to the U.S. South or to evangelicalism and encourages readers to consider how a tacit agreement among White people to find and protect common ground is chipping away at the promise of democracy, one seemingly insignificant interaction at a time.

# 1

# The Welcome Plant

The map app on my phone announced, "You've arrived." Convinced that Google had made an error, I pulled over to double-check the address. There was no way, I thought, that Sunday Group could be meeting in Maple Hill, an upscale neighborhood of huge brick homes and impressive mature oak trees. Most of Welcome cannot afford to live there. This was a six-figure salary neighborhood, and the majority of Welcome has a household income of less than $75,000 per year. Again, the app announced, "You've arrived," prompting me to notice the assembly of midsized SUVs and pickup trucks parked in the grass, on the shoulder of the road, two of which had the WC (Welcome Church) logo on the back bumper. Unable to coax my car over the curb, I ended up parking on the street alone out in front of the modern farmhouse home where Sunday Group meets. I grabbed my tray of grapes, took a deep breath, and rehearsed my lines—"Thanks for having me! For those who I haven't met, I'm the one who has been studying how you do church in the community. . . ."

Cora, a familiar face, answered the door. I knew her from the Women's Book Club. Cora was the one who told me about Sunday Group. After a brief but warm greeting, she led me to the kitchen and left me with Vicki, a sixty-something-year-old with short-cropped hair and a smoky voice. Vicki was in charge of food and beverages. She took the grapes and asked what I wanted to drink. "Unsweet tea would be nice," I said. "We've only got sweet," she countered. "I'll take water, thanks!" Vicki got down to business. She took a red Solo cup, filled it with ice and water, and firmly set it on the counter beside me. Her demeanor caused me to doubt my drink order. I slipped out of the kitchen and into the adjoining dining room with a paper plate of bean salad, pickled okra, and green beans with bacon. I don't particularly favor bacon, but I took it to compensate for my otherwise conspicuously vegetarian plate in a house full of meat eaters. Lynn, another friendly face from book club, yelled,

"I got you a seat right here!" The ten-seat table was full of sweet tangy accents and loud bouts of laughter. Cora's husband, Zach, a tall man in his thirties with an athletic vibe, and Ray, an elder man in a crisp pastel polo shirt and shorts, were doing the talking. Zach was excited about having group for another semester, and Ray said that he had missed the food that comes with it. When supper was over, we stuffed our disposable plates, plasticware, and Solo cups into the trash and found a place to sit in Frank and Joan's capacious living room, the official meeting space.

Twenty-seven participants attended small group that evening, not counting the kids who were playing out of sight upstairs. All but two White. Twenty-four of the twenty-seven were married couples paired off on two plush sectional sofas and oversized chaise lounges.

I knew Frank was the leader as soon as I saw him. He reminded me of Billy Graham, a spiritual powerhouse with a measured smile. He was the only man there in khaki slacks. The others were dressed in shorts, jeans, or cargo pants. After a warm welcome, Frank got a few introductions out of the way. He started with the Terrys, a married couple who work for the city, and then turned to me, "a special guest from Ole Miss" who is studying how they "do church," as he put it. One of the participants shrugged, "You ain't bothering me none!" and another shouted, "You're welcome here, we're a friendly bunch!" The room was electric with broad smiles. I had their approval and that felt good. Frank nodded approvingly and then moved the group's attention to Javier and Lucía, a Latino couple who were seated next to Gary, a Sunday Group regular. Gary straightened up in his chair and gestured toward Javier, "He's a colleague from work—they've been to our church a few times." Javier presented himself and then motioned for his wife to do the same. When she said "Lucía," two different people asked, "Can you repeat that?" Her eyes shifted from the ground to her husband, and then back to the packed room again. "Lucía," she said quietly. A voice from the room finally exclaimed, "Oh okay!"

Frank leaned back on his heels and asked, "What should we do this semester? Should we do Matt Chandler's study again?" Chandler is an influential evangelical pastor and Calvinist who adheres to Christian hedonism (the belief that the deep human desire to be happy can only be satisfied through the glorification of God). He is also a major player in the church plant movement.[1] Among other accomplishments,

Chandler grew The Village Church that he pastors in Flower Mound, Texas, from a congregation of 160 to a multiple campus ministry of over 10,000 congregants, and has led Acts 29, a global organization that adheres to Calvinist theology and trains evangelical leaders how to take an "entrepreneurial attitude" to church planting.[2] *The Explicit Gospel*, the Bible study by Chandler that Sunday Group finished the semester prior, teaches that Christians need to be clear on what the gospel says about the life, death, and resurrection of Jesus Christ and committed to sharing that gospel with others. That call to share reflects the mission of Acts 29, which derives its name from the twenty-eight chapters in the Book of Acts, making the movement to multiply church in the modern era the "next chapter" in the church's history.

Sunday Group playfully dismissed the idea of repeating Chandler's study, but church planting remained a mainstay of its agenda. The following week, Frank stood tall at the front of the room and held a bright yellow dish sponge up in the air. "What happens when a sponge sits in a bowl of water too long?" he queried. Junior, who was relatively new to Welcome, and to born-again Christianity, was the first to speak up. He tilted the bill of his blaze orange hunting cap back and giggled, "It gets nasty." Others giggled along, shouting, "Moldy!" "Yucky!" Frank paused for a few seconds and then slowly expelled water from the sponge into a small ceramic bowl. "I have to make use of it," he smiled coolly. "I have to squeeze it out." The room fell quiet. No one was scrolling on their phone. Frank had their attention.

Frank launched into a lesson about what historian Grace Elizabeth Hale describes as "the imagined beginnings of Christianity."[3] He walked over to a dry-erase board at the front center of the living room and sketched out two churches with steeples on top. After drawing the first church, he encircled it with arrows that were pointing inward. The Church (i.e., mainstream churches) is "too inward focused," he said. It pays too much attention to what goes on at church, how much a church can grow, and how to retain members for a lifetime. Then Frank moved over to the second church, drew a circle in the middle of it, and added arrows that were pointed out and away from the circle. He asked those who had Bibles with them to turn to Ephesians, the tenth book in the New Testament. "The early church" in the city of Ephesus was like ours, Frank said while pointing to the circle in the middle of the second

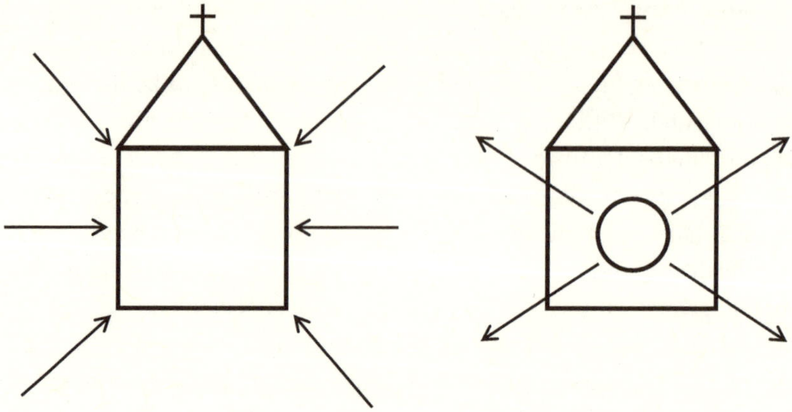

Figure 1.1. Replication of the purpose of church small groups that Frank drew on a whiteboard at Sunday Group. The church on the left is "inward focused." The church on the right is "outward focused" and activated by small groups that spread the gospel.

church on the board. It was "outward focused." People would gather in small groups in each other's homes, and at first, there were only a few groups meeting. But within only fifty years, he continued, those small groups had multiplied into thousands that converted Ephesus, "a city of sin and sex goddesses," into a city of believers.

Frank erased the churches and replaced them with a circle diagram on the board. He guided us through it with a black marker. God is in the center of the circle, he professed, before asking, "How do we show love for God?" Sunday Group members shouted their answers with pride, "Obey Him!" "Trust Him!" "Show love to others!" "Spend time in the Word!" and "Tell others about Him!" Frank squeezed the sponge again. Droplets of water fell to the bowl. "Truth and life are transference—transfer what you know to others."

***

Nearly every Sunday, Bird tells the church that their number one job is to plant the seeds of Bible-believing Christianity in the nation and around the world. And while Bird and the church he leads would never use "activist" to describe themselves, their collective interest in church planting expresses what anthropologist Omri Elisha terms an "activist orientation."[4] They believed that they have a special responsibility to be a church that appeals to everybody, especially those who are tired or wary of the traditional church, and they placed that belief at the center of their religious lives. In fact, being a church for everybody is the stated goal that most consistently tethered the core of Welcome together. No matter where they came from, or how they found Welcome, churchgoers agreed: the seeds of biblical sameness have to be planted in multiple communities and they were eager to do that planting.

This chapter examines how Welcome planted those seeds in pursuit of national salvation.[5] Welcome presented itself as a plant for "regular folk," to use their words, that contrasted with what other churches in the local scene were offering. That is, they positioned themselves as distinct from the liberal Mainline Protestant churches that progressive professors, students, and alumni of higher education attend; as well as from what they considered stuffy Baptists churches, and the impersonal evangelical church plants that had popped up in Oxford. Welcome was on a mission to establish church plants that "match," which for them meant reproducing Christians who acquiesce to a few key beliefs (i.e., men and women are naturally distinct and have different roles; abortion is immoral; homosexuality is sinful; the Bible depicts factual events; God is in control of all things; and the job of evangelicals is to multiply the church and its influence). Small groups are where church leaders, informal and formal, taught regular folk how to match, and the members of Sunday Group developed an interactional routine that strengthened those matches.

## Plants That Match

In his book *Church Planters*, sociologist Richard Pitt writes that while church planting is nothing new, the model looks different nowadays. Whereas older denominational churches created clones, the new ones "take on the character of the religious communities that form them or the charismatic entrepreneurs they form around."[6] Further, according to Pitt, church planting is on the rise in the United States because it has become easier to plant a new church than to change or expand on an old one. Planting a new church is an easier gain for a few reasons. First, older churches that pivot to new audiences run the risk of losing long-standing members who pay the bills. Second, changes in the population can make a new church necessary. Third, church plants are better at attracting newcomers than are established churches. Finally, new churches appeal to young adults more than do older churches, and can also make younger people feel like they can be involved and take charge without the old guard in their way.

Welcome is a "seed plant" that received financial resources and people power from what church planters refer to as its "mother church," a Southern Baptist congregation that is almost exclusively White. Bird touched on Welcome's germination one spring morning when he expounded on the mustard seed in the Gospel of Matthew. That mustard seed, he preached, grew into a tree that supports the birds that sit on its branches. Welcome's origin story is like that mustard seed, he said. "It's a story of an idea and a meeting between men" that transformed into a big tree, almost overnight. That meeting evolved into the decision to plant Welcome, which made Bird, the approachable youth pastor, the founding figure of his very own church.

When Welcome first opened, it was listed as "Other/Nondenominational" in the local church directory, but the church is connected to the Southern Baptist Convention (SBC), an annual two-day convention and collection of nearly forty-seven thousand Baptist churches across the United States that share the SBC's core beliefs and ministry practices.[7] Welcome's governing structure reflected a growing trend in the Southern Baptist tradition to shift from congregational governance to an elder-led polity that gives elders, who are exclusively men and usually appointed by the pastor, outsized decision-making power. That structure of governance, according to columnist Rodney Kennedy of *Baptist News Global*, is a byproduct of a Calvinist "conservative resurgence" in Southern Baptism that elevates the role of the pastor, stresses order and stability over democratic governance, and diminishes the voices of women in the church (since women cannot be elders and are therefore formally excluded from the decision-making process).[8]

The Welcome plant began with its roots more firmly in the ground of the SBC than it let on, which proved appealing to churchgoers who were looking for a church that felt familiar without being dull and out of touch with the modern world. Members of the church who were at Welcome from the very beginning told me that over one hundred people showed up to Sunday worship on opening day. They were stunned by that turnout. Electing to have church on the gym floor of the Recreation Center was unusual in Oxford, and they were surprised to see the overwhelmingly positive response to that choice. Bird was ecstatic, but he also worried that the attendance might wane once the "swelling" went down, a term that one of Pitt's interviewees used to describe church plants that lose that hot-new-thing feeling.[9] Those worries ended up being unfounded.

Within a year, the number of regular attendees shot up to over three hundred. The church had attracted what social scientists and religious leaders call "church shoppers," or those who are in the market for a church experience that suits their sensibilities, beliefs, and taste in music. Some of those shoppers were "hoppers" who bounced between a number of churches, always on the lookout for what each had to offer week to week.[10] The other group were "transfers," or believers who had ties to a neighboring congregation in the region or the parent church.

After its first two years in operation, the Welcome regulars had settled into their new church home. The ones who stuck around had arrived by one of two paths. One path was made up of White Southern Baptists who had grown tired of their old church's lackluster gospel hymnals and aging, disengaged pastors. Most from this path were White married couples ranging from thirty to seventy years of age who had lived in Mississippi for most or all of their lives. Many of them knew Bird and Anne, or knew of them, before they visited Welcome.

Transplants were the other main group at Welcome. They were new to Oxford, or to Mississippi, and had found the church through a Google search or Facebook post, or from an acquaintance at work. Some were in their forties, but there were just as many transplants in their twenties and thirties. Unlike their elder Southern Baptist peers, the transplants did not have preexisting ties to Oxford and were at Welcome to make new friends. Most transplants were White, but there were Black, Latino, and Asian Americans who came to Welcome on this path, too. To many at Welcome, the church was clearly more diverse than the church's peer institutions in Oxford, but in terms of racial makeup, Welcome is not multiracial. A multiracial congregation is defined as a congregation in which no one racial or ethnic group comprises more than 80 percent of the participants, and Welcome did not meet that definition.[11]

Welcome was one of a handful of church plants that had caused a buzz in town. Two others, Lakeshore and The Vine, had opened in public, transitory venues that had a feel similar to that of the Recreation Center where Welcome met.[12] And like Welcome, both pledged to be a different kind of church than the congregations that planted them. In fact, several of the people I interviewed had visited or been part of either Lakeshore or The Vine before settling on Welcome. These plants were Welcome's biggest rivals, a position that Bird made clear when he told the church, in a tone of sarcasm, that they "will not hurt" his feelings if they "go check out one of those other churches." But those other churches, Bird warned, are nothing like Welcome.

Being a church for regular folk was the unofficial brand of Welcome, and it was a brand that my sociology of religion students picked up on when they carried out participant observations of religious congregations in the area. Every single student, every semester for three consecutive semesters, described Bird and the church he leads as "friendly" and "laid back." One student wrote, "They don't care what you wear, they just care that you're there," and another described Bird as "an outgoing guy with a good nature." The field notes from students who attended Lakeshore and The Vine, by contrast, were less about a warm vibe and more about middle-class signifiers. White "fraternity looking" college students, wrote one student, dominate Lakeshore, the satellite church that is based on sermons recorded and broadcasted from the mother church's location. And The Vine, students wrote, is a mixed-age, "clear spoken," and "studied" congregation of mostly White, middle-class people who dress well.[13]

Bird is proud of how his church compares to other plants in the community, but he wants it to stay midsized. Becoming a megachurch is "not the point," he told me. Welcome was planted to be a community where Christians learn to "do life together," he said. Indeed, Bird made clear on my many Sunday mornings that Welcome does not aspire to be like Lakeshore, which was on the brink of going mega. Lakeshore, he said from the church stage, offers an "amazing service," but he cautioned, "the pastor isn't even there!" "After three visits, you might still think he's there," Bird chided, "but he's not!" That pastor is live-streamed from another location. Bird shouted, "I'm here! I want to know *you*!"

Bird wants to see Welcome build more, not bigger churches. This means, as one perspicacious churchgoer, Ryan, explained, "Once the church gets too big, it's not going to go to two services or three more services every Sunday. It's going to stay at one service and start another church plant." Ryan was also clear about how the church planting philosophy differs from that of the emergent church. Emergent churches are unconcerned with preserving the "basis of church," he said. An emergent church might break off from another church because they don't agree with its interpretation of the Bible or because they want to explore a new set of beliefs or practices.[14] Welcome is not a church of exploration, he clarified. Welcome and its "mother church" match. When the mother church planted Welcome, it did so to pass a specific set of beliefs and values down to a diversifying community.

## A Plant for Regular Folk

When Bird and Anne first tossed around the idea of Welcome, they had one thing clear: they wanted it to be a church for "regular folk." They wanted it to be, in Anne's words, a "different Oxford than the one you find in *Invitation Oxford*," a local, glossy lifestyle magazine that covers high-profile bridal showers and the latest trends in fashion and food. That magazine, Anne implied, is not for "regular" people. *Invitation Oxford* features the kind of people who acquire party houses for football weekends and who can afford to live and attend church downtown. The folks that Welcome reaches are working people, not *those* people.

Planting a church for regular folk can feel like a radical undertaking in Oxford, a town that unabashedly caters to "legacy families," or White wealthy families with a history in one of the university's esteemed racially segregated sororities and fraternities.[15] Its downtown "Square" is a magnet for these families. It's the part of town where White sorority sisters spend their daylight hours shopping at expensive boutiques; where White fraternity brothers congregate in sports bars for big screen TVs, stiff mixed drinks, and cold beers; where White families socialize and stroll their babies around colorful storefronts, a colonial-style courthouse, and a Confederate monument that harkens back to Mississippi's antebellum, slave-owning heritage.

There were many at Welcome who felt disconnected from the Oxford scene, and that disconnection consistently took on an anti-elitist tone. When I asked Cora, an active member who was directing the children's ministries, what she thinks about living in Oxford, she touched on how it has changed: "Back when we first moved here, it was just real small, tight knit. And now it's grown. It's just totally different now." But, she clarified, "There's not anything just horrible about it. Jobs are good. [Welcome's] good. Schools are good." The thing that she doesn't like about it, she told me, is "the keeping up with the Joneses perspective of Oxford." Housing is unaffordable, she noted, and "it's hard as a woman here." She feels pressured to stay fit, nicely dressed, and forever young:

> You've got college girls. You've got stay-at-home moms—it's very in your face. It's almost like a "Real Housewives" feel. I know that sounds crazy but just, like, the Botox, the plastic surgery. . . .

White southern beauty standards are, without a doubt, legendary in Oxford, and these standards, according to interdisciplinary scholar Elizabeth Bronwyn Boyd, represent and act out a "bygone South" that upholds racial hierarchies and class privileges.[16] White girls and women, young and old, feel pressured to perform a particular, elite variety of femininity to fit in with the "It" crowd (i.e., White wealthy crowd), and Cora felt that pressure ease up at Welcome.[17] She doesn't feel like everyone is scrutinizing her clothes and makeup. "They are just happy to be there," she said, and that feels good.

Leah, a young White woman who was in Oxford for graduate school, reflected on the Sunday morning scene downtown: "Everyone is so concerned with what bag you're carrying; with the brand you're wearing." In California, where Leah grew up, "people cared about that stuff, but nowhere near as much as they do here," she said. "It's all about who you know and how much money you have—even the churches have paid parking!" she exclaimed. "I'm not against religion," she continued, "but it's upsetting that a church has reserved parking for members who can pay for it." Parking is free downtown on Sundays, but Leah was either unaware of that or was referring to game day weekends when churches rent out parking spots to football fans on Saturdays for extra cash.

Like others at Welcome, Leah appeared annoyed with what she considered the formal churches downtown, most of which are historic Mainline Protestant congregations that are part of church bodies that affirm LGBTQ+ people and ordain women into the priesthood (Episcopal, Presbyterian, and United Methodist). Leah described how between 9 and 11 a.m., women, men, and children filter into well-kept cornerstone churches in brand-new Sunday best outfits, implying that the liberal churches downtown cater to a different class bracket than Welcome. She was engaging in a form of indirect signaling that sociologist Lydia Bean charts in her book about the building blocks of evangelical political identity and support for the Republican Party.[18] Bird participated in that same kind of signaling on Sunday mornings.

One Sunday he preached that "The Church" with a capital C, not his church, is an inhospitable place to be. The Church has neglected working people, he said, and has spent too much time on "minor" issues like the clothing brands that people wear to the house of God. Welcome, he lectures, is unattached to this minor stuff. Welcome focuses on the major stuff—creating a church in which everyone, of every age, income, race, and ethnicity, feels equal in the eyes of God. Or, as Bird announced one Sunday at the top of service:

> Come as you are.
> Blue jeans, sweatpants!
> We don't care!
> This place is for regular folk like you!

Sarah, a White registered nurse in her thirties, mimicked what Bird preached, almost verbatim, when we met to talk over cold sandwiches and iced tea in a box store bakery. "A lot of people at church are just stuffy and stuck up," she said. "We're not stuffy," she smiled. "We have a 'Hey, come on in! We're glad to have ya' kinda thing going on." It "isn't about tithing, or about your Sunday best," another churchgoer explained. "It's about reaching out to people that need hope and love."

Angie, a newcomer to Oxford, chose Welcome because she appreciates its "come as you are" attitude. Welcome, she said, passes her litmus test for evangelism: she could invite a stripper to join her for service on

Sunday morning. Before moving to Oxford, Angie was part of a ministry that focused on sex workers in Dallas, Texas. From that experience, she embraced the evangelical narrative that "90 percent" of strippers are in that line of work because they have been raped, molested, or abandoned, or are single moms desperate to make ends meet.[19] "You know, no one just wakes up and says, 'I'm going to take my clothes off for a living,'" she attested. Getting to know strippers, praying for them, feeding them, talking to them in the locker room, changed her relationship with church. "I don't think I'll ever be able to go to a normal church again," Angie said. Angie thinks Welcome is unprepared for sex work ministries, but she believes that the people who lead, organize, and serve it have their heart in the right place. "It's young, and it's going to get there rightfully," she affirmed.

Churchgoers attribute the "come as you are" feeling to Bird. He is far from stuffy. He never wears a suit and tie, and "he doesn't try to put himself above you to make you feel like he's better than you," one of the church's founding members said. The church lovingly regards Bird as an "everyman's man," or as one churchgoer put it, "like Norm from Cheers": unpretentious, reliable, and good-natured. He has a knack for making working people feel seen, be it his infectious relatability, or how he delivers The Word in plain-spoken English. He also embodies muscular Christianity, or a mode of Christianity that places emphasis on manual labor, strength, and fearlessness.[20] He speaks kindly about blue-collar workers and shares anecdotes about his own working-class roots in the Mississippi Delta where his father, a man who "never wore ties," worked with his hands as a repairman.

On top of trumpeting his working-class roots, Bird preached that blue jeans were acceptable, even encouraged, at Welcome. During one service, he told a story about a funeral he attended in blue jeans. "Everybody was dressed better than me!" he yelled, "Some people were lookin' at me like 'huh?'—it was awkward." Bird cocked his head and clicked his tongue, a sound that signaled the moral of the story to come: "What you wear doesn't matter!" he yelled. "What matters is that you're covered in Jesus!" Bird ended his remarks about the funeral with a brief tangent about how "cool" it is to watch his wife Anne dress their kids in T-shirts and ball caps for church on Sunday. "If you have a problem with that, get over it."

Dave, who has fallen in and out of work and in and out of love with church, likes that Bird is a regular guy in jeans. He was uninterested in trying out a new church, but his wife Sharon convinced him to check out Welcome. She heard that a church was at the Recreation Center and wanted to see what that was like. "I didn't feel like an outcast," she explained. "It wasn't snooty." When Dave finally agreed to give it a try, he wore blue jeans and a T-shirt, thinking to himself, "if they can't accept me like this, this isn't the place for me." To his surprise, several people went out of their way to greet him. That small gesture of kindness was important to Dave, and he was comforted to see others wearing jeans. The bonus, he added, is that Bird preaches in blue jeans. A pastor who wears jeans is a pastor who says, "I don't care *who* walks through that door, and I don't care what they're wearing." Dave and Sharon have been at Welcome ever since. They even joined the Sunday Group that Frank leads in Maple Hill. Dave likes that he and his wife can wear what makes them comfortable, and they appreciate that Welcome brings people from a variety of social standings together.

## Small Seeds

Regular folk have to be coached into sameness, as well as be convinced that they should be doing more to help the church thrive. Much of that coaching takes place in small groups, the social branches of church where churchgoers forge an identification with one another and with the larger church plant enterprise to produce churches that match.

To obtain full membership at Welcome, churchgoers were expected to attend or facilitate a small group. Some small groups met to have informal Bible studies. Some were organized around a particular Christian ministries study, such as those of evangelical superstars like Beth Moore or David Platt. Some had a specific topic or theme on the agenda: for example, a group for parents about raising believers, a racial reconciliation group called Be the Bridge, and a group for individuals in recovery from drug and alcohol abuse. The topic of the small groups varied, but the structure and objective of each was to create space for churchgoers to get to know one another and fortify a Bible-believing identity together.

Ryan, a college graduate who grew up Baptist, always had something sophisticated to say about small groups. He was the one who had explained that the whole point of Welcome is to multiply, not to relocate to a larger facility and become mega. Small groups, he said, are integral to that multiplication. This is why Ryan thinks, "It'd be awesome if there were like twenty small groups going on every Monday night of every week, or some going on Wednesday night." It's simple math, he said: "If you have ten people in each of the twenty groups, you could have two hundred people in church that are meeting each week to build each other up and start other groups."

The people I got to know at small groups were adamant, like Ryan, that American evangelicalism needs these groups if it wants to protect traditional religious values from decimation. A few even suggested that small groups are essentially the lifeblood of Welcome and proposed that these are the spaces in which churchgoers are made into "disciples" who can protect the biblical foundations of evangelical Christianity. In what follows, I examine how Sunday Group bolstered enthusiasm for the church and its evangelist cause. I show how their discussions about salvation and the afterlife endorsed biblical sameness, or the performance of a uniform belief in the Bible that discourages critical contemplation.

### *Planting the Seeds of Sameness*

Sunday Group, the group where the bright yellow kitchen sponge took center stage, was the most well-attended meeting at Welcome. It had a reputation for being a place where churchgoers could learn about the Bible, eat good food, and have a good time. It was also the group where churchgoers conducted what sociologist Randall Collins refers to as "interaction ritual chains" that solidified and sanctified biblical sameness.[21] From week to week, Sunday Group came together face to face to engage in conversational routines that either culminated in the collective acknowledgment that God is omniscient or in deliberations about what else they could do to share the gospel with nonbelievers. These rituals proved to be as important to the maintenance of a Bible-believing identity as was prayer or a Sunday morning service—through these interactions, participants came together in the same space to focus on concerns that led to an enthusiastic identification with evangelical Christianity.

One Sunday, the group had a discussion about eternal damnation that had all the elements of a successful interaction ritual: it got the group to focus on being part of Welcome, and it spawned strong feelings of moral superiority that could be translated into action when the meeting was over. Ryan, who was known as the smart intellectual one, kicked off the ritual when he posed a rhetorical question about free will. "Are we predestined or not?" he asked. Before anyone could answer, Ryan answered his own question, describing it as a "circular answer." God is "omniscient and we humans understand time in a linear fashion. God sees time differently." This is why we cannot fully grasp His plans, he concluded. Humans have a limited perception of time, and this limitation explains why God already knows what will happen to us. He knows our will because He designed it, Ryan professed.

Sarah took the floor next and asked a question that struck me as provocative, which was unusual at Welcome. While peering in Ryan's direction, she inched forward in her seat and asked, "But does he know why I am here, but not in another country?" She stuttered before continuing, "What if, what if we don't get to *them* [in another country]?" Visibly pleased by the question, Ryan went on to assure her that "everyone will be given a chance [to be born again] before they die." They may hear about God from someone else, he reasoned, or something might happen "inside them." God will give them an opportunity, he assured her, and it will be on that person to decide if they accept His invitation. Sarah leaned back in her chair as if struck by big important news. "Ah ha!!" she yelled. "They don't need someone to tell them! God can do it! I had never thought of it like this! It totally makes sense!"

After an energized back and forth about how Ryan's view of predestination "makes sense" from around the room, the group carried on with their discussion of evangelism. The animated exchange that follows is an extension of the shorthand notes I took on how the ritualized "interplay," to use sociologist and symbolic interactionist Erving Goffman's term, unfolded.[22] The pace of the interplay quickened, and group participants often overlapped in their utterances and finished each other's sentences. It was a dynamic that made jotting every single word down impossible, but the gist of what was expressed is here:

SARAH: What about hell? Does God know who is going to hell before they know—

NATHAN: Already knows—

SARAH: Then why evangelize?

(Sarah looked around the room and others watched her looking)

ANNE: He can present himself [as Ryan said earlier], but—

SARAH: But that's our job—

ANNE: There's beauty in that, in doing our job. We get to be part of the story.

NICOLE: Does he already know that they're not going to change their minds?

JOAN: He wants us to reach people.

NICOLE: When you're born, does he know—

RYAN: He knows everything. He's already seen the map. It's nuts!

When Ryan yelled, "It's nuts!" smiles spread like wildfire across the room. A few cackled in a gesture of delight. The interaction ritual had reached its climax. Order was restored. The group had found release from that tricky question—why evangelize?—on what Goffman terms the "front region" of church life, or the social arena in which they were paying close attention to what each other said.[23] In this front region, they maintained and embodied certain standards that actualized the idea that they were all in agreement.[24]

Ryan's remark that God's ability to know everything is "nuts" was akin to the amen of a prayer. It gave the group an opportunity to close the ritual with a response that safeguards sameness: God knows everything. He knows who will go to heaven and who will go to hell. He knows who will be introduced to the gospel. There is no reason for Christians to worry or feel guilty about those who end up in hell. Christians evangelize so that they can be part of God's story. Those aspects of evangelicalism, according to the group's informal leaders Ryan and Anne, are biblical and therefore indisputable.

That same evening, another lively deliberation about heaven, and who they might see, recognize, or know once they get there took place at Sunday Group. Vicki, who lost her father when she was a teenager, was the first to pose a practical question that had been on her mind: will her father know her, and will she know him? Nathan, a fairly quiet participant who comes to group with his wife Sarah, scanned the room before assuring Vicki that her father will recognize her in her older age. "They can see us," he said. Several group members nodded agreeably.

But Anne challenged Nathan on that point. "God doesn't want the deceased to see or worry about their loved ones when they get to heaven," she said resolutely. Ryan spoke up in confidence, "We'll know them, but how, I don't know."

"What if you've been married twice? Will you have two husbands [in heaven]?" Nicole, a mom in her thirties, inquired hesitantly. After someone muttered that marriage is obsolete in heaven, the back and forth grew sharp and swift.

VICKI: You'll know. I think you'll know.
RYAN: The question is—will we care?
NATHAN: Exactly!
FRANK: These discussions are from our—
RYAN: Finite human lives.
SARAH: I'm going to love everybody like I do my husband and my kids. Maybe even better.
[short pause]
CINDY: We're going to be so busy singing at his throne—we won't notice who is around and who isn't!

After Cindy's remark, which functionally dismissed Nicole's sensitive question, Lynn, who had been silent the entire time, intervened with a joke about the homework that Ryan needs to do before the next meeting. "Three pages, double spaced!" she teased. Others in the room giggled with her. No one mentioned the verses in the Gospel of Mark that speak directly to Nicole's question.[25] The subject was dropped. The group arrived at the unspoken consensus that the discussion had gotten out of control and that it was time to move on.

The dialogues about "major" issues, such as the afterlife, were among the most energizing interaction rituals of Sunday Group, and these rituals unfolded more or less the same each time. First, one or two people would take it on themselves to make a statement for the group to respond to. Following this, another person (usually one of the women) would make a request for guidance about what to believe about the topic at hand. When this moment arrived, the attention space grew focused and electrified. Even the shyest members participated in the game-like rush to pose questions or make statements that deflected collective reflection and uncertainty. The swell of participation reinforced the importance of the subject in question, making it, by consequence, one of authority for Bible-believing identity itself. But before the ritual could become unmanageable or unpredictable—such as the conversation about whether a person will have two spouses in heaven—informal leaders of the group (the ones considered most knowledgeable or connected to church leadership), stepped in and ended it. They directed the group toward an answer. God has a plan. Humans cannot understand His plan. To be a believer is to believe that.

The act of spreading the seeds of Bible-believing Christianity was another major issue that routinely held the attention space of Welcome. Like the emotionally charged interplays that transpired at Sunday Group, the next section shows that talk about growing the Welcome plant was a key source of biblical sameness in the church.

### *Spreading the Seeds of Sameness*

When Frank held up the sponge at our Sunday Group meeting, it was not wearing blue jeans. But we all knew that the sponge was the church and that the droplets of water symbolized the boundless acts of evangelism that can turn America back in a Christian direction. Those droplets, the group determined, can take many forms. They can be a church invite, a short prayer, a Bible verse, a healing hand on a hospital floor, a warm meal for a neighbor in hard times, or an entirely new small group ministry.

Doing more to expand church was a mainstay of Bird's spiel on Sunday mornings. Occasionally Bird's tone about what the church was doing, or should be doing, was encouraging. He might tell the church that he was pleased to have a good turnout at a particular outreach event or express gratitude to the volunteers who made it happen. Most of the time, however, Bird's tone was harsh. He criticized Christians who, to use his words, "just clock in and clock out of church" and he consistently preached that he expects *his* church to step up and do more for God.

Bird had a talent for making churchgoers feel unproductive. I heard churchgoers wonder aloud about what else they could do for the church, especially the ones who were already involved in small groups. Hannah, a stylish woman in her early forties with long wispy hair and a pronounced southern drawl, was anxious one day after church let out. Earlier that morning, Bird had preached about the "debt" we owe to Jesus. "Jesus was beaten beyond recognition," he said, and if the church wants to repay that debt, it has to "run after" people. Hannah loved that sermon, she told me, but she had doubts about how to go about the running part. I didn't have any advice to offer, so she turned to Maura, a core member of the church who was sweeping the gym floor with us. "I want to do something, but I don't know where to start or what to do!" Hannah cried out. Maura looked at her with sympathetic eyes. Hannah's pitch grew irritated, "I just want to do something!"

The pressure to do more for the church, and for the cause of evangelism, even had me contemplating what more I could do. I prepared dishes for potlucks, volunteered at outreach events, attended small groups and Sunday services, and yet still felt like I was missing a chance to be more involved. "Maybe I could volunteer to do the church set up at 7:00 a.m. on Sunday mornings, or run the Connect table, or make coffee for the early morning crowd," I wrote in my field notes. Welcome was a greedy institution that sought to develop high levels of routine organizational participation.[26] The options for service to the church were endless. Some were eager to do more. Others felt guilty about not doing enough.

Doing more was a regular focus of attention at Sunday Group. It was the focus of the very first meeting of the semester—the one when the group playfully decided to skip Chandler's book—and it stayed on the agenda for the entirety of the semester. At that first meeting, Zach, Cora's husband, initiated an interaction ritual about doing more when he voiced what he considers the purpose of a small group: to create new leaders in discipleship. After sharing a little about the "van ministry" that he and his wife do with Bird (they pick up drunk college students from downtown bars and give them a ride home in the church van free of charge), Zach reminded the group about the evangelist message that Bird preaches: go out and seek people, get to know someone new, and share the gospel with them through a relationship. That message, he told the group, "slides in one ear and out the other." Zach's face turned a dark shade of pink as he admonished churchgoers who are "clocking in and clocking out" on Sundays. It bothers him that people will go to church or participate in small groups but do nothing else.

Zach's observations about apathy in the church stirred a spirited debate about breaking out of one's comfort zone, how a believer will know when to do it, and whether everyone can or should be doing more. Big Green, a tall, sturdy man who assists Bird with a working men's ministry lunch on Mondays, spoke up in defense of the Sunday Christians who are, in Zach's words, "just clocking in." We all have our roles, he retorted. If someone isn't doing something new, then God has not asked them to. Big Green may be right, Zach admitted, but some people are lazy and ignore the voice of God. Plus, Zach argued, being idle and waiting to hear Him speak is an excuse to be "deaf to the message."

Zach choked up, and through tearful eyes announced that he and Cora had decided to organize a new small group. Glancing over at the first timers, Javier and Lucía, Zach said that if he were in their shoes, he would not come back. The group was too large, he said, and that can make it hard for newcomers like them to feel like they belong. The space fell silent. It was one of the most charged small group moments I had ever witnessed at Welcome. Then, practically one by one, members of the group took turns expressing what founding sociologist Emile Durkheim referred to as "collective conscience" in his theory of religion, the division of labor, and social order.[27] They told Zach and Cora that they would be sorely missed before reassuring them that they were right for wanting to take church elsewhere.

By that point, it was past 8:00 p.m. and the study needed to come to a close. Bird suddenly appeared at the front door, mumbled something about there being "a bunch of lost folks at church," and then bragged about a bouncer he saw at a downtown bar donning a Welcome T-shirt. "Someone asked me, 'Can you believe that a bouncer at a bar was wearing your shirt?'" Bird looked around the room grinning ear to ear. "Things are accepted in Oxford that aren't accepted in other parts of Mississippi." There is an arts community, there's drama, theater, and a film festival, he said. Oxford is like the city of Ephesus, which leaders of Sunday Group had earlier described as a city of greed and sexual immorality. It's a city that needs to be saved.

To close the meeting, the group shifted away from Bird and back over to Zach and Cora, the youngish married couple who want to turn a city of sin in a Godly direction. Frank asked the couple to come up for prayer, and without more direction, Zach and Cora knelt near an oblong footstool at the front of the room. Everyone stood up and laid hands on the couple, or on a person who could reach them. Frank thanked "the Lord for all that they do for the community" and asked God to guide them as they carry out their ministries. Others, both men and women, took turns praying for the couple, describing them as "courageous" and "brave." That prayer was long. Long enough for a few arms to go numb.

## The Microsociology of Plants

Thousands of churches close annually due to waning attendance, and many more struggle to keep their doors open.[28] White Mainline Protestants struggle the most, but White evangelicals have experienced drastic drops in their numbers too. According to a 2020 Public Religion Research Institute (PRRI) census on religion, there has been a 9 percent decline in the population of Americans who identify as White evangelical since 2006.[29] Even the Bible Belt is losing churchgoers. An estimated 30 percent of Southern Baptists seldom or never attend church, and in 2018, the General Social Survey found that 45 percent of White Southerners only attend church about once a year.[30] "If 'lapsed evangelical Protestant' were a denomination, it would be the largest religious body in the South," historian Daniel K. Williams writes in *Christianity Today*.[31]

Churches in Mississippi are faring better than most. It's the most churchgoing state in the country, and more than 60 percent of its churchgoers attend almost weekly. Yet despite the favorable conditions, there are pockets of the state, such as Oxford, where evangelicals have lost ground. The Welcome response to this loss was to plant a church for regular folk, have the church match its mother, and train people within it to be the church in their respective communities. This strategy mimics the national evangelical call to expand their beliefs and influence into as many different shapes and sizes of church as possible.

Previous research on the relationship between interaction rituals, social solidarity, and congregational vitality finds that congregations that create opportunities for individuals to be performers (i.e., through dancing, praising, or praying out loud during service) are more likely to increase emotional energy, or what Durkheim calls "collective effervescence," which in turn increases congregational attendance and retention.[32] But research on the recent wave of church plants has missed how the ebb and flow of a conversation about belief, or about "running after the lost," can make or break a church's ability to replicate its ideological franchise. This chapter has shown that interactional rituals in small groups are what produce and retain conservative religious beliefs within a corporate model of church that capitalizes on replication.

At Welcome, the interaction rituals of small groups energized and mobilized churchgoers to scatter the seeds of Welcome. This is because, as anthropologist James Bielo puts it, small groups are much more than where "just talking" happens."[33] Small groups are where churchgoers act out and build what Goffman refers to as the "interaction order" of their existence.[34] Through ritualized talk about eternal damnation, reaching the lost, and the afterlife, the participants of Sunday Group established a working consensus that what is—as well as what is not—communicated in these groups should be the basis of their faith, their church, and their community.[35] They obliged one another to accept the project of sameness without question, and habitually returned to the consensus that critical dialogue is incompatible with what Southern Baptists deem biblical truth. That is, they created a situation in which each of them was to appear as if they agreed, even if they didn't. Or, as Goffman might say, they engaged in a project of "impression management" that regulated the meaning of biblical truth and how to conform to it.[36] The most authoritative figures in the group facilitated that project. They were the ones who set the parameters on what was up for debate, what sorts of questions had gone too far, as well as how deep a conversation could go before going over an invisible yet powerful line.

Small groups also strengthened the Sunday morning message that "believers" are supposed to take church into everyday life. Small groups, then, were sites of evangelical mobilization or where an activist orientation could take shape. Hence, the people who attended small groups were also the ones who were most likely to volunteer for the church's outreach events, set up its Christmas party, station themselves at the Welcome booth on Sunday mornings, make coffee for staff, and organize the annual vacation Bible school. Their voices dominate this book. They were the ones who believed that there was always something more, something else, that the church could be doing to bring America closer to God.

The next chapter examines how the church implemented "welcome talk" that emphasized extending its table of love and acceptance to racially marginalized communities. It shows that while welcome talk made Welcome churchgoers feel more open and inclusive than other churches in town, it gave White congregants the best seats at the church's allegedly longer table.

2

# We Don't Build Walls, We Build Longer Tables

Bird looks serious when he preaches about walls. He'll tilt his head to the side, peer out the corner of his eyes, and holler out a message like this one I heard on an ordinary Sunday:

> I'm about to say something that might make some of you hot under the collar.
> But just hear me out now—
> God doesn't tell us to build walls!
> He calls on us to build longer tables!

I was stunned the first time I heard Bird bring up walls. It was 2016 and Trump was headline news for his campaign to "build a big, beautiful wall" along the U.S./Mexico border. I was also perplexed by the "hot under the collar" line that Bird had used—an idiom that refers to being agitated, uptight, or annoyed by something. Was this a cautious objection to the White evangelical support for Trump's xenophobic border patrol policies? Or was Bird simply encouraging churchgoers to let their guards down, fellowship, and have a meal together?

One day after church was over, I stopped Bird in the corridor outside to talk about walls, trying my best to make a politically neutral comment about how it brings Trump's campaign to my mind. Bird bent towards me and whispered that he disagrees with Christians who say that *all* Mexicans need to "go back home." A member of Welcome had posted "Build a wall!" on Facebook, and Bird recounted that he pulled this man aside and had a long talk with him about it. "You can't be doing that," Bird had explained. "We have Hispanic people at our church—we're a multiethnic community." He has to handle these incidents carefully, he told me. "If someone feels like they're being attacked, they're not going to listen to you." For him, being careful means addressing racist behavior on a case-by-case basis in private. Not at the structural level in front of the church for everyone to hear.

Bird shouted, "We don't build walls, we build longer tables," on subsequent Sundays, but never disclosed his criticism of the proposed U.S./Mexico border wall. One time, he asked the church to pray for a married couple from Mexico. The couple, he explained, were members of Welcome and were about to embark on a trip to Mexico to renew their visas. They were "going through the proper channels" to immigrate, he said, and needed prayers for a safe return. This couple, by Bird's account, were loyal to America, and to Welcome. They believe that America is the greatest country in the world and are helping the church "reach other Hispanics," he attested. They had, in other words, passed what sociologists Glenn Bracey and Wendy Leo Moore describe as a "utility-based race test," which is a test that White people use to ensure that incoming people of color are willing to serve the interests of White people in a space.[1]

When I prompted churchgoers to reflect on what they hear in the "walls" message, national borders or the immigrant members of their church seldom came up. For them, the walls metaphor stood for how close-minded churches behave—too quick to judge, too stuck on tradition, too cliquish, too uppity, and too segregated by race. Sarah explained that when Bird preaches "We don't build walls, we build longer tables," she hears "Y'all come on! Everybody can come!—It doesn't matter your background, where you're from, what mistakes you've made in the past. Everybody's welcome." Other churchgoers made the exact same point. Welcome is laid back, they insist. Nobody is better, or holier, than another. All are sinners. All are welcome. Or as Bird preached one day:

> We're a church of all nations!
> We don't build walls, we build longer tables!
> No matter your race, your gender.
> No matter how broken you are.
> Even if you don't believe in Jesus, we want you to be here.

***

Church of all nations is a theological phrase that has roots in the Great Commission. Yet when said in the contemporary context of a White church, it takes on a deterministic understanding of race that conflates race with ethnicity and national origin.[2] White evangelicals invoke the church of all nations motto to make the case that racial inclusion is part of a divine plan to spread the gospel around the globe.[3] But scholars of race and religion have pointed out that evangelicals are steadfast in their commitment to protect the church's standing as an all-White space, or a space where White people use their authority and control to decide who can be in the space and what actions, sensibilities, and beliefs are permissible in the space.[4]

Regardless of what evangelical churchgoers and their leaders intend to get out of their pledges to diversity, *how* they put their practice of diversity into action is significant. The organizational pursuit of diversity in everyday interactions, church teachings, and sermons can either chip away at racial dominance in multiracial spaces, or to the contrary, make the scaffolding of White dominance hard to see and therefore impossible to remedy.[5]

This chapter examines how Welcome puts its promise to build longer tables into action. It shows how the church staged "welcome talk," which I define as a twist on diversity talk that amplifies a commitment to and success at achieving racial and ethnic diversity, while eclipsing reflective dialogue about what diversity is, what diversity achieves, or why it matters.[6] Welcome talk is akin to what sociologists Joyce Bell and Douglas Hartman term "happy talk," or talk that makes it difficult for people to consider troubling social inequalities in a meaningful way.[7] Yet different from happy talk, my concept of welcome talk specifies how talk that exaggerates diversity circumvents critical reflections on what it takes to meaningfully work toward racial inclusivity. Further, welcome talk works in tandem with small talk. It makes it easier to evade conversations about race, even when the situation calls for it.[8]

The next section shows how churchgoers think about the cause for multiracial unity at Welcome. It examines how they perceive the walls of a Black/White racial binary in their everyday lives and shows how churchgoers embrace the idea that Welcome is ready to "build longer tables" in a town that they believe is ready to move past racial divisions.[9]

## The Walls of Race

When I asked churchgoers what being a church of all nations means to them, they almost always brought up that Welcome is trying to bring different races, especially Black and White people, together. Bringing different races together under the same roof to worship God is hard, they point out, but the church tries.

Claire, a White woman in her early twenties who had been church shopping, chose Welcome for its diversity. She visited shortly after moving to Oxford and, of all the churches she tried, Welcome was the most racially and ethnically diverse. She reflected on that first visit:

> I sat down behind a couple, and it was a biracial couple. And I thought, that's cool. I just thought, "I think they probably would have been uncomfortable at the church I was in last Sunday." And so that kind of put me at ease, and I thought maybe this could be the place for me. I just looked around and I saw, I think I saw Natalie and Earn [a Black couple], and I just saw people like interacting with each other. I think I heard two different languages spoken that Sunday too. I think I heard someone speaking Spanish, and a language I didn't recognize. And I thought, you know, that's a sign for me. I could give this place a chance for a few weeks.

Welcome was the closest thing Claire could find to the multiculturalism she had grown accustomed to abroad while in South Asia working for the Peace Corps. By the time we did the interview, she had been at Welcome for a little over two months and had been participating in its racial reconciliation group, Be the Bridge, for most of that time. She appreciates the multiracial mission of Welcome, even though she was unsure of what exactly it was or meant. To her, the most important thing was that the church believes, like she does, that interracial worship in the church is what God intended.

Benjamin, a lawyer in his forties who identifies with his Indigenous heritage, transferred to Welcome from another Southern Baptist church. He also thinks it's "cool" to be at a church that recognizes the biblical reasons of interracial unity.

> We visited and we felt like that—even if that it was not already attained at that point, it was something that at least commonly we agreed on. We believe that if Christians of all ethnic groups were going to be worshipping Christ in heaven eventually, we ought to be doing it here, too. And that it doesn't make sense that we're divided in the way that we are.

After noting his reasons for joining Welcome, Benjamin brought up racial segregation and said that when he arrived in Oxford for college in the early 2000s, he felt like he was stepping back in time. Black people "weren't particularly welcome on the Square—the White community was over there, and the Black community was over there [on another side of the Square], and that was pretty much it." Benjamin was referring to the Black churches and neighborhood located near the Square in what was historically called "Freedmen Town," the part of Oxford that African Americans developed after being released from slavery at the end of the Civil War.[10] There was no mixing at the bars, at restaurants, at church, or even on campus. "It just blew me away," Benjamin said.

Benjamin's recollection of racial segregation was echoed in what Ray, an elderly White member of the church, observed when he was growing up in Mississippi.

> Back in our little hometown, there were central railroad tracks right through the middle of the town. And on one side, simply speaking, were like six thousand Blacks. On the other side, six thousand Whites. And the business community right by the railroad tracks on the White side. During the day, there was tremendous crossover. All the Blacks would cross the tracks to work at the White businesses, or to work as domestic help in White homes. And back then, since the Black population was so poor, they were glad to have any work, including domestic help. So even poor White families tended to have a nanny.

Ray paused and cautioned against people who pass judgment on the South: "That's just the way life was," he said. "Nobody even really questioned it. . . . The Whites just thought that the Blacks preferred it that way."

Ray attended the University of Mississippi (UM) when the Civil Rights Movement was taking shape. He was there in 1962 when the Supreme Court ruled that it was illegal to bar James Meredith, a young African American U.S. Air Force veteran, from the all-White university. Mississippi Governor Ross Barnett was vehemently opposed to racial integration, as were many White students at the segregated university.[11] In the lead-up to the Court's ruling, Barnett avowed in a statewide televised broadcast that the state "will not surrender to the evil and illegal forces of tyranny . . . [and] no school will be integrated in Mississippi" while he was governor.[12] President John F. Kennedy sent a small contingent of U.S. deputy marshals to ensure the safety of Meredith as he registered for classes, but the marshals were blocked by state politicians and troopers who were under the direction of Barnett. Kennedy had to increase the number of federal law enforcement substantially. When Meredith registered for classes at UM, White Mississippians were incensed. They held riots on campus for several days. Two bystanders were killed and more than two hundred soldiers and marshals injured.[13]

Ray thought it was odd that civil rights activists were demanding change. It was normal for a university to be segregated, he said, and African Americans "seemed happy" at the Black colleges in the state. Reflecting on the events surrounding Meredith's enrollment, Ray recounted:

> No Whites—I mean almost none—were excited about the concept. After a few weeks of being frisked three or four times on the way to class every day, and the tear gas had washed away through the ether, and the violence had settled down, it was business as usual again. But it took a few weeks for the marshals and the National Guard to quit having a tight lockdown on the town. You'd still go to class, but it was different. Being searched and frisked on the way, to and from.

Ray acknowledged that White resistance to basic civil rights was an unchristian thing to do, but he didn't feel that White students were the main culprits of the violence. White students were simply defending the life they had always known, he insisted. One separated by what a founding figure of American sociology, W. E. B. Du Bois, termed "the color line," a line that legally dictated where Black people could be, when, and under what circumstances.[14] Ray concluded his version of racial integration at UM to underscore a point that others were making: Oxford has made progress and a racially "mixed" church like Welcome, to use his words, is moving the community in the right direction.

Sampson, a delivery driver in his late 30s, joined Welcome because he wants to overcome racism in the state. He explained:

> I had a White guy tell me, "If we want to see change in Mississippi, it has to start here in Oxford." So many things have happened in Oxford that

> influenced the rest of the state. If we could just grasp that—that okay, if we really want unity, we can start unity. And others can see it.

Bird invited Sampson onto the leadership team, almost immediately. Sampson had reservations about it at first. He was unsure about being the only person of color in a room of White leaders. But racial discomfort is familiar territory for Sampson. In a tone of exasperation, Sampson explained, "I've gone places where I was the only Black person in two or three hundred people. I've had White Christians refuse to shake my hand." The way he sees it, racialized discomfort is a tiny price to pay for interracial unity. Sampson continued, "There are areas in Mississippi, to this day, where I wouldn't be welcomed to go . . . simply because I look different." He wants to see that mindset change, and he was proud of being part of a church that wants to usher that progress forward.

Sampson believes that Welcome is that place where racists can "come in, hear the gospel message, and open up to the spirit of God." He shared the following scenario:

> Let's say you didn't like Black people and you come to [Welcome] on a Sunday that I have to preach. Now you have a choice. You can stay and listen, or you can get up and leave. Why?—because they've got a Black dude up there preaching.

Sampson took on the voice of a hypothetical churchgoer who would be angry about having him, a Black pastor, lead a service but stuck around:

> Maybe the way I was thinking about Black people, or Mexican people, or whoever. Maybe I had it wrong. Maybe I need to reevaluate myself. Maybe they aren't so bad after all.

Sampson knows White people who "didn't even like Black people" before attending Welcome. Now those people go out of their way to shake his hand. "Some even hug me," he added optimistically. Sampson explained that the spirit of God has made them "self-aware," and that he feels blessed to be the one who lights that spirit. Plus, he added with a touch of confidence, "No one has gotten up and walked out the door when I'm preaching." Welcome is a White church, he said, but not the Whitest or most racist space he's ever been in.

White churchgoers credit Welcome for showing them that God calls them to be a "church of all nations." Sarah, for example, admitted that hearing the church of all nations motto made her cognizant of her racial biases. When she thinks of her kids growing up and being married, she still envisions them with White partners, never with people of color. But through Welcome, she has come to accept that she has a Christian duty to open her heart to people regardless of skin color or nationality. That change of heart, she said, made her realize that her daughter could, hypothetically, fall in love with a man of color. Understanding that possibility, and learning to accept it, is what being part of a "church of all nations" had given her.

Maura, one of Welcome's first Black members, values the mission of Welcome but she also understands why Black people are wary of a predominantly White church. In our private interview, she recounted how she used to stay away from the downtown Square and from churches like Welcome. She was trying to avoid the slights, insults, and indignities that take a disproportionate toll on Black Americans. Since joining Welcome, Maura has been venturing out into White spaces and has even taken her kids to shop downtown. Most of the time she has a pleasant experience. White people speak to her, and some are familiar faces from church, she said. But White people still make her uneasy. They made her feel that way on a recent trip to an ice cream shop with her kids.

> My kids were having so much fun, laughing and talking. They could care less about what was going on around them. But me being me, I'm always observing what's going on. I could just see [White] people staring at them, frowning.

Those looks made Maura feel like she had to leave the ice cream shop earlier than she wanted to. Situations like that, she said, are ordinary, and they are the kinds of situations that remind her of why she attends church with White people. She wants to stimulate change for her children's sake, and she thinks she can do that best in a church where Black and White people come together under the same roof to worship God.

Amani, who I met in the church's racial reconciliation group, liked Welcome's all nations mantra for a related reason. She and her husband came to Welcome on a spiritual quest for what she called "racial healing" in a white supremacist world. Her husband Brian was less than enthusiastic about doing that healing at Welcome. In our private interview, he recounted having a "blah" feeling when Amani showed him a picture of Welcome on Facebook. "I wasn't really feeling it," he laughed, but he agreed to give it a try. There were hardly any Black people there, but he met enough people of color to feel safe. When he and Amani joined the racial reconciliation group (Be the Bridge)—or what Brian jokingly referred to as "the Black group"—he grew fond of Welcome. Now he thinks "it's cool."

Welcome was less hostile than the other White spaces that Amani has to be in. The school where she taught didn't even attempt the talk of racial inclusion. It was, by her account, an unapologetically White school in every sense of the term. It overlooked Amani for promotions, excluded her from work parties, and repeatedly asked her to explain herself to White parents who were "upset that a Black teacher with natural hair was in charge of a classroom." That school wore her down. It twisted her hard work into an object of discrimination, and that was frustrating. When Trump was elected, her frustration morphed into downright anger. Welcome, she said, has soothed that anger. She has met nice White people there who sit next to her on Sundays and who greet her and her children with warm, friendly smiles. A few of them even signed up for what her husband called "the Black group." They might be uninterested in having deep discussions about race, but still, she reasoned, they were showing up to a group about improving race relations, which was above and beyond what other White people in her life have done or will ever do.

***

Across the board, the people who make up Welcome are pleased to be part of a church that purports to tear down the walls of race, but they seldom carved out space to come to a shared understanding of what tearing down those walls could look like. For churchgoers of color and a handful of White allies, tearing down the walls of race was a project of racial repair oriented toward lessening the pain that racism causes and changing the hearts and minds of racist White people. For most White churchgoers, however, tearing down the walls of race was largely a performance of welcome talk. They talked about wanting to be diverse, about how Welcome is more diverse than most, and about the biblical foundations of multiracial worship. They focused less on diversity in recruitment and inclusivity, and more on how being in a church that says it wants to be diverse makes them feel good about themselves and the image of God they worship.

The next section shows how churchgoers made sense of falling short of their goal to be a multiracial church. Some argued that the church is doing all it can to make racial minorities feel welcomed, but that segregation is, on some level, inevitable. Others had an entirely different take on why the church is incapable of fulfilling its "dream" to be a multiracial community of believers. They suggested that the church puts emphasis on its image as a welcoming congregation but neglects the hard work of rectifying racism.

## The Walls of Welcome Talk

Talk about diversity being "appealing," "fantastic," or "a great idea" was widespread at Welcome. But churchgoers were unable or unwilling to articulate what, exactly, diversity is or what White people can do to make diversity "happen," as several put it. That is, instead of focusing on concrete transformation in how the church conducts itself, the church did what the university in sociologist James Thomas's study did: it practiced diversity rhetoric that sees "minority representation as the final, rather than first, step toward a more just and fair society."[15]

Welcome repeated that it wanted to tear down the walls of race, but its White congregants were averse to addressing how White Christians in the South built and maintain those walls. Only one interviewee raised the report that the Southern Baptist Theological Seminary released in 2018, which acknowledges that the SBC was formed in 1845 by slaveholders who had broken from abolitionist Baptists in the lead-up to the Civil War because they were theologically and economically invested in upholding an institution that brutalized human beings who were racialized as Black.[16] Further, no one addressed how White Christians sustained Jim Crow segregation, the legal enforcement of racial segregation in the South, which began immediately after the Civil War and continued until civil rights activists determinedly mobilized for change in the 1960s.[17] Instead, when I prompted interviewees to reflect on what the church could do to actualize interracial harmony, they suggested that the church was doing the best it could and argued that segregation is inevitable.

Matthew, who directs praise and worship, brought up the inevitably of racial segregation when I asked what the church can do to achieve its dream to be racially diverse. According to him, the church isn't diverse because "birds of a feather flock together."[18] In an attempt to validate that point, he recalled that Rev. Dr. Martin Luther King Jr. had "said something" about segregation being unmistakable on Sunday mornings, and then explained that "there are some studies that show that in our social world, we're attracted to people who are similar to us, who have similar ideologies and views."[19]

Other White churchgoers maintained that segregation is hard to dismantle, especially in the South. Cora, who likes seeing people of different ethnicities at Welcome, thinks that racial segregation is a custom born from habit. In the South, she said, "You have your Black church, you have your White church, you have your Korean church, you have your Hispanic church, and I don't know that people are comfortable enough to come together as one." People get in their "comfort zone," she insisted, "and it can be weird to leave." Emma, a recent college graduate, touched on a similar theme:

> There are African American churches, and there are White churches. Not because African American people don't invite White people, and not because White people don't invite African American people. It just ends up being that way.

"It's a vicious cycle," her husband added. "People are just stuck in their ways."

There were, however, a few White churchgoers who refused to accept that segregation is unavoidable. Those churchgoers used terms like "white supremacy" when they grappled with the root causes of racial segregation and were also the ones to offer solutions that stretched beyond welcome talk—or talk that exaggerates the church's stated commitment to inclusivity.

Brooklyn, another recent college graduate, said that being a multiracial church has to be done with intention and that Welcome was not being intentional enough. "Instead of coming into a community, setting up a church, and saying, 'Everybody fit into this,'" the church has to be "students of its context." It has to do its research on how white supremacy and racial segregation have been state sponsored, financially driven, and church sanctioned. It has to be thoughtful about how it addresses current high-profile racist incidents.

When Brooklyn heard that Bird was opening a multiracial church in Oxford, she was thrilled. "I was like, 'I'm there, that sounds awesome!'" Bird had been Brooklyn's youth pastor at Welcome's parent church, and she knew that he had traveled the world on mission trips. It made sense to her that a multiethnic church "was his heart." Plus, at that point in her life, she thought that building a multiethnic church was simple: get White, Black, and Brown people together in the same building to worship God.

Brooklyn's perspective on what it takes to achieve multiracial unity changed in the student-led Be the Bridge (BTB) group that she did with other students on the university campus. In that group, Brooklyn and her peers went through Morrison's BTB guide together, discussed it at length, and came to the realization that White churches produce "a lot of hurt" that White Christians ignore.[20] Brooklyn credits her change in perspective to the deep conversations—sometimes difficult, sometimes painful—that she and her student peers of different races had about systemic racism. They had hard conversations in that group, about Trump, about mass incarceration, and about anti-Black police violence. Those kinds of conversations about race were absent at Welcome.

Brooklyn started to doubt Welcome's authenticity when Donald Trump ran for president. She was shocked to learn that her churchgoing peers could boast about being a racially and ethnically diverse church and then show their support for Trump on social media for everyone to see. Trump encourages the church to sin, she said. Those posts made Brooklyn feel associated with sin, and it made her question Welcome's multiracial platform. On top of that, she pointed out, there were cops who were coming to church in full uniform. She asked rhetorically, "We've got a lot of Black people coming to the church who are actually quite terrified of cops, right now. Is that really the best thing for the members of our church?"

The welcome talk that punctuates the church, Brooklyn and others implied, had made it difficult for a race consciousness to blossom. In fact, it had the opposite effect. It allowed the church to neglect Black congregants in the name of a "play nice" rule, a pervasive, albeit unspoken, communication practice that perpetuates what sociologists Anne Warfield Rawls and Waverly Duck term "tacit racism." The church discouraged honest talk about what the church can or should be doing to end racism.[21]

Welcome talk also gave White churchgoers permission to be ambivalent or confused about the point of diversity itself.[22] For example, Chancey, a White homeschool mom who attended BTB, told me that it was unclear why, exactly, the church should care about diversity. When I asked her opinion of multiracial inclusion, she stumbled through her answer, shifting from "I like the idea" to "I'm not sure why it matters." She explained,

> I don't know. . . . I'm not really—I mean, I think it's something that's appealing to me, but I can't tell you why. Does that really matter, you know what I'm saying? Like is that *really* important? Is it really? Like, where do we feel comfortable? Why does it matter if we are in a place where we're comfortable? It's hard to mix, it's hard to change people.

Chancey's challenge to the mission of diversity might be troubling to some churchgoers, especially those who want to believe that racial progress is a goal shared by all at Welcome. But her rhetorical questions about whether diversity is "really" necessary to me, another person racialized as White in the church, underscores the trouble with welcome talk. It made clear that Welcome had overstated its commitment to diversity and that this overstatement had hollowed out reflective thinking about why it matters.

Rather than consider how the church could combat racial inequality, the church did what Thomas terms "staging difference"—it cast a spotlight on its racial minorities to boast its image as a diverse and inclusive organization.[23] This staging came up when I asked Claire if she had recommendations for how the church might improve on its dream to be multiracial. "Don't single people out for being different. Don't use them as a token of diversity in the middle of a service," she said. When I prompted Claire to elaborate, she sighed out loud and told me that she hesitates to criticize Christians who are trying to do better, a remark that others made when critiquing the church. However, she continued,

> It makes me uncomfortable when [Bird] points out all of his like Spanish-speaking friends in the front row—I don't know if that should make me uncomfortable, but I just wonder how that makes them feel. Like being singled out for that reason.

Claire's observation that Bird draws attention to what he calls his "Hispanic brothers and sisters"—whether or not they want that—resonated with a church service I had attended prior to our interview. It was the first week of the fall semester. Bird was excited about students coming back. "They bring something new to town," he beamed. "They bring energy." Then Bird turned to the woman with dark brown hair standing next to him on stage. "This is María." She's from Oaxaca, Mexico, he told the church, "Just South of town," he joshed. "I love my Spanish-speaking neighbors," he avowed. "They cook good food—they are amazing people." The church chuckled louder than usual, a sound that made Bird grin. Following that comment, Bird gave the stage over to María.

María, one of a few Mexican-born individuals in the room that day, was there to talk about her mission in Oaxaca. Growing up, María said, she never thought she would be a missionary, but as she got older, she "realized that God had another plan." María started out by serving people who suffered addiction and trauma, but now works in a Christian school that serves kids who live with their missionary parents. María teaches English there, but the schools are "terribly understaffed" and "in need of rescue," to use her words. She ended her short talk with a plea to the church—she asked them to support her mission work and to get involved in "rescuing" others with the English language. Bird came back on stage, led a quick prayer, and encouraged the church to visit the Connect table at the back of the room where they could learn about the ministry in Oaxaca.

María's guest appearance occurred two Sundays after the "Unite the Right" rally took over Charlottesville, Virginia in August of 2017. Widely considered the most dangerous and hate-filled rally to unfold in recent memory, the rally brought hundreds of neo-Nazis and white nationalists together for a terrorizing protest that ended in severe injuries and death. The worship team transitioned from María's talk to Bird's sermon with a peaceful song titled, "The Church," originally by Elevation Worship. The version of the song that we sang was posted on the projector screen for all to sing. In part, this is what we sang:

> Now's the time for us to rise
> And carry hope and let love shine
> *And show this world that mercy is alive* [emphasized in italics on the projector screen].

As we sang "The Church" in unison, I wondered if the catastrophic events in Charlottesville would come up in the sermon or if the congregants would be left to make sense of the tragedy, the racism, and the hate all on their own. At the close of the song, Bird shouted amen, told us about the solar eclipse that was to happen the next day, and said he "hopes the world doesn't end," before reassuring us that if it does, "it's going to be okay because God is in charge."

That song "The Church," Bird explained moments later, urges us to remember that "Church is more than an event you attend. It's a people you're a part of." Bird then prompted the students to consider how they could activate a church of all nations in college. There are over ninety nations at the university, he said, and some of them have never heard of God. In the past week alone, Bird bragged, he's met students from Tennessee, Georgia, and Louisiana—"There's probably some Yankees there too." Then, in an abrupt shift in subject, Bird broached the rally for white supremacy in Charlottesville. He and the elders had met earlier in the week and decided that they "really" want to be a multiethnic church, not just say that they are.

Bird's face was stern, and his posture defensive, when he cried out, "If you profess to know Jesus and have hate in your heart, you're just dumb!" The church fell quiet. You could hear a pin drop. There were a few mutters upfront, likely amens. No shouts back. Bird's right leg shook as if releasing anxious energy. Meanwhile, I was writing notes in my field book: Who exactly is he calling dumb? Is he talking about the Proud

Boys, the group of white supremacists who claim to be in God's favor? Did someone from the church post a hateful message on social media for others to see? Or express support for the rally?

Other than call people who are hateful "dumb," Bird said nothing else that could be directly tied to Unite the Right. He did not offer to counsel those in distress and he neglected how the violent attack in Charlottesville could make members of racialized groups, like María, feel unsafe. Instead, Bird fell back on his common refrain. He preached that the church has to "be a church of all nations" if it wants to stop hate.

The next section shows how Welcome carried out its dream to be a church of all nations at its Spring is Here outreach event in a low-income Black neighborhood. White churchgoers boasted about Spring is Here almost every time that I asked them to elaborate on the church's efforts to achieve multiracial unity. Even if they had never attended Spring is Here, they knew that, as one claimed, "it has something to do with diversity."

## The Walls of Small Talk

Spring is Here is a treasured outreach ministry at Welcome. It's a family-friendly affair that the church held in Rolland Residential, an affordable Black single-family subdivision on the outskirts of Oxford, for at least two years in a row. The developer who established Rolland Residential in the 1970s started selling the lots at a discounted price after going bankrupt, and according to local news reports, the slump in pricing gave Black residents a chance to invest in a home. By the 1980s, all but one of the White families had left, a change that one Black homeowner attributed to what social scientists call the "racial tipping point," or the point at which White people pack their boxes and leave after "one too many" Black residents have moved in.[24] Once the White families were gone, Rolland Residential got a reputation for being "bad" and "dangerous," terms that Welcome churchgoers used to describe what they've heard or think of the neighborhood.

When Welcome brought Spring is Here to Rolland Residential, its volunteers stationed themselves with their hot dogs, hamburgers, and bubble wands underneath white canopy tents they had set up on the edge of the parking lot. About sixty kids, mostly middle-school aged, came out for the food and games. Once the event got moving, kids were throwing balls and sprinting around, having a grand time. A few men from the church stood on guard near a bright colorful bouncy house to monitor the horseplay, bantering with the kids in between shouting "Slow down!" Women were in charge of handing out the food, and the kids kept them busy. One volunteer served hot dogs, nonstop, for almost an hour. "Time flew by," she bragged. "Once the kids figure out that they can have as much as they want, you can't keep them away!"

On the Sunday that followed Spring is Here, Heather, my graduate research assistant, attempted to find out why churchgoers want to bring church to Rolland Residential. She had volunteered for the event and therefore was in the best position to ask them what they took from the experience. I asked Heather to "find out what motivates churchgoers to volunteer. Find out why they think that outreach is important." At the time, I didn't think much about my instructions to Heather. I assumed the assignment was simple. I was wrong.

Heather was unable to get past the wall of small talk. Churchgoers deflected her queries at every turn of every interaction. First, there was Sampson, a church elder. After some benign remarks about the success of the event, including that they, in his words, "had a lot of food," Heather asked him how Spring is Here is different from the other church outreach events. Instead of answering the question, Sampson smiled at a family coming through the church doors, picked up their small child, and spun him around. Heather took the cue, walked off, and tried to chat about it with Brad, a White volunteer from the event that she knew fairly well.

Brad ended the conversation about Spring is Here within a few seconds. After sharing that he uses "jokes to break the ice and minister to people," Heather asked if he did that at Rolland Residential. Brad chuckled at the question, "No, I was cooking all the meat!" Then, Brad brought up another, unrelated topic: he took out his phone to show Heather photos of his new house. "My wife is really excited to move everything out of storage. We've been living in an 800-square-foot apartment for two years now." Once their conversation about storage units and dining room sets fizzled out, Brad excused himself to go find his wife.

Determined to talk about something other than food, Heather cornered Cheryl at the coffee stand where they volunteer together at church on Sunday mornings. Heather asked Cheryl if she thought the event was successful, and if Cheryl thinks the people from Rolland Residential will visit Welcome. Cheryl, like everyone else, concentrated on the food—"We practically had to beg people to take food because we had made so much!" The point of the event, she said, is to "let them know that if they need a church, ours is open"—with "them" in this scenario referring to Black residents that the church sees as in need of salvation, and "ours" referring to Welcome, a church dominated by White people, like her, who offer that salvation.

Cheryl felt good about what Spring is Here accomplished. But she was unable to say what the residents of Rolland Residential thought about the event. She barely spoke to anyone from the neighborhood. She is, by her own admission, "not very good at talking to people," especially in places that she is unfamiliar with. On top of that, she added, the adults from the neighborhood tended to stay away from their church tents. They were "just so shy," she observed. She was, however, thrilled to report that she handed one resident a church pamphlet and told them, "Now you know where you can find us."

Before Heather could ask a follow-up question, Cheryl took charge of the conversation, "Did you hear about what happened about two days before we came? There was a shooting!" It involved drugs, she said. It happened right down the street from where Welcome had set up in Rolland Residential. "Those houses are a bit dumpy. . . . Those houses are going to be taken over by the county soon," she continued. "It's sad, but it will be a good thing in the end."

Bird was the only one to comment on the Spring is Here event without prompting from Heather. Welcome, he preached the following Sunday, prioritizes "the community" over numbers on Sunday morning. They had canceled church last week for Spring is Here, and they will do it again, he bragged. From there, Bird called out a college student from the church, "a sorority girl," he clarified, who emailed that she felt the church could do more for its Black and Brown neighbors. Shaking his head, Bird affected an African American vernacular English accent as he told the church, "It was like she had sucker punched a brotha through the screen." This college student, he noted, is from a nicer end of town. "She was blessed, amen?" Bird posed the question back to the church, "What more can we do for that community?" Then he shouted, "It's time for someone else to rise up!"

The residents of Rolland Residential may never step inside Welcome, Bird admitted. Still, the event was a success. The people in that neighborhood have been introduced to Welcome and now know it as a place of accepting, friendly people. If they go out looking for a loving church, they know where to find them.

***

Spring is Here is characteristic of what I and my colleague Kelsy Burke call a "diversity project." It was an event that made the church feel good about what it provides to people of color "living in dire circumstances."[25] Rolland Residential is only a few miles from where the church meets on Sundays, but it felt like foreign land to Welcome. The kind of neighborhood where, as one churchgoer said, "you start to realize that we have people living like a third world country right here in our own backyard." A place where another grasped that "you don't have to go all the way to Oaxaca" to be involved in a ministry for the bottom rungs of society.

Diversity projects are an evangelical enterprise of church plants, conferences, blogs, workshops, and best-selling books centered on the goodwill of (White) Christians who give up their advantaged lifestyles to reach the racially marginalized and economically dispossessed.[26] The evangelical preoccupation with diversity is especially predominant in the newest wave of evangelical women's ministries, ministries that quietly critique some aspects of white supremacy and, to a lesser extent, patriarchy. The IF: Gathering, a live-streamed women's conference that evangelical superstar Jennie Allen spearheaded, is one of those ministries. Its first meeting was in 2014, and by 2018, IF had become the largest Christian assembly of women in the United States. In addition to its live audience in Austin, Texas, IF was broadcast at nearly two thousand locations in forty-nine U.S. states and seventeen countries.[27] When I attended the live-streamed IF event with the women of Welcome, we watched it at a neighboring church auditorium one year, and then at a churchgoer's home the next.

From year to year, IF showcases White women doing ministry work in marginalized communities. One of the videos it features is about a White woman who rekindled her relationship to church after she and her husband relocated to a midwestern city that, according to the narration, had been ransacked by economic downturn and racial division.

In the video, we watch her, the narrator, alongside seemingly poor Black women at a kitchen table having a meal or helping her guests fill out forms or pay bills. As these images pass by, she tells viewers that the church she planted made her the happiest she has ever been. She no longer cares about being in the best or fanciest church anymore. All she cares about is saving souls.[28]

The outreach to Rolland Residential was not as involved as the outreach ministries I learned about at the IF conference, but the motive behind it is similar. Both are part of the evangelical mission to attract more Americans to born-again Christianity, and both are diversity projects that evangelicals perform in place of substantive conversations about race. When Heather asked churchgoers about Spring is Here, they pivoted to small talk about food, and in turn knocked race out of the conversation, even as they signaled race in their remarks about "letting *them* know *we're* here." And in the absence of naming who attended the event, or who the event was for, churchgoers evaded talk about what it means for White Christians to hand out hot dogs to Black children and call that action "church." Instead, talk about the event was restricted to welcome talk. They now know where to find us, churchgoers said, and that knowledge alone builds longer tables.

## The Problem at the Table

White Christians, especially but not exclusively evangelical Christians, are more likely to deny the existence of structural racism than are White people who are religiously unaffiliated.[29] They are more likely to claim that the killing of a Black man by the police is an individual disaster, more likely to see monuments to the Confederacy as icons of southern pride, and more likely to negate the fact that generations of slavery and racial discrimination have made it hard for Black Americans to climb out of intergenerational poverty.[30] And when confronted with terms that challenge or call attention to white supremacy—such as White privilege and Black power—they become more distraught than other groups.[31]

Welcome talk is one way for understanding how evangelicals neglect their complicity in white supremacy and structural racism without having to resort to anger or conflict. Rather than tackle racial inequality head on, welcome talk removes these subjects from the allegedly longer table. It does this by prioritizing the perspectives and comforts of White people. As this chapter has shown, Welcome presumes that people of color will spiritually benefit from White people who welcome them into White spaces, and it promotes the colorblind racial ideology that diversity can be pursued without having to address how evangelical Christianity has historically endowed people with differential forms of agency based on race.[32]

Welcome talk advances what critical race scholars call "white ignorance." It distorts the reality of racial inequality, evades "moral and practical implications of critical racial consciousness," and perpetuates the corporate power of Whiteness—institutionally, organizationally, and in the everyday.[33] Here, I list how welcome talk prevents reflective dialogue that could stimulate critical awareness of what it takes to achieve multiracial unity.

Welcome talk maintains that:

- Allowing people of color in a White space resolves racial division.
- Hospitality is the main ingredient of multiracial unity.
- Multiracial unity is being actively pursued if not already accomplished.

Spring is Here was an on-the-ground manifestation of welcome talk. By holding the event, the church could defend the idea that White evangelicals want to racially integrate, and that the church was doing all it could for that to happen. Through persistent talk about the spiritual import of such a ministry, the church overstated its effort in a way that made it easier to look past the root causes of racial division, even as they came into contact with the results of anti-Black racism in a low-income neighborhood in Mississippi.

Churchgoers of color were attracted to welcome talk too. Some joined Welcome because of its professed racial diversity, and others admitted that while Welcome needs to approach inclusion differently, they appreciated the church for saying it wants to be racially integrated. Indeed, according to these churchgoers, the White people at Welcome were less aggressive than the White people they encounter at work, at school, and in other White Christian spaces. The language of White racism, as anthropologist Jane Hill describes it, is ubiquitous and infects all corners of our everyday lives.[34] Welcome talk provided churchgoers of color refuge from that language. When they walked through the doors of Welcome, they entered into a gentler White world—a world in which White people are warmer. Or, as sociologist Leah Glass might point out, a world in which White individuals at least say that they are trying to not be racist.[35]

Yet regardless of what churchgoers liked about Welcome, the hard truth is this: while Welcome promised to build longer tables, it gave White people the best seats at the table. It did this through welcome talk that appeals to White people.[36] When someone brought attention to the arrangement of the table, the church retreated to small talk that both catered to White sensibilities and cut meaningful dialogue about the eradication of inequality short.

The next chapter examines how the church recoiled from discomfort in other seemingly minor but profound ways. It elaborates on how the sticky subject of white supremacy and other polarizing subjects were contained at church. It shows how, in the name of unity, the church neglected pressing issues that were riveting the nation and their local communities at the time.

# 3

# America Is Divided (But the Church Cannot Be)

Judy, a cheerful person with big blinking eyes, kicked off our introductions at the Women's Book Club with the proclamation, "I am different." She scanned the fellowship room of six friendly faces and chortled at herself. "I'm really weird. Really weird." Lynn, a friend of hers who organizes the book club, tilted toward Judy from across a white plastic folding table, smiling wide, "Yeah, she's weird!" Judy blushed and explained herself: "I like history. I'm passionate about it," she said. "I like reading about the Third Reich and World War II—I like learning about all that stuff." Judy exhaled loudly. "I just cannot believe that people would do such horrible things—that ordinary people would let such catastrophic things happen to a group of human beings."

Judy was the only one at book club to raise war, conflict, or dehumanization in the presence of others as an issue, and I was eager to see where her comments might take us. Other than a few awkward laughs, no one engaged Judy. I decided to seize the silence that had blanketed the room. I followed up by asking Judy what spawned her interest in WWII. "It was Anne Frank's diary," Judy said. She read the diary when she was young and was disturbed that people could "behave that way." I was struck by the ambiguity of her comments. She never used the words Jew or Jewish or Holocaust or Nazis to describe the contents of Frank's book. She did, however, exhale loudly again before proclaiming, "Oh my Goodness—something like this could happen again!" In that moment, my mind leaped to the alt right movements that were taking to the streets, to the rise in anti-Semitic and anti-Muslim hate crimes, and to the xenophobic rhetoric that electrified Trump's "Make America Great Again" campaign.[1] No one said a word. No one explored what Judy feared could happen again. We were momentarily locked in silence. Then, within seconds, the conversation took a sharp, unexpected turn to Muslims.

Anne, the preacher's wife, interceded to tell us that she, like Judy, loves to read and that she was reading *Seeking Allah, Finding Jesus*, a testimonial about a Muslim convert to Christianity. Her intervention reinvigorated the group, giving them a means to relate to one another. One participant shared that she "loves testimonials" before another took the group down the path of casual Islamophobia.[2] One White woman who had come to book club directly from work in blue jeans claimed that Muslim men beat women in their homes, and another donning a pressed blouse and full makeup affirmed, "They don't have the freedoms we have!" Cassie, who has a degree in religious studies and was the only person of color present that night, added that Muslims are "extremely committed to their faith" and "never leave it." Several went on to affirm that Muslims who convert to Christianity are among the most dedicated. "They give up everything for God," Cassie smiled in delight, even their own families.[3]

This chapter opens with the conversation that did *not* happen at book club alongside the one that did to shed light on how the potential for disagreement and thoughtful dialogue is suppressed at church. The book club dodged subjects that could expose their perspectives on fascism, or in Judy's words, what could happen again. They also steered clear of talk about racist practices and incidents that could be used to hold the church accountable for the reproduction of white supremacy. Instead of engaging discussion about polarizing subjects that are tied to their faith, they performed sameness. They projected attitudes and opinions that matched what others projected—in this case, the racist stereotype that Muslims are barbaric, religious fundamentalists who would be better off as Christians.[4]

In this chapter, I show how the church observed the unspoken rules of biblical sameness: 1) they kept their political differences to themselves; 2) they drew attention away from divisive or racist atrocities; and 3) on the rare occasions that churchgoers did unleash a conflicting point of view, they were ignored, interrupted, or dismissed.

One of the most consistent acts of sameness that I observed involved Trump. Churchgoers held diverging opinions of Trump, but for the sake of unity, the church tacitly agreed to stay quiet about him, even in a racial reconciliation group that was started to promote healing and reunification in the aftermath of the volatile 2016 U.S. presidential election.

## Keep Politics to Yourself

Broaching the subject of Trump was taboo, so much so that I could only learn what churchgoers thought about him in private, confidential interviews. White Protestant Christians are accustomed to keeping a safe distance from political discussions at church, especially those in the U.S. South where politics are equated with movements for civil rights.[5] Still, the silence surrounding Trump surprised me for two reasons. For starters, the dearth of conversation about him concealed what every pollster had shown: White evangelicals love Trump, especially in Mississippi. I assumed that churchgoers might bring up how they or others were responding to the election, even if they decided to keep their vote to themselves. Plus, Trump arguably made national headlines more than any other political figure in U.S. history. To keep quiet about him, churchgoers had to neglect almost everything that had been covered in the news.

From the outset, I had to think carefully about where to place questions about his presidency in my interview guide. I had to keep the lines of communication open once I brought him up. I already knew most of my interviewees from small groups, but I still needed ample time to deepen our connection before touching on a subject that was deliberately avoided at church.

I eventually settled on moving questions about Trump toward the end of interviews, just before I ask what outsiders get wrong about Christians. That strategy worked, as evidenced by the opinions they expressed about him within the context of our private conversation. After the first round of interviews, I added a question that could shed light on my observations of avoidance: I asked *if* churchgoers talk to others about Trump at church.

Thatcher, a family physician and lifelong Christian, echoed what other churchgoers said about keeping politics to themselves. After telling me that he has always voted Republican but had decided to do a write-in when he cast his ballot for president, Thatcher shared that he is uncomfortable with being candid about his political views.

AMY: Did you talk with anyone about not voting for either of them?
THATCHER: My wife and I did.

AMY: But outside of that?

THATCHER: I think it's come up a little bit—with those that I know well. I feel like politics in church can sometimes cause problems. I feel like we are at a very white or black place in politics right now. Like, it's almost not okay to be in the middle, or in some gray area. I feel like you have to be completely pro-everything, or completely anti-everything.

Asking churchgoers like Thatcher how they voted—a churchgoer who made clear that he only feels comfortable talking about politics with people close to him—could get tense. It was through this tension that I learned that churchgoers were quiet about Trump because their views of him and his presidency differed, sometimes dramatically.

Dave and Sharon, a married couple who claimed that racial hatred swelled during the Barak Obama presidency, helped me see what other interviewees alluded to. When we met for an interview at a sandwich shop, I shared my observation that churchgoers seldom dabble in politics at church and that I wanted to understand why. Sharon folded her arms and reflected on my asking for whom she voted earlier in our conversation. "Some people might get plumb ugly with you for asking who they voted for," she scowled. "That's none of your business." I vividly recall thinking, "Uh oh—this is not going well." Dave teased, "Yeah, that's none of your business who I voted for!" He was letting me know that he, and by extension they, were not mad at me. People get offended too easily these days, argued Dave. "It's hard to judge how people are going to take a question, or not take a question," he continued. After that, Sharon explained that she voted for Trump because "he doesn't sugarcoat" the truth. He can be "rough about it," Dave added, but at least he is honest.

Trump's bad manners, and his bad morals, were raised by almost everyone I interviewed, but the pro-Trump churchgoers downplayed how racism electrified his presidential campaign.[6] "He's a good businessman and he's good with money," Gary, a diehard fan of Trump professed. "He isn't that good socially," he laughed awkwardly. Gary was not alone in his assessment of Trump's social skills, as many described it. Churchgoers admitted that Trump "says things that are completely stupid," "hurts people's feelings," and "acts like a junior high kid." But they seldom mentioned the content of what he said or how he acted. Instead, interviewees drew on the rhetoric of colorblind racism to describe how he treated people, then later in the interview claimed that Trump does not treat people that badly.[7]

Dave was the only Trump supporter to touch on racism directly. He complained that the media had been unfair to Trump in its coverage of the wall that he promised to build along the U.S./Mexico border. Mexicans, he said, could come over here "as long as they do it legally," and the proposed wall was merely, in Dave's opinion, a way of enforcing that requirement. The liberal media is critical of Trump, he surmised, and was ignoring the hard truth about immigration. Later in the interview, Dave and Sharon dismissed the charge that Trump encourages racism and racist movements for white supremacy. From their perspective, racial conflict was the worst during the administration of President Barack Obama. When Obama was president, Dave and Sharon feared that a "race war" would erupt if he got assassinated, meaning they were afraid that Black Americans would feel outraged enough to start an armed conflict with the White side of America. Those fears vanished when Trump was elected. They were confident that Trump, a White candidate who had support from the far Right, could keep that from happening.

The few churchgoers who voted Democrat, or hadn't voted at all, or called Trump "an idiot," were less guarded about Trump's racist rhetoric. In our private interview, Claire, a young White college graduate who had recently moved to Oxford for a job, told me that a vote for Trump was a "vote for White privilege," and Amani, a Black churchgoer who teaches at a predominantly White middle school, said that she was scared when he won the election. "He pushed the country back a few decades," she said, and his election irritated old "racial wounds" that she suffers daily.

Other churchgoers who opposed the Trump cabinet took issue with how he disrespects women. One of these individuals was Brian, a Black father of two who attended the church with his wife and their kids. Through occasional bursts of uneasy laughter, he contended that Trump was terrible, but that Mike Pence, the vice president during his first administration, "is probably the devil." The Mike Pences of the world, he explained, claim that if a rape caused a woman to get pregnant, she enjoyed the rape and, therefore, does not have a right to an abortion. Brian found this argument "repulsive." Brian accepted the anti-abortion sentiment that the unborn are sacred, but he also believed that a woman who had been raped or molested was under no obligation to follow through with an unwanted pregnancy. Christians who supported Republicans like Pence made him suspicious of people who use religion to support their political positions. Some of those people, he asserted, are evil.

Brian's remarks stood in direct contrast to what Gary said about abortion in our interview. Gary liked Trump precisely because he stood behind the pro-life movement, a movement that claims God, and only God, determines when a life begins and ends.[8] Gary told me that cases of rape and incest were hard, and that it was really "sick" that someone would do that. But, he continued, "That child didn't do it—and if you abort that child, that child might've been a future president or someone who cured cancer. So, who are you to say that that life should end?" Unlike Brian, Gary was proud of the work that Republicans were doing to make his view on abortion the law. His assertion that an aborted fetus could have been someone important resonated with the rhetorical platform of the broader pro-life movement.

Brian and Gary attended Welcome every Sunday, participated in its small groups and men's ministries, and had mutual friends. Yet their diverging views on Trump and reproductive rights were off the table of discussion at church. Brian got "the vibe" that there were, in another interviewee's words, "a fair amount of Trump supporters" at Welcome, and Gary presumed that the people who oppose Trump could get their feelings hurt if his name came up.

Christians who were critical of Trump detected that churchgoers like Gary were in the majority at Welcome. Lynn, an active and founding member of Welcome, never talked to others about the election, but assumed that most at the church had voted Republican. Republicans, she said, know how to manipulate Christians. If they "say a candidate on the other side is devil worshipping, the Christians hear it, and they run for it." Benjamin, who described himself as a Libertarian with anarchist leanings, also thought that the church had voted Republican, even congregants of color who he had mistaken as moderately liberal. Benjamin never heard that directly, but he had gotten that "feeling" at church leadership meetings.[9]

The presumption that the Welcome majority had voted for Trump pushed the ones who hadn't, as well as the ones who had, to stay quiet about it. Claire, who liked Welcome for its racially diverse mission, never talked to anyone at the church about the election or about the racism that it inspired. She assumed that Welcome was Republican, so she kept her opinions to herself. She "didn't want to initiate that conflict and have to have that conversation." She opted to keep her opinions to herself since her opinions might provoke a heated exchange about race.

Brooklyn, a White college student who had launched Be the Bridge (BTB) at Welcome, remembered feeling stunned that Christians at her church had supported Trump without hesitation. Trump had explicitly dehumanized people, she said, and his election had made churchgoers of color wonder whether the person sitting next to them supported their dehumanization. "That's where something has to be said, and needs to be said," she asserted. Brooklyn, however, didn't speak out. Like other White people, she didn't know how to confront her racist White peers. There was no model for that in the church, or in her life, and she was afraid of what might happen if she spoke up. "We were all so torn and had such strong convictions and feelings that I feel like we couldn't even talk about it."

The evangelical support for Trump was the elephant in the room, an "open secret," to use Zerubavel's phrasing, that spiraled into the active denial of who Trump is and what he represents for the church.[10] An elephant that symbolized a glaring incongruity: Welcome claimed to be a racially inclusive church where "all are welcome," yet congregants declined to engage in conversations that could have roused critical reflections on the reproduction of racism or even acknowledge the demonization and racialization of Muslims, a religious minority that the Trump administration had attacked repeatedly.[11] This elephant loomed large in every relationship at the church, even among those groups and relationships formed to talk about race.

When I asked Brooklyn if BTB attendees talked about the election, she sighed heavily, took a long pause, and said that she had gotten a "sense" that talking about it could make its members angry at one another. She did, however, reach out to the group after the votes were counted with a text that read, "No matter how you voted, today there are people waking up who are really disappointed, really disheartened, and even scared. And so, I hope that our group will be the light today."

No one responded to Brooklyn's message. The group avoided the subject, even as one of its own members tried to bring attention to it.

About a year later, I asked Maura if Trump had ever come up at BTB when I was not around. Maura had been part of BTB since the very beginning and even took over the group after Brooklyn moved off for seminary. She was the right person to ask. Maura raised her eyebrows: "No, we don't go there," she said firmly and with a hint of regret in her voice. I understood the cue. If I wanted to fit in with the group, I had to go along with BTB's unspoken rule: keep politics to yourself. Don't bring him up.

One of the most revealing "keep politics to yourself" moments of the BTB group happened in January 2017, when Trump was under international scrutiny for describing Haiti and several African nations as "shithole" countries. Our Sunday evening gathering kicked off with its usual form of fellowship: we chitchatted about food, weather, and school on Maura's sectional sofa. Chancey, a White homeschool mom, shifted from the weather to parents, or what she might call absent mothers. She lifted her chin high, bit a tortilla chip, and grumbled about parents who complain about snow days. "They're your kids! If the school has to close, you should be able to take care of them!" Maura, a mother of two who works full time at a public school, smiled warmly, took a long deep breath, and told us that it was time to get started with the lesson.

"I want us to start by talking about what's been going on in the news," she announced. I couldn't believe it. The group was finally going to confront the elephant in the room—Trump! But Maura didn't say anything about him. Instead, she took out her phone and pulled up an H&M advertisement of a little Black boy wearing a green hoodie that read, "Coolest Monkey in the Jungle." Several in the group shouted, "I saw that ad!" and carried on about how the image *could* be offensive to *some people*. Within a few minutes, the group settled on the idea that the ad was offensive, but that the offense may have been unintentional. From there, its members pivoted to lighter topics such as where they shop for their kids, which companies have the best deals, and finally to White members facetiously asking Black members when it will be okay to shop at H&M again. Trump's high-profile racist comments about Black people from around the world were never explicitly addressed.

***

The church's silent agreement to ignore Trump made critical reflection on the evangelical vote for him inaccessible.[12] That is, the church did not simply fail to hold the same political perspective or opinions of Trump; how they were "doing" church entailed a deliberate effort to refrain from acknowledging those differences.[13]

The conservative, pro-Trump supporters believed that more liberal members of the church were delicate and might "be offended" by their vote. They kept quiet about him because that was the polite Christian thing to do, not because they feared backlash or thought their vote jeopardized their standing with other evangelicals. The more liberal-leaning members of the church, however, said they chose to be silent about Trump for a different reason: they did not feel comfortable enough to declare their views at church. They were worried about getting into a fight, or "getting yelled at" if they questioned the Christian vote for Trump. In an effort to avoid such hostilities, they kept their opinions to themselves. Besides, they granted, church was not the place for conflict. Church was a place to be united, to be the same, and that sameness perpetuated the White status quo. Bird also steered the church away from politics that could incite friction or change. The next section shows how he relied on ambiguous language to remark on racial divisions and White racist uprisings from the church stage.

## Don't Call It What It Is

Bird modeled what sociologist Mikael Klintman calls "strategic ignorance," or the active calculation of the costs and opportunities associated with additional (e.g., inconvenient) knowledge.[14] He neglected to name and acknowledge high-profile issues that were impossible to miss, especially when those issues jeopardized the church's standing as a unified body of believers who oppose racism. Days before the 2016 election, a historic Black church in the Mississippi Delta was torched and vandalized with the words "Vote Trump." On the Sunday that followed the attack, Bird used a small part of his platform to mourn the church's loss. He reminded the church that Jesus loves everybody, "of every color, of every nation." Then, after a short lesson about breaking bread (i.e., sharing a meal) with different communities, Bird contended that "they" are his brothers and sisters and that an attack on "them" is an attack on "us." After this nod to Christian unity, Bird remarked that "some people say it was political," before shouting, "I don't know if it was political!" But if it was, he chided, "I hope Jesus solves that!"

Focusing on the political motivations of the church burning was a distraction, he preached. The church needs to focus on Jesus, he said, and on letting their African American brothers and sisters know that they are welcomed at Welcome anytime. My heart raced the whole time Bird spoke. I was hopeful that Bird, and the church, would face the violent uprisings that Trump fueled and why. That reckoning never materialized. Instead, Bird insinuated that merely describing what had happened could lead to division. And the doubt he expressed over the "political" motivation of the crime was revealing. It not only directed attention away from the atrocious defacement of the church and what it read. It was also reminiscent of a "false flag" conspiracy theory that the church burning was plotted by the Left to vilify White conservatives.[15]

Bird was ambiguous about other racists events. In 2019, two neo-Confederate groups, Confederate 901 and The Hiwaymen, came to Oxford to protest the proposed removal of the University of Mississippi's thirty-foot-tall statue of an unnamed Confederate soldier that then stood on a pedestal at the front entrance of campus.[16]

Over the previous decade, the university had made slow but steady progress away from its Confederate brand, and that progress had stirred up a debate about the statue. In 2003, the university retired its antebellum South mascot, Colonel Reb, and in 2015, NAACP (National Association for the Advancement of Colored People) students pushed for the faculty, student, and staff senates to pass resolutions that resulted in the removal of the state flag from campus, which at that time included the Confederate battle symbol. Then in 2016, UM Chancellor Jeffrey Vitter formed an "Advisory Committee on History and Contextualization" comprised of administrators, alumni, and faculty (primarily from History, Sociology, English, and African American studies). This committee created and installed a "contextualization" plaque in front of the statue that stated that the "defeat of the Confederacy actually meant freedom for millions of people." Two years later, that same committee unveiled six new contextualization plaques on campus that

Figure 3.1. Students from the Black Student Union protest a 30-foot-tall Confederate statue and the neo-Confederates who revere it, University of Mississippi, February 23, 2019. Photograph courtesy of Michael Fagans.

Figure 3.2. Neo-Confederates rally for the Confederate statue and oppose the university students who want to take it down, University of Mississippi, February 23, 2019. Photograph courtesy of Kerrigan Casimir.

acknowledge the slave labor involved in building the university and that provide information about the racial segregationists and slave-holding White men behind several of its building names. By 2019, the Associated Student Body voted unanimously for the statue to be moved to the Confederate Cemetery, a less prominent place on campus, prompting more community members to stand in solidarity with the movement to "Take it Down."

After much sustained pressure, the university removed its Confederate statue from the front entrance of campus and transferred it to the less contentious location. Before its removal, the neo-Confederates requested a permit to rally on campus at the statue, which was also the rallying point for the Ole Miss Riot of 1962, during which White students violently attacked the campus in response to James Meredith becoming the first Black student to enroll at the university. Student activists from SASI (Students Against Social Injustice), who were leading the charge to take down the statue, heard about the permit and responded with a plan for a counter-protest. Those changes are what mobilized the Confederate 901 and the Hiwaymen to meet for a rally in Oxford. They were tired of students "crying on and on" about Confederate iconography and were determined to "draw a line in the sand," as their Facebook post about the event put it.

Oxford was tense that weekend.[17] The neo-Confederates arrived on Saturday for their "Mississippi Stand" rally, paraded through town, then assembled on campus to oppose what they called "cultural genocide." Students showed up, too. Tucked behind a barrier of foldable steel gates and armed police officers, they chanted and waved signs that read, "Y'all Lost" and "A Heritage of Hate is Nothing to Celebrate." One sign in particular took issue with silence: "It is Not Enough to be Quietly Non-Racist. You Must Be Loudly Anti-Racist." The lines were clear. Oxford was being pressed to answer: Which side are you on? For white supremacy or against it?

On Sunday, the day after the neo-Confederates vacated town, Bird told the church how he was feeling about being a pastor that day:

> I'm anxious this morning!
> I'm nervous this morning!
> I'm a little overwhelmed this morning!

> I believe right now—to be a pastor of the U S of America, the United States of America, is one of the most difficult responsibilities ever!
> [Volume shifts from shouts to a soft whisper]
> Let me tell you why—*man, there's lines drawn everywhere.*

Bird was right. Lines are being drawn everywhere. Racists are fighting for a world in which White people dominate the history and future of America.[18] Anti-racists are struggling for one in which people of color have the opportunity to live free of deprivation, violence, and fear.[19]

Despite the seriousness of the weekend protest, Bird failed to take a firm stance against white supremacy or make the terms White, racism, or Confederate part of church vocabulary. Instead, he used his time on stage to imply that conflict, not racism, is the problem, and that activists who expose or acknowledge the lines of division are in the wrong because they put politics before God.[20] It was an impassioned testament to biblical sameness. It denied blatant anti-Black racism in the church's very own community, and it gave the church an opportunity to ignore how white nationalists commit more violent crimes than any other subgroup associated with domestic extremism.[21]

Bird's reluctance to confront race and racism head-on is widespread in evangelical communities. White evangelical pastors commonly choose to focus on what unites Christians and to avoid what could divide them.[22] Further, the uptick in political extremism has had a chilling effect on pastors and what they preach.[23] In a 2022 story in the *New York Times* titled, "Pastors Are Being Driven Out by Trumpism," journalist Ruth Graham reports that evangelical pastors have been quitting, or at least considering quitting, in huge numbers and that some of the motivation to leave is driven by the conspiracy theorists and far right evangelical churchgoers that venerate Trump.[24] If a pastor appears to question or contradict Trump, she finds, they risk backlash from their parishioners, even harassment in some cases. The pastor that Graham spent the most time with for her story, Kevin Thompson from Arkansas, had to relocate to another state after being threatened for taking positions that mildly challenged right-leaning perspectives on Trump, Black Lives, and QAnon conspiracy theories.

For many pastors, a decision about how to lead the church through the muck of deep division can turn out to be a dreadful career choice. It can, in other words, feel impossible to strike what theologian Leah Schade terms "the Purple Zone," which she defines as "the place where the boundaries of red and blue merge, mix, and produce another shade altogether."[25] Indeed, as Schade's research reveals, pastors feel unprepared to preach about divisive subjects, and of those surveyed, almost 80 percent said they wanted guidance on how to facilitate such dialogue with their congregation. Schade also finds that churchgoers can be quick to accuse pastors of being "too political" and that pastors are wary of this label—a label that can be used to discredit or disparage how they lead the faith.

***

A year after the white supremacist groups stormed through Oxford, and in the middle of the 2020 global pandemic that shut down the world, I drove past an assembly of ten folks—nine White, one Black—ranging from thirty to eighty years old holding signs that read, "Love thy Neighbor" and "God Loves You" in the old courtyard of the downtown Square. Their rally, if you can call it that, caught my attention. They had gathered off to the side of the Confederate monument near the area where Take It Down activists had started demonstrating when a worldwide wave of Black Lives Matter protests erupted to demand justice for George Floyd, Breonna Taylor, and Ahmaud Arbery, all of whom had been murdered that year. Credited as possibly the largest collective demonstration in U.S. history, Black Lives Matter pressed businesses, universities, and political leaders to condemn racism and police brutality. Academics made collective pleas for the dismantlement of anti-Black racism.[26] A small group of church leaders in the Southern Baptist tradition signed petitions calling for racial reconciliation.[27] And local activists organized their communities to campaign for the removal of racist iconography, as Take it Down had in Oxford.

At first, I mistook the small Love Thy Neighbor demonstration for Take It Down, but quickly realized that their signs said nothing about the statue or Black Lives. These signs were different. They were made of white posterboard instead of recycled cardboard, and every single one had the word love on it in red or blue lettering. Within minutes, I learned that the love they were declaring was unconcerned with dismantling symbols of white supremacy. It was not the vision of love that I learned from bell hooks, a Black feminist who conceptualizes love as the act of relinquishing power and control to the benefit of the most marginalized members of society.[28]

Bird was among the group, and when I saw him, I brought my car to a sudden stop and yelled out, "Bird!" He did the same in return, "Hey Girl!" I was surprised, and genuinely happy to see him. It had been a while. Bird ran over and told me about the protest, how he had gotten involved, and what it meant to him. The demonstration had been organized by a young woman at his church, he told me. He hadn't announced it. There would be hundreds of people there if he had, he said. They wanted it to be "more intimate" than that. Bird spread his arms out wide like wings and cried, "There's too much division in this country right now, Amy!" Everybody is hating on everybody, he moaned. I nodded and muttered a puzzled mmm hmmm, pushing the record button in my brain. Bird was there to "remind people to stop focusing on their differences and to start focusing on their similarities." Then he leaned toward my car and softened his voice to tell me about a guy from Black Lives Matter who had stopped by earlier and had asked Bird to join forces. Bird let him know, and then let me know, that he "isn't taking sides." He was there because he wants people to love each other. He was there to push for sameness. To make the case that we are better off when we push our differences to the side. He was not there for Black Lives. That would be choosing sides, and Bird doesn't believe in choosing sides.

Bird neglected to call out white supremacy. He ignored the roots of the racial conflicts that were stirring in his hometown. He used ambiguous language to describe treacherous organized racism. Yet Bird was not the only or main culprit of silence and denial at Welcome. A suspicion of open and honest conversation was evident in all corners of the church, even within BTB, the church's only racial reconciliation group. BTB did approach delicate subjects (i.e., race and racism), but its members were constrained by the church's very own speech norms, norms dictated by White people in all types of white spaces (not only church spaces).[29] They habitually fell into the routine of either speaking into a void or sticking to subjects that were less charged.

## Speak into the Void

Unlike at other small groups, race and racism were topics of discussion at Be the Bridge (BTB). Its Black members were candid about their personal experiences of racial discrimination, and they voiced concerns about racial profiling and policing. But at every turn of every conversation, members of BTB also cautiously avoided references to structural racism, the term "white supremacy," and talk about escalating racial unrest.[30] This was glaringly evident in how the group pushed Trump, the racist alt right, and local conflicts over Confederate iconography out of the conversation.

When Maura took over BTB, she made clear, from the very beginning, that we should embrace discomfort. Her comment reminded me of a line from Jodi Skipper's book about curating public history exhibits on slavey in Mississippi: "Discomfort is a necessary feeling for people considered White who are seeking to do antiracist work."[31] Tackling taboo subjects can feel risky, Maura cautioned, and she wanted us to take those risks. To make the point, she followed the advice of Morrison, the author of the BTB study. She brought a small glass elephant to our meetings. The elephant, she reminded us, symbolized the things that were hidden or difficult to talk about. By holding it when we speak, we were to feel encouraged to be forthright in our observations of race and to be heard without interruption from others. Her strategy worked, to some degree. Once the elephant made its appearance, group participants spoke up often and were more attentive to the dynamics of the conversation. Yet, unlike the ritualized interplays about an all-knowing God that transpired at the Sunday Group meetings, there was still little back and forth with the elephant in hand. Group members would pass the elephant around the room, but rarely touched on what another had said when it was their turn to speak.

More often than not, participants of color in BTB spoke into the void, meaning they spoke without being heard or taken seriously by other members of the church.[32] Follow-up questions, responding comments, or requests for clarification about what they said were rare. This was especially true if a matter concerned the church directly. At one BTB meeting, group members took turns sharing disturbing news about fellow churchgoers who had said or done something racist. In a pained voice, Maura told us about a church family that had painted themselves in black face for the world to see on Facebook. Kelly, a White college student who was involved with campus ministries, shared that she had heard churchgoers joking about how they "go packing" (carry a loaded gun) to Rolland Residential, the Black neighborhood where Welcome puts on Spring is Here. And Natalia, a Latina member, leaned forward and lowered her head to tell us about the insensitive things that had been said on the church's mission trip to Mexico, "Things like, be prepared to be around dirty kids." A few of the White participants let out moans of annoyance on behalf of Natalia and the other women who spoke up that night, but that was it. The group failed to entertain Natalia's suggestion that churchgoers should have to have cultural sensitivity training before going on mission trips, and the subject of what church leadership could do or should do about racist incidents involving black face and guns vanished from the conversation.

On the few occasions that participants did build off what another said, it regarded scripture, finding grace, the weather, or individual acts of racism—topics that were safe to return to if and when the conversation started to veer in a prickly direction. Public school teachers, in particular, were a recurring source of blame for anything and everything, including individualized racist behavior. On the first day with the glass elephant, we kicked off the discussion with a news story about a teacher in a neighboring school district who had been terminated for a racist post she made on Facebook. She had written that Black people were lazy and should "move back to Africa where they will have to work for a living." Gwen, a White woman who told us that she was suspicious of the phrase "White privilege," was the first to speak up. "Good, that teacher needs to be fired!—It's hateful," she lamented. Gwen then did what other White women so often do when confronted with the subject of racism—she turned the conversation away from racism and onto her own personal hardship, in her case, as a parent.[33] She jumped to the subject of a teacher at her kid's school who "has a mouth," a phrase she used to convey the teacher's allegedly rude and bad attitude.

Amani took the elephant from Gwen and gave advice from her perspective as a mother and as a teacher: "For your kids to be treated right, you have to be the crazy person sometimes." Gwen and another White mother in attendance liked what Amani had to say. They raised their right hands up to the sky, gesturing in agreement, something that never happened when the criticism turned to White privilege. Gwen grabbed the elephant back, excited to share her opinion that teachers are arrogant and entitled. Talk about the racist post and what it implies fizzled out. Teachers were easier to be upset about.

On the rare occasions when a group member's remarks pivoted toward institutional racism, their observations were unheard, trivialized, or dismissed. The week after a Minnesota police officer was acquitted in killing Philando Castile, Brooklyn's BTB group met for its end-of-the-semester finale in a family-friendly sandwich shop. The group was quieter than usual, and it was evident that Charise, a BTB regular in her twenties, was feeling down. I sensed that Charise was upset by the group's failure to grieve Castile or to call attention to the corrupt criminal justice system at this and other meetings.[34] In previous meetings she had noted that as a biracial mother of a Black son, she was disturbed by the murder of Castile, a 32-year-old Black man who was shot and killed by a police officer in front of his girlfriend and her four-year-old child.

Brooklyn, the group leader, looked over at Charise with an empathetic smile. It was her way of gently recognizing Charise's feelings. She then pushed forward, asking how the group was feeling about what was going on in the nation. An eerie silence grew heavy in the room. Then Anne leaned up and away from her sandwich to inform us that she was behind on the news. "I have no idea what's going on in our country—I haven't had time to," she said. The room fell silent again, prompting Brooklyn to change the subject. How Charise was feeling and why, and what exactly was going on in the nation, was one of many contentious matters that carried on unaddressed. If the racially privileged churchgoers were to ask penetrating questions about that, their knowledge might induce an obligation to act on behalf of Black lives.[35] They did not ask a single question.

Confederate monuments to white supremacy and their place in the public sphere were a hot topic at the time of my study. Activists on the side of Black Lives were organizing all across the U.S. South to remove symbols of the Confederacy from university campuses, public parks, and government buildings, and the movement had reached a record-breaking height after the murder of George Floyd in 2020. According to the Southern Poverty Law Center, 160 symbols of the Confederacy were removed in 2020, the highest count within one year in U.S. history.[36] I remember driving to BTB on Sunday evenings contemplating how I might react, or how I should respond, to those in the group who supported or opposed the public display of Confederate iconography in Mississippi. Repeatedly, I learned that my worries about what to do or what to say were unfounded, as such topics rarely came up at BTB.

Politically conservative men of color in Maura's mixed-gender BTB group were the only ones to speak up about Confederate symbolism, and they argued that change was unwarranted, un-Christian, and dangerous. Joe, a military man who introduced himself as racially "mixed" with "White Dixiecrat grandparents," was the first to express his opinion on movements to take down Confederate imagery in Mississippi. He leaned forward into our large circle and spoke forcefully. The university was "wrong to take down the state flag the way they did," he said. "It's up to state legislatures to put the [state] flag up for a vote." Joe's remarks inspired Marcel, a member of the church who identifies as "Christian before Black," to speak up, too. "If you're trying to take down flags and statues," he said, "you're just agitating—all that does is *agitate* people." He then brought up a name that had never been uttered at our meeting before: Black Lives Matter. Taking his hand to his forehead, Marcel shouted, "That's the worst thing that could happen right now!—Three women—three women started this thing!" Marcel told us that he had done research and found out that those three women want to "get rid of the heterosexual males in society." "Their values are way off," he warned, and are not to be trusted.

Joe and Marcel's criticisms of leftist "agitators" who, in so many words, brought violence on themselves, were touchy. Amani, one of the most candid members of BTB, later made a fleeting comment about how it's unfair to "lump everyone into the same box." She was the only one to offer a counterpoint. No one else challenged them, nor attempted to dive into a discussion about the merits of collective demonstrations for racial justice. Everyone else kept their thoughts to themselves and moved on to topics that diffused tension. Several White members swapped stories about their mutual mistrust of teachers and took turns complaining about older racist family members who, in their words, "were never going to change." Their allegiance to sameness was restored again.

***

BTB's approach to racial reconciliation is common in the Southern Baptist tradition. Jemar Tisby, president of The Witness: A Black Christian Collective, argues that the recent wave of racial reconciliation programming in the evangelical church is more concerned with the appearance of diversity than with changing mindsets or racial justice.[37] Other scholars have made similar points about evangelical efforts to reconcile race relations. Robert P. Jones of PRRI writes that racial reconciliation is "a strategy for making peace with the status quo"; it asks White Christians to confess their sins in exchange for Black forgiveness.[38] Nothing else, Jones argues, is required of White Christians from the racial reconciliation mission. On a similar note, sociologist Michelle Oyakawa argues that racial reconciliation programs may be doing more harm than good in multiracial evangelical churches. In an article on how pastors use the rhetoric of reconciliation in their ministries, Oyakawa describes racial reconciliation as a "suppressive frame" that prevents critical dialogue about racial justice and White cultural dominance.[39]

Racial reconciliation programs like BTB have their flaws, but conversations about race in any form or fashion at Welcome were understandably hard for Brooklyn, Maura, and the other BTB participants. They were taking on a subject that others avoided at the majority White church—they were opting to discuss race. Indeed, at the beginning stages of the group, many of its participants, of every color and every political position, took pride in BTB's reputation as the unusual small group at Welcome. Over time, however, in private conversations, a few of its members voiced reservations about the group's waning numbers. The group was violating church norms and they were unsettled by the loss in White membership that came with that violation. Within less than one year, BTB had dwindled from fifteen to seven participants: four Black and three White. Soon thereafter, a few of the remaining members convinced Maura that it was time to disband. In its place, they launched an alternative group that some participants of BTB, present and past, had in common: parenting.

Amani was sad to see BTB turned into a group about parenting. Honest conversations about race were on the horizon, she said, and she was troubled by the choice to abandon the issue. Maura, the group's leader, was also disturbed by the sheer number of White people who had dropped out of the group, and she was saddened that the church had done little to support their efforts. In private conversations with her and a few other members, I learned that members of BTB had suggested that Welcome let them host one of their discussions about race on the Sunday morning stage, and they had pitched the idea of its leadership team going through a racial reconciliation program. Bird, as well as

Welcome's governing body of mostly White male leaders, allegedly ignored their requests. Black members of BTB were speaking into the void. BTB was unable to gain traction in the church, and by the time I terminated my research, it had not been restarted again.

## The Politics of Sameness

Welcome stood behind a common refrain that punctuates American evangelicalism: The United States is divided, but the church cannot be. To this end, Welcome routinely ignored politically charged events that could rouse disagreements, even in circumstances when their very own community felt like it was under fire. They did not bring up Trump, one of the most polarizing figures in U.S. political history. They did not name or talk about Confederate iconography or White racial domination, even as neo-Confederates marched through Oxford. And they repeatedly circumvented critical dialogue about race and white supremacy, even in a group that a churchgoer organized in response to Trump's race-baiting presidential campaign.

Welcome is not unique in its choice to evade uncomfortable truths that could cause friction within Christian communities. Silence and denial are salient practices of church in the evangelical tradition, and these practices gained momentum in the Trump years. The fallout over silence at the 2017 Southern Baptist Convention's annual meeting provides a telling example.[40] At that meeting, Dwight McKissic, a prominent Black minister who founded Cornerstone Baptist Church in Arlington, Texas, submitted a resolution that demanded that the SBC denounce the racist ideologies and "totalitarian impulses" of the alt right that are infecting "the minds and actions of its violent disciples." SBC leadership dismissed the resolution's "wording" as too contentious, decided against raising it for discussion, and shifted to lighter topics. Outraged, McKissic went to the mic and requested additional time; he wanted his resolution to be heard. It took his protest, as well as other Black voices in the SBC, to have the resolution deliberated and passed. If it were not for McKissic's persistence, the SBC would have quietly avoided the issue. One of Welcome's BTB members reflected on how the SBC main stage mirrored what happens at churches across the country in a social media post:

White Christians are careful not to "rock the boat," they wrote, even as the boat runs over their "brothers and sisters of color."

Avoidance structures biblical sameness. In the context of Welcome, as in many other evangelical churches, "difference" was synonymous with "disruptive." Consequently, those moderately closer to the left side of the political axis were likely to report feeling pressured to keep their opinions to themselves than were conservative members. These churchgoers inferred that if they wanted to stay in good standing with other Christians, they had to observe an unspoken yet powerful rule of engagement: keep politics to yourself, do not name the elephants in the room, and if you do speak up or ask questions about a divisive issue, do not expect dialogue. Expect to speak into the void.

There is a hegemonic ideal in American evangelicalism that being White, cisgender, heterosexual, conservative, and Republican is what makes a person good.[41] Those who deviate from that ideal, on one axis or another, must manage their deviation by hiding what they think and emphasizing what makes them the same as others at church.[42] Put another way, they have to put on a convincing Christian act. Emphasize their status as a mother or father, as a husband or wife, as a critic of nonbelievers, as a churchgoer. The next chapter examines how gender factored into that act. It shows how the church communicated that biblical unity depends on men's authority over women in home and nation.

4

# Back to Basics

In the aftermath of Brett Kavanaugh's controversial appointment to the Supreme Court, Bird was joined by his wife Anne on stage to preach the Word on gender. In the weeks leading up to their sermon, the nation had been following the Kavanaugh hearing which involved an accusation of sexual assault from Christine Blasey Ford, a fifty-year-old psychology professor who attended high school with Kavanaugh. In a grueling testimony before the Senate Judiciary Committee, Blasey Ford tearfully described how a drunken Kavanaugh and another boy pushed her into a bedroom and attempted to rape her at a small house party when they were teenagers.[1] Two other women accused Kavanaugh of sexual assault while the hearing was underway, but the evidence lodged against him did not sway the majority Republican Senate of wrongful doing.[2] Kavanaugh became a justice of the Supreme Court on October 6, 2018, the day before Bird and Anne's sermon.

Bird and Anne started their remarks with a verse from the Bible on men's dominion over women in marriage: 1 Peter 3:1–7, which they referred to as "Lessons from the Rock." They read the passage that tells "wives, be subject to your husbands, so that even if some do not obey the word, they may be won without a word by the conduct of their wives, when they see your respectful and pure conduct."[3] Following this, Bird mentioned Genesis 2:24, a verse that he uses when he does weddings because it calls men and women in marriage "one flesh." This morning on stage, he continued, he and Anne are like "one person." The church should assume that Anne agrees with whatever he says, and vice versa, and that whatever they share is rooted in a biblical marriage under God.

The Bible's instructions for marriage can be hard to digest, Bird warned, and it might upset the "ladies in the house." This is God's Word, and their job is to preach it. America is in shambles because men are allowing women to lead, Bird continued. God made men the bosses. Wives can make a positive impact on men—their bosses—through

Figure 4.1. Depiction of the umbrella of protection and authority that Bill Gothard developed when he founded the Institute in Basic Life Principles, a Christian fundamentalist organization. The umbrella places God at the top, men/husbands second in command, and women/wives at the lowest position just above children.

"Godly submission, conduct, and . . . fear of God." "We all have bosses, but we don't have a problem with that," Anne added in a defensive tone. God is a God of order, she countered. If you picture an umbrella, Christ is over the top, then the husband, then the wife, and then the children. What Anne referred to was, in fact, as Bill Gothard had popularized it, a descending hierarchy of three umbrellas of authority, as seen in figure 4.1. Gothard, an influential Christian minister who is associated with the Duggar family and its sexual crimes, came up with the umbrella of authority concept when he founded the Institute in Basic Life Principles.[4] That umbrella is a safe haven for women, Bird said, and women should want to be protected by the umbrella that God designed. "Let all that stuff hit them first!" Anne tittered.

Bird and Anne never gestured toward the political fallout that was unfolding across the country over Trump's nominee for the highest court in the land. They did, however, tell women to get their "priorities" straight. Stop trying to be like men, stop nagging on men, and stop dressing in revealing clothes. It's okay for women to dress well, Bird clarified, but they should not "use that to attract away from God." Like other influential evangelical leaders, Bird was preaching that men are unable to control their lust, and that the responsibility falls to women to ensure that men steer clear of sexual sins.[5] And "the Men," he resumed, have to get better at supervising their wives and daughters. It's a man's job to protect women, he preached.

Bird and Anne's remarks followed the playbook of "gender complementarianism," the belief that men and women are inherently complementary, and that God created men and women to complete one another in heterosexual marriage.[6] Bird told men to take care of their wives, and Anne described men as a "blessing" that fills in women, which she referred to as the "weaker vessel," a phrase she quoted from 1 Peter 3:7. But they pushed evangelical beliefs in gender complementarianism further: they preached that men should have complete dominion over women and implied that gay and lesbian people violate God's design for marriage. It was a hard spin on "soft" patriarchy, a brand of patriarchy that Christian ministries use to legitimate men's headship in the home, church, and society. Yet slightly different from the ministries that ask men to be leaders who balance firmness with care, Bird and Anne said little about what men could do to rid America of moral decay.[7] Women were the problem.

One churchgoer I interviewed told me that Bird and Anne's sermon made her so uncomfortable that she almost got up and walked out in the middle of service. Bird and Anne looked uncomfortable too. Their voices were teeming with hesitation. They expressed regrets as they spoke and warned women that their remarks on submission might be upsetting. But Bird and Anne insisted on pushing past the discomfort and preaching what they refer to as the Word.

Welcome was committed to implementing its Southern Baptist planter church's belief system, and White male supremacy defines that system.[8] However, holding onto that belief system in a new inclusive church plant could be challenging. It took work, and that work was persistent at Welcome. This chapter examines that work. It shows how multiple levels of church life proactively squelched progressive understandings of gender before those understandings had a chance to emerge. The church preached that men are the God-given bosses of women. Men in the church encouraged each other to be politically incorrect. And women in the church pressured each other to stay quiet about the gender arrangement in marriage, especially if their views countered or contradicted the Word.

## Men Are the Bosses

The Rock, a men's group at the church, was invested in the idea that men are the God-given bosses of women. Pace, my graduate research assistant, attended The Rock for its monthly meetings at the church office on my behalf. It was for men and for men only. Guest speakers referred to "The Men" when they wanted to call attention to a specific aspect of leadership. Church leaders yelled out "Men!" when directing other men where to go or what to do next (e.g., "Men! Start the lineup for the buffet," and "Get in your groups, Men"). And "these Men" and "the Men" were featured in prayers and prayer requests before heavy meals of meat and potatoes.

Most of the participants who showed up for The Rock were White, but there were also Black, Latino, and one or two South Asian men at almost every meeting, and they, like the White men in attendance, sat together or near one another. Apart from a handful of retirees, the participants ranged from thirty to fifty years of age and came to The Rock meetings directly from work. Some arrived in button-down shirts, crisp slacks, and spotless polo shirts. Others wore work T-shirts and muddy jeans. The turnout ranged from about 25 to 40 people. More than half of those were regulars.

The attendance was higher than usual when James, the director of a reputable facilities management business, came to give a talk on leadership. "Raise your hands if you've ever felt like a leader," James directed at the top of his presentation. Every single one of the fifty or so attendees raised their hands. "First impressions matter," James professed. Men who work in hard labor don't know how to shake hands, he claimed. "They either give you a death grip or a dead fish hand." James beckoned a young White man in a polo shirt to stand up for a demonstration. "Make eye contact," he instructed, as they shook hands.

After the handshake demo, James began a lesson on work ethic that appeared as if it had been pulled from *The Protestant Ethic and the Spirit of Capitalism* by social theorist Max Weber. In that foundational early twentieth-century text, Weber explains how the Protestant theology of predestination, or the belief that God has preordained who is going to heaven and hell, fueled the idea that a person is "called" to a specific job (e.g., gardening or maintenance) and are obligated to fulfill that calling with a good work ethic.[9] That calling, according to Weber, is the moral engine of capitalism that made the United States. It turns exploitative labor into a spiritual asset, and rewards competition, specialized labor, efficient production, and hard work.

James stood out in front of a blank PowerPoint screen and peppered his audience with questions: "What's your purpose? What's your passion? Men, what's your legacy?" James clicked on his PowerPoint slide show: "In the same way, let your _______ shine before others, so that they may see your good works and glorify your Father who is in heaven." This is from Matthew 5:16, James clarified. "Y'all know it," he assured them. James waited a few seconds and then filled in the blank himself. The answer was "light." James clicked to the next slide that had replaced light with the words "waffle fries." "In the same way, let your waffle fries shine before others, that they may see your good deeds and glorify your Father in heaven." The owner of Chick-fil-a (a fast-food giant that has a reputation for being anti-gay and ultra conservative) gave him the idea, he said.[10] "Whatever you do, just fill it in that blank." The work that men do, no matter how hard or low paying, is valuable when it serves God. "Every day. At work. At home. Men, you set the thermostat," and the thermostat has to be oriented toward God.

Men who view work in "this worldly" terms are not real leaders, or even real men, James said. Those men are miserable, he continued, because they refuse to see how each and every job gives praise to God, country, and family. Those men are, in his words, "drama mamas," "know-it-alls," and "whiners" who demand better wages or take academic stabs at economic exploitation.[11] Christian men should avoid those kinds of men, James advised. And women, he implied, were never meant to be leaders. They were put on earth to work under the direction of good Christian men and should see that work—especially the unpaid stuff—as a gift from God.

The notion that men are the God bosses of women was accentuated in the church, especially when guest speakers came for a visit. Johnny Flynt, a retired baseball coach and former Baptist pastor, preached about men's dominion over women when he spoke at Welcome on behalf of Families First, a nonprofit organization that wants to, in his words, "rid the family of Satan." His stop at Welcome was part of a tour he was doing in churches, community clubs, schools, and prisons to teach "misdirected mothers" and "failing fathers" how to rekindle their relationship with God.[12]

"If you have a copy of God's Word with you," Flynt instructed, "turn with me to Colossians 3:18–20—we're going to look at the blueprint for a Godly home." Before reading Colossians, Flynt made the church roar in laughter with a playful digression about how his grandkids thought that Adam and Eve got kicked out of Olive Garden (an Italian restaurant franchise) for eating the forbidden fruit. He lingered for a moment, letting the laughter die down, and then summarized the verse in a forceful tone, "Wives, submit. Husbands, love. Children, obey. And parents, do not exasperate your children."

Husbands are the head, wives are the heart, and children are the hope, Flynt preached. "We don't have any excuses—we have the B-I-B-L-E: Basic Instructions Before Leaving Earth," and the instructions are clear. Women are supposed to "complete men," not "compete" with them, Flynt charged forcefully. "You don't complain, don't fight, don't fuss," he advised. The women who do, he continued, are the ones who invite Satan into their home. "Stay on alert to Satan!" Flynt shouted at the close of the sermon. "He's gonna get after you!"

Ray, an elder member who participates in The Rock, had the same blueprint for a Godly marriage as Flynt. When I interviewed him and his wife Nancy, Ray told me that he has had to have several conversations with his wife about male headship. Those conversations, he assured me, have been good for her. His wife sees male authority differently than "the world" does[13]:

> Unsaved people in this society can't understand that greater blessings flow upon the home when it's a Godly home. It doesn't mean [that the

> Godly home] will be pain free. But the love, and the joy, and the peace will flow freely and easily when there's not a contesting over authority, the husband's authority, in the home.

Nancy, his wife, had been quiet the entire time that Ray talked about his dominion over her in marriage. Once she spoke up, she made a vague comment about how all marriages are hard and then concluded that, "It is, so, uhhh—we certainly have an anchor." That anchor, according to her husband and church teachings, is unrivaled male authority in the home, at work, in the church, and in larger society.

## Women Are Almost Feminist

Men's headship anchors the evangelical church, but Welcome could not leave that anchor alone unattended. There were ladies in the house (to borrow the phrase from Bird and Anne) who wanted to be their own bosses and who objected to male supremacy. Claire, who referred to herself as "almost feminist," was one of those people.

The way Claire sees it, women who sign up for marriage are signing up for a round-the-clock boss. She wasn't looking for a boss.

> I was always around strong women who were leaders, and I wanted to be that. I didn't like being told that I couldn't have a certain role just because I was a woman. But all these people around me were telling me, "This is in scripture. This role is a man's role. There are roles that a man should have and roles that a woman should have. There are characteristics that you should display and characteristics that he should display." It never sat well with me. It still doesn't.

It has been difficult for Claire to reconcile her resistance to male headship with church teachings on marriage, but she told me she thinks she may have found a solution: just stay single. In defense of singlehood, she told me about her Christian mentor from college. This mentor, Claire explained, was a single mother for her entire adult life, independent, and very happy. That mentor told Claire to never apologize for her power, but also, ironically, that if Claire were to ever marry, she had to submit to a Godly marriage. "Swallow your pride and respect your husband," her mentor advised. Claire decided to remain single like her mentor. Staying single in a religious subculture that pushes hard for young women to find a husband has been difficult, but it has been worth it to her. The alternative is just too bleak, a point that the ex-Christian fundamentalist Tia Levings effectively makes in her memoir, *A Well-Trained Wife*.

Sarah, a self-described "strong-minded and strong-willed woman," was also uncomfortable with the church's gender arrangement in marriage. She joined Welcome because she wanted to be part of a church that was less extreme in its views on gender. Her previous church taught that women should treat their husbands like kings—"It was a wait on a man hand and foot kind of a thing"—and she got tired of it. Taking on a deep aggressive tone, Sarah mimicked the preacher of that church and repeated the sexist jabs he made from the pulpit: "I'm the man, the wife should go and fix my plate," and "All women do is talk and spend money." She has never had to sit through those kinds of crude jokes at Welcome, and she loves it for that.

When Sarah joined Welcome, she felt listened to, and she established a playful, sibling-like relationship with Bird. But Bird and Anne's sermon on gender made her angry. Bird spoke more than Anne, she said, and he made women sound less important than men.

> I am very "Go woman!" Not that I think women can do everything that men can do. We are made differently to do different things. They can't give birth. I don't have a penis. I mean, you know, I know there are differences, and I know God gave us different capabilities, and I completely respect that. And I do know that the Lord made the husband the head of the household, but that doesn't mean that he can't fix my [dinner] plate just as well as I can fix his. . . . I do feel like I struggle with the entire Bible when it comes to . . . women and men's roles.

After elaborating on how the sermon made her feel, Sarah talked about how her beliefs in gender essentialism correspond with and in some ways contradict evangelical teachings. She believes that men and women play different roles on the same "team" in marriage but struggles with the belief that men should have the final say in everything. That message makes her "feel insignificant or silly, or incompetent, or uneducated," and she doesn't like feeling that way.

Plus, Sarah pointed out, the church appears to have replaced gender complementarianism with a more incendiary message about men having irrefutable authority over women. Sarah's perception of the shift to patriarchal extremism is not unfounded. Investigative journalists and "exvangeligal" women (post evangelical women who left fundamentalist Christianity and their domineering husbands) alike are sounding the alarm about the malicious antifeminist platforms that have taken over White conservative Christianity[14]—platforms that are powering the new and growing "trad wife" (short for traditional wife) phenomenon on social media. Trad wives post content of themselves dressed up, pretty, and smiling while doing household chores and taking care of children in the service of patriarchy.[15]

Sarah reflected on how the church presents scripture and said:

> Sometimes it's portrayed like "I'm the man, hear me roar!" kind of thing. Like, is the woman supposed to bow down to her husband? Maybe that's how it['s] supposed to be, but I feel like the Lord took the rib from the side of Adam to come alongside him and be his helpmate, and to be equal, you know? I know that sounds so juvenile and petty, but I really struggle with that.

Ironically, after making this statement, Sarah cut herself off and said, "If that's what the Bible says, it's legit." But that even if it's legit, she "can't promise" to be obedient. Sarah, in other words, cannot promise to do gender in the way that the church prescribes. She is a self-described "very opinionated" woman who has a hard time with what sociologists Candace West and Don Zimmerman term doing deference and passively watching men do dominance.[16]

Sarah's remark about Bird and Anne's sermon during her interview was extensive. My transcription of it was almost two pages, single spaced. She rarely had opportunities to ponder biblical womanhood, and she was using the interview setting to do that. Notably, Sarah was fully aware of how her discomforts contradict church teachings and her awareness of that contradiction is what made her reaction to my inquiries about gender messy: I cannot obey but will try to if God says I should. I am not sure if that is what God says. I can't promise I'll do it. I don't think I can do it.

Sarah, like other women in the church, seldom had a chance to reflect on the gender arrangement in the church and she understandably had a hard time formulating, much less explaining, her opinion on gender when I asked her. Her point of view had been pushed so far to the margins of church that it felt taboo, destructive, even flat-out wrong to voice it. Sarah asked me if she was making sense, admitted that she was "having a hard time explaining it" and then sighed, "I struggle with it. Significantly."

Maura also struggles with what the church expects of women. When I asked her, in a private interview, what being a woman of God means to her, she sipped her iced soda and said point blank, "It's like you can't slack. You can't slack. You got to be on top of it at all times." Maura told me that she tried giving "everything" to God for a long time. She put her family first, and she put herself "on the back burner." Over the years, she has finally come to realize that she is just a human, to use her words, and that she can't do everything for everybody all the time. She has to take care of herself too.

> It's so easy to just get lost and totally forget about you. And I've done that for so long. By the time you're done, you got a stack of stuff like this [holds her right hand high] and you're on the bottom. It's hard to crawl out. [. . .] This year, I made it a point to start doing stuff for me again.

When we sat down for an interview, Maura said she was still trying to figure out how to give herself time, and without bringing negative attention to herself. Maura was an active member of the church and volunteered in its children's ministries program. She was also the primary caretaker in her family even though she worked full-time outside the home at a school. But now she no longer signs up for "everything," or lets her husband make her feel like she has to.

Claire, Sarah, and Maura reject the idea that women are inferior to men, but none of them were openly critical of the church's directives for gender and marriage. They were scared to speak up. As far as they could tell, everyone else in the church believes in male supremacy—a belief that takes the form of a God-given truth in part because women like them are too afraid to express their grievances.[17] The next section underlines how vocal critiques of political correctness coerced women to stay quiet about the church's hardline stance on gender. It shows how men in church leadership persistently avowed that the Word on gender is offensive and that true believers are offensive.

## The Bible Is Politically Incorrect

Less than a year after Bird and Anne's sermon on gender, Welcome launched "Back to Basics," a study that met Sunday nights at the church office for a month. Nearly 120 churchgoers attended the first meeting. Bird, visibly pleased with the crowd, stepped onto the small platform of the worship room and thanked "The men" and "The women" for coming. He was, to use his phrasing, "nervous" about doing Back to Basics and he imagined that others were too. When you mention biblical manhood and biblical womanhood, he said, "some warning signs begin to pop up." Then, without elaboration on what those warning signs are, Bird promptly deterred any critical thinkers who might be present from speaking up. He reassured everyone that God created an order and that those who embody that order are "aligned under the Lordship."

Bird kicked off the event with a parable that underscored the basics that the church wants to get back to. The parable began with a man driving somewhere he has never been to before. Lost, he opens a map app on his phone for directions. He eventually grows tired of "that woman's voice" and switches the app to mute. The man drives forward, still looking at the map app, and as he does, the estimated time of arrival escalates from "eight minutes to thirty-eight minutes, to forty-eight minutes, to an hour and seventeen minutes," Bird chuckled. "Surely y'all know where I'm going with this! You've all heard that voice announce 'Recalculating, Recalculating!'" he exclaimed to a room of light laughter. Bird deepened his voice to communicate the seriousness of the matter. The church is lost. It needs to pull over, turn around, and find the right directions. Stop letting "the culture" (i.e., women) tell the church what to believe about gender. Put the church (i.e., men) back in charge.

"Who did He create first?!" Bird yelled. "Adam" and "The Man!" participants shouted. Bird nodded agreeably, explaining that the gender order is glory to God. Some Christian men and women are dismissing that order, he chided, because they are "afraid of offending people."

Bird paused for a minute and then told the church that Adam in Genesis was also responsible for the fall of humankind. Eve felt free to listen to a snake, and not him. Adam ate the fruit that she offered, and he allowed her, a woman, to eat the fruit as an autonomous agent of her own body, independent of the man that God created first. "He should've stepped up and showed some leadership and told Eve not to eat the fruit," Bird said. Biblical men "reject passivity." That is basic, he preached. Adam failed the basics of masculinity. He failed to take charge of Eve. She took charge of him.

Once Bird was done emasculating Adam, Sampson took over and directed "the ladies" to the adjoining kitchen and asked "The Men" to stay where they were and divide into small groups of four to five. Pace was assigned to Sampson's table along with three other White men.

Sampson skipped the introductions and jumped right to the subject of what he and Bird termed accepting responsibility.[18] "Adam was a punk," Sampson grinned. He let "another man" (the snake) speak to his wife and tell his wife what to do without intervening, he said. Sampson relaxed back in his foldable steel chair and asked the group to reflect on how they accept responsibility in their homes. Before anyone had time to answer, Sampson described how his wife grumbles at the term "submissive." "It's just so harsh," he admitted. "I don't want my wife to be my slave" and just have babies, cook, and clean, he said. Yet regardless of what he expects of her, he countered, he has to be the one to decide what she does and does not have to do. Taking ownership of decisions in the home is what accepting responsibility means in the evangelical faith, he lectured.

Men have become too afraid to lead, Sampson cautioned. Too afraid of offending somebody and being charged with "toxic masculinity," a phrase that had been trending on social media to refer to men who use aggressive means to assert their power and control, and too often eagerly misheard as the suggestion that all men are violent and cruel.[19] "Toxic—what is toxic masculinity and all that madness?" Sampson quizzed rhetorically.

Wayne, a White man with silver cropped hair, clasped his hands on the table and smiled wide at Sampson's comment. All the "problems" started in the 1960s and '70s when middle-class White women entered the workforce, Wayne asserted. Men and women started cheating on their spouses and "stuff started coming over from California," like drugs. On top of that, according to Wayne, the news from New York—which he called "fake news"—had made it seem as if Black people were being terrorized down South.[20] "I was there, I lived it," he claimed. "I saw Dr. Martin Luther King Jr. walking through the streets of Memphis, past Black and White people, and everyone was just fine." Integration was forced, Wayne moaned. "Not that it's a bad thing," he added, as he lightly touched Sampson's arm, the only dark-skinned man at the table. Wayne had a Black woman working for him in his home back then, he assured him, and he was kind to her. She "was good as gold." Wayne paused as if waiting for confirmation. Sampson seized the moment and pivoted away from race and over to an issue that he and Wayne could agree on: God's rules for gender are politically incorrect. Men of God have to be politically incorrect too.

"Can anybody remember how God punished women after Eve ate the fruit?" Sampson probed. God warned Eve of the punishment after He stipulated that childbirth be painful, he clarified. One participant shrugged his shoulders, unsure of the answer. Sampson hurried to the punchline: the punishment is for women to want to be like men. To want to have what men have. To want to lead like men lead. The church should be unafraid of women like that, and of "backlash," he declared. Being in line with the Word, even if it offends women, is praise to God.

My head spun the first time I read the field notes from Back to Basics. It was hard to comprehend how a church that usually evades contentious issues could be so up front about male supremacy.[21] American evangelicals have a reputation for supporting and protecting white supremacy and patriarchy, but recent studies had found that evangelicals feel pressed to communicate their beliefs about race, gender, and sexuality in less aggressive terms. If they want to attract young people, they cannot come across as judgmental bigots. They have to, in the words of sociologist Sarah Diefendorf, work on their messaging and offload the "ugly" stuff—racism, sexism, homophobia, transphobia—to elected officials like Trump.[22]

Welcome leaders were clearly concerned about how some people might respond to their directions for women and men, as evidenced when Bird said he was "nervous" about doing Back to Basics. Yet different from how church leaders and small group participants handled other polarizing issues (the Confederate flag, border walls, the election of Trump), the leadership team at Welcome were "ugly" about gender. Rhetorically, they paralleled what the Republican Party was doing in its "politically incorrect" campaign to Make American Great Again. Rather than try to make patriarchy appear less threatening, they got offensive, and their offense paved the way for churchgoers like Wayne to downplay social hierarchies of race and gender that put Black women, such as his Black nanny, at the intersection of multiple systems of oppression.[23]

## Men Are Offensive

The Reasoned Defense group was a small group at Welcome that took enormous pride in being offensive. Bob, a college-educated biblical literalist, launched the weekly group on the heels of the 2017 Women's March, the largest recorded women's demonstration in U.S. history.[24] When he and Pace met for fried chicken at the university dining hall, Bob described evangelical apologetics as a coalition of believers that use archaeological and scientific evidence to develop a "robust academic" argument that the Bible should be the moral bedrock of America.

One Reasoned Defense meeting, which Bob framed with scriptures in Genesis, drove home the idea that Christian beliefs about gender are offensive and that believers should root their identity in the offense. Four men and two women showed up to that meeting, which took place in an unkempt room downstairs from the fellowship area where Back to Basics was held. All the participants were White, and with the exception of Pace, in their thirties or older.

Bob, the group leader, pulled on his short beard and remarked on the time—6:30 p.m.—and joked that his store-bought honeybun is "the dinner of champions." Pam, one of two women in attendance, glanced over at Bob affectionately and promised to bring him freshly baked brownies next time before asking sarcastically, "So, do women need to leave the table tonight?"

Bob had alerted everyone via group chat that they should expect to cover, "Is the Bible anti-woman?" Reflecting on Bob's message, Clayton, who was accompanied by his wife Bev, brought up a rumor he heard about a Baptist church with a female pastor. Pam mentioned that she thinks the church is in Chicago and that "they" (assumingly the female pastor and her husband) were going to be referred to as "co-pastors."[25]

Bob cut Pam off, "Are the co-pastors even married?" Before Pam could answer, Bob interrupted her again to stress that women are not preachers. They are teachers. And a woman who teaches the gospel, he added, should only be allowed to do so under the direction of her husband.

Bob ended the conversation about women who preach on a prayer. He noted that "people are starting to have multiple interpretations of the Bible" and asked God to help him defend the truth. After the amen, Bob read Genesis 2:18–22, word for word, the part of the Bible that describes how God took a rib from Adam to create Eve. He ended on verse 23, which quotes what Adam said:

> This is now bone of my bones
> And flesh of my flesh;
> She shall be called Woman,
> Because she was taken out of Man.

Without elucidation of the text, which Bob believes speaks for itself, he brought up feminists who "diss the Bible" as misogynistic. The previous waves of feminism were not as bad as the third one, he said. Those waves fought for the vote and were not centered on the idea that gender is socially constructed. Third-wave feminists believe that "men and women have zero differences," which to Bob is "absolute craziness" and "divorced from reality."

Tanner, a member of the group who often jostles for the lead with Bob, selected another verse from the Bible that "proves" women are supposed to submit to men: 1 Corinthians 11. Excited by the call, Bob read two verses out loud from a New King James Version of the Bible: "For man is not from woman, but woman from man. Nor was man created for the woman, but woman for the man" (1 Corinthians 11:8–9). Bob then asked the group to flip to 1 Corinthians 14:34: "Let your women keep silent in the churches, for they are not permitted to speak; but *they* are to be submissive as the Law also says." The group snickered lightly, and Tanner, smiling, looked at Pam with his right index finger up to his lips and shushed her, prompting her to tap his thigh playfully as they both giggled. Bob attempted to lighten the severity of the verse: "people have different functions," he said, but that does not make them of unequal value to God.

Bob followed up with another scripture, pulled from Ephesians, that tells wives to submit to their husbands. This verse, Bob claimed, clarifies that marriage is not just about theology. It's about "biology." Men are "chemically addicted" to women, and Christians must observe "gender differences" if they want to respect the bodies that God gave them.

One of the quietest men in the group, Clayton, spoke up in support of biological determinism. The "chemical bonds" that men release (his voice lowered) when they orgasm is what makes pornography addictive, Clayton said. Men compulsively screen pornography, he explained, because they are hardwired to "bond" with women sexually.

Audibly electrified by Clayton's remark, several of the men in attendance started debating what hormone exactly—is it serotonin or dopamine?—releases when men ejaculate. They eventually concluded that the specifics of the hormone were irrelevant. The "bottom line," as Tanner put it, is that "something chemical" happens. Men have insatiable appetites for the "opposite sex" and women, the group surmised, derive pleasure from other acts of intimacy like caring for children. Not from sex.

Clayton, Tanner, and Bob's assessment of men's addiction to pornography fits with what Protestant Christians have been saying about it since the mid-1980s, when evangelical leaders started to claim that good Bible-believing Christian men become addicted to pornography because God made women for men.[26] It is, as sociologists Kelsy Burke and Trenton Haltom point out, a claim to addiction that skillfully puts a religious spin on the sex/gender/sexuality system, or a set of social arrangements rooted in a gender ideology that claims that there are only two sexes (male or female), that people are born male or female, and that the sex of a person determines their gender identity and sexual orientation.[27] As Clayton, Tanner, and Bob joyfully argued about what hormone "finds release" when men ejaculate, they made the case that God created an order that puts men in charge of sex.

Pam, who sat quietly through the lively exchange about pornography, changed the subject from chemicals back to what she called "The F Word" (feminists). "Do they even read the Bible?" she probed flippantly. Clayton responded by wondering aloud how Christians should share their views on sex and gender with *those* people, and raised a practical question: "How do you get on the offensive without being offensive?" How, in other words, can evangelicals advocate for male supremacy without sounding misogynistic and backward? In previous meetings, the group had studied Greg Koukl's "tactics" workbook, which teaches evangelicals techniques for winning arguments with skeptics, and for them, feminists are among the most despicable skeptics. But Clayton's question about how to share their views with nonbelievers went nowhere. Instead, "somehow," Pace wrote in his field notes, Bob brought up the Free the Nipple movement, and before he could explain what it was, the conversation took a dark turn.[28]

> TANNER: And then they ask why they're getting raped—
> CLAYTON: At that point, they're asking for it.

Tanner, who works in the legal field, added that he has watched many "beautiful girls" come through the county courthouse to file complaints of sexual assault. Those girls are actually the ones to blame, he smirked. They "make nine bad decisions and the guy makes one."

Tanner's nonchalant remark about rape invigorated the group. Clayton, Bev, Tanner, and Pam all started speaking over one another about women who drink, get high, and blame men for what they regret later. "Being under the influence is a surrender of your sovereignty," Tanner asserted. Men get "confused," Clayton added. "Some people say we're a rape culture. We're not a rape culture! We're an over-sexed culture!" Tanner exclaimed. "Africa is a rape culture. They have to use bear traps to stop rapists," Bob added.

The lively exchange about rape abruptly circled back to women pastors. Clayton argued that the Bible says that if a woman can't lead men in their own home, then they certainly shouldn't be allowed to lead men at church. Pam followed up on Clayton's comment by drawing a parallel between women pastors and women in the military, "Women can't protect men. . . . How are we supposed to believe that women can fight?—blows my mind!" And Bob claimed that whereas male pastors base their sermons on fact, women base theirs on emotion.

The movement to be "P. C." (politically correct) in the church is the problem, Clayton asserted. The church has become too tolerant of same-sex marriage, and pastors have got to "stop dancing around this stuff," he said. "It's the young people!" Pam and Bob shouted almost simultaneously. Pastors are scared of offending them.

The meeting was at high volume. No one seemed to notice that it had gone half an hour over its scheduled time. Everyone was shouting over each other, eager to express their outrage at "P. C. politics" that they and other conservatives feel censor their views and religious freedom. Pace decided it was time to leave. The comments about rape were disturbing, he wrote in his field notes, and he needed some fresh air.

One week prior to this meeting, U.S. actress Alyssa Milano had posted #MeToo on Twitter, a phrase that activist Tarana Burke coined in support of women and girls of color who had endured sexual assault because she too had experienced this violence.[29] Milano's #MeToo post went viral overnight. Reasoned Defense never addressed #MeToo by name, but the group made clear where it stood on the issue: rape is a woman's fault. Men are chemically destined by God to crave women sexually (often leading to sexual addiction to pornography) and women are making choices that confuse the insatiable impulses of men.

***

The misogynistic stance that Reasoned Defense took on sexual assault may seem extreme, but it is widespread in U.S. culture.[30] A survey study by PRRI found that 41 percent of Republican men (compared to 24 percent of Democratic men) think that men being falsely accused of sexual assault or harassment is a bigger problem than are the unreported incidences or disbelieved experiences of women.[31] PRRI also found that Republicans, especially Republican men, are the most likely to vote for a political candidate who has been accused of sexual harassment by multiple people.[32] The White evangelical support for Brett Kavanaugh and Donald Trump prove that point. Except for a few vocal critics, evangelical leaders overwhelmingly stood up for Kavanaugh after multiple allegations of sexual misconduct emerged against him, and also for Trump after his comments about the sexual violation of women went viral.[33] "Grab them by the pussy," Trump had said. Beautiful women are "like a magnet" he quipped, and like the men that the Reasoned Defense group described, he has no control over how he responds to women. He "just starts kissing," them. It was a statement that epitomizes what sociologist Jane Ward terms the "misogyny paradox, wherein boys' and men's desire for girls and women is expressed within a broader culture that encourages them to also hate girls and women."[34]

The group's disdain for women pastors reflects the evangelical mainstream too. In the summer of 2023, the Southern Baptist Convention made headlines that would make Bob's Reasoned Defense group feel the rush of victory. The SBC voted to expel several women-led congregations from the organization, and it approved an amendment to its constitution that explicitly prohibits women from holding pastoral titles. In a *New York Times* article about the vote, two religion correspondents, Elizabeth Dias and Ruth Graham, argued that the "crackdown" on women "stems from growing anxieties many evangelicals have about what they see as swiftly changing norms around gender and sexuality in America."[35] The pastors who voted to expel Rick Warren's Saddleback Church, among other churches, didn't want children to be "confused" about what God intends for men and women, and were concerned that women-led congregations create a slippery slope that, in the words of one Michigan pastor, leads to "homosexuals" marrying each other and becoming pastors in the church.[36]

Groups of men like Reasoned Defense are setting the blueprint for biblical sameness in the evangelical church, and their guiding principle is a social arrangement with White men in charge. Indeed, when the sexual assault of women came up at Reasoned Defense, a few in the group claimed that women are to blame for their rape, a claim that only White people can safely make in a state like Mississippi where White men have a violent history of accusing and executing Black men for allegedly raping White women.[37] (White) men don't rape, they just get "confused," an outspoken member of the group concluded. Africa by contrast is a rape culture, the group leader had said. It is a place where women have to fight off what he implied are the voracious sexual appetites of Black men.[38]

The solution to the "confusion" that White men experience, the members of Reasoned Defense indicated, is simple: get back to the basics of gender that the church prescribes. Put White Christian men back in charge of sex, dating, and marriage. Kavanaugh, a Supreme Court justice who has a history of ruling in favor of religious objections to contraception, and who voted to overturn women's reproductive rights, helps conservatives obtain that solution. And Trump, a president who vows to protect the "religious liberty" of White Christians, and who nominated Kavanaugh for the Supreme Court, is a solid ally to the movement to put White straight Christian men in control of women's bodies, choices, and livelihoods.

Reasoned Defense, however, does not represent the entire church. As the previous pages have shown, there were women in the church who opposed the idea that men should have absolute dominion over them and who believed that women can lead. But the Reasoned Defense group had no incentive to acquiesce to these women, or even try to empathize with their point of view. In fact, as indicative of the fervent back-and-forth about rape, it was biblical to *not* empathize. As Bird indicated when he spoke at Back to Basics, listening to women endangers the church. It thrust the church in the wrong direction. Christians have to restore the old map of gender, he had preached. The men of Reasoned Defense were convinced that they had the right map, and they were ready to share it.

In the next section, I show how a small group meeting of women promoted patriarchy too, but from another direction. Rather than make aggressive comments about feminism and gender, they nudged each other into silence about the immediate impact that male domination has on their lives. They conveyed to each other "don't complain."

## Women Don't Complain

Book club was a space for women to talk without men in the way. The participants, who were few in number, valued that space. They liked having a night off from their family obligations and connecting with other women from church. Some arrived with their books marked up and dog-eared. Others arrived having only read part or a few pages of the assigned books.

For the inaugural semester of book club, we read three books published by evangelical women. Two of those books were about women and the Christian men who took care of them. The first book, *Hope Heals: A True Story of Overwhelming Loss and an Overcoming Love*, by Katherine and Jay Wolf, is about a young married couple that struggled to regain a normal life after Katherine, the lead author, had a sudden massive brain stem stroke. The second book, *Redeeming Love* by Francine Rivers, is a novel set in the 1850s about Angel, a sex worker, and

Michael Hosea, a Christian man who obeys God's call to save her from prostitution in California's gold country.[39] The third book we read, *Falling Free: Rescued from the Life I Always Wanted* by Shannan Martin, was not about marriage, or about men who look after women in hard times. Yet it was the book that prompted participants to open up a little bit about their own marriages.

*Falling Free* essentially asks White women to share the gospel with people in impoverished communities.[40] Martin writes about the kids from the "other side of the urban tracks" that she has cared for and mothered as the basis for making that "ask." One of those kids is Robert, a young Black teenager who she and her husband "adopted" from a neighborhood "racked with addictions." In a racially charged tone that perpetuates the stereotype that Black men are wild and animalistic, Martin tells readers that Robert has the "volume level of an entire kindergarten class combined with the physical presence of a moody, fire-breathing circus acrobat."[41] Having him around, she continues, has been tough. She has gone to bed crying "quiet, salty tears" of exhaustion, and has wondered aloud whether she can rally herself to make pancakes for him and her family, "Again."[42] But Martin insists that the sacrifice has been worth it. Robert calls her "mother" now, and that is freeing. Freedom, she clarifies, is "letting go" and putting her "fist-pumping, raucous-laughing barn burner of a dad" (i.e., God) in control.[43] When Robert came into her life, God took over.

The book club convened to discuss *Falling Free* at Chancey's house. Seven women, counting me, between the ages of thirty and fifty (all but one White) showed up. Chancey, a former schoolteacher turned homeschool mom, had plenty of room for us in her large two-story brick home, and she was excited about showing us her sitting room in the loft. That room is where she hides from her family. It has everything she needs. Comfy sofa chairs, a television set, and a door that she can lock, she laughed. At the time, I didn't think much about Chancey's comment. But that changed when I reviewed our assigned chapters from *Falling Free*. Self-care is toxic to faith, the book charges. "If I hear the oxygen mask analogy one more time (save yourself first!) I might poke shish kebab skewers into my ears," Martin writes.[44] That loft where we sat in the comfy seats was Chancey's oxygen mask, and Chancey was proud of it.

Anne facilitated the discussion. She started us off with a question from the discussion guide that came with the book: "How do you feel about the life you have compared to the life you thought you wanted? Resentful? Relieved?" It was a question drawn from Martin's argument that women should stop planning out the life they want and open themselves up to the one that God wills for them.

Chancey was the first to speak up. She feels disappointed with the way her life turned out, and she attributes that disappointment to her marriage. Chancey enjoys the outdoors, and she always thought that she would have a husband who likes to travel and take long hikes. Her husband Ed is not that husband. She rarely sees him. All he likes to do is play golf.

The other women at book club deterred Chancey from saying anything else negative about her marriage. As soon as she finished speaking, another participant named Jill made clear that she is nothing like Chancey. "I actually never thought about the life I always wanted—I'm perfectly happy with where I am." Two other participants added that they are also content and that, like Jill, had not put much thought into what they wanted from marriage. One described her marriage as something that "just happened" to her, and another said that she had always thought "practically" about marriage, and never about what she could gain from it.

Chancey's less-than-ideal marriage was momentarily cleared from the conversation, but she brought it up again when we discussed *Falling Free* for the second time at Anne's house, a ranch-style cabin in the sticks along a narrow stretch of paved country road. After a few minutes of friendly chit chat about pastries, where to sit, and where I am in the research process, Anne had us turn to a chapter about "sacrifices," or the comforts that White middle-class Christians give up for missions in marginalized communities.[45]

Anne kicked off the discussion by asking if we had any reactions or "general thoughts" to share. The room fell silent for a solid ten seconds. Chancey straightened up in her armchair, "Okay, I guess I'll go first." The book made her think about her marriage, and about how she and her husband "don't have the same vision." She wants to do "more," which for her means bringing church to poor, orphaned, and homeless children. Her husband Ed does not share her vision. "They're [Martin and her husband] on the same page—we're not on the same page." Several of the other participants vocally agreed with some aspects of what Chancey said. Martin has a "wonderful marriage," one said. "She's lucky!" another shouted.

I stayed quiet, as I usually did during the discussion. I was having a hard time understanding how they had reached the conclusion that Martin, the author, was so lucky. Martin says little about her husband in *Falling Free*. It is unclear if her husband pitches in on preparing pancakes "Again" for her ministry of a welcoming table, and she neglects to specify how he reacts to her tears of exhaustion. In the instances where Martin does write about her husband, she depicts him as a spiritual leader of old and forgotten friends, not as a helpful hand in their extended "family" on the other side of the tracks.

Gwen, who had missed our first meeting about *Falling Free*, circled back to Chancey's comment about husbands. Her husband is nothing like Martin's, she said. "I need my husband to be happy. If he's not happy—good grief," Gwen moaned in annoyance. Hearing this, a few others nodded in agreement. One let out an animated "mm-hmm."

Gwen rolled her eyes and reiterated the church's commandment for marriage with a sarcastic twist: "Marriage is not about being on the same page. It's about keeping one person happy." In her house, a happy husband is the only way anyone can have a "peaceful life," she laughed in exasperation. Chancey, who was nodding yes, voiced annoyance with her own husband again: "I struggle to even hear God's plan without getting my husband on board first." She cannot "unplan" in the way that Martin advises, and she blames her husband for that. He gets in her way. He gets in the way of God.

Just as the heat was turning up on husbands, Anne intervened. She prompted us to turn to another page of the book and asked what we could give up in order to devote more time to God. The answers varied, ranging from turning off the "smut" on TV, to shutting down their phones, to the to-do lists and stuff, "So much stuff!," that clutters their minds and homes. From there on, the group stuck close to subjects that were tenuously tied to Martin's idea of "living small." There was talk about retirement, about dreams to minister to the poor, and about how important it is for people to take pride in what they do, even if what they do is flip burgers for minimum wage at a fast-food restaurant.

The subject of marital discontent had been contained, but not for long. Jennifer, the youngest stay-at-home mother in the group, initiated the talk about husbands again later that evening. She shared that when it comes to her mother-in-law, she "struggles with grace," a term that evangelicals use to describe the practice of being kind and compassionate to others. Her mother-in-law makes her feel like a bad mom and a bad wife, and her husband never defends her. Gwen, the one who feels obligated to put her husband's needs first, nodded in agreement. "I don't feel supported by my husband either—it's frustrating."

"Okay!" Anne interrupted. "We have to get to the last chapter—it's getting late." Under Anne's direction, we flipped to the next chapter, which was less charged. The participants talked about community and the importance of making time for people, and boasted about how Welcome is, in Anne's words, an eclectic gathering of people with "all the money in the world" as well as people "who can't make ends meet." Husbands were squeezed out of the conversation again and the women who complain about them were too.

***

In *The Tragedy of Heterosexuality*, Ward argues that the culture of straightness normalizes and revels in bad marriages.[46] It is common, for example, to hear women endlessly complain about their husbands and to build community with other women from those complaints. Welcome was invested in straight culture but talk about marital problems was minimal, even among women. Wifely submission to men, the church directed, is the glue that locks families and faith together. Women who complain about that arrangement, or try to get out of it, the church warned, are at odds with God's plan for them.

Women are deterred from complaining about men for a very practical reason. When women see other women duck out of the umbrella of authority that Bird and Anne preached, they may come to see the gender arrangement differently. Complaining is an aspect of that ducking. Complaining can lead to revolution, just as it did in the 1960s and '70s when women joined feminist consciousness-raising groups to talk candidly with other women about sex, sexual abuse, marriage, and family life.[47] A few members of book club edged the group closer to those types of conversations, and when they did, they were swiftly nudged back into what political scientist Elisabeth Noelle-Neumann terms a "spiral of silence" that made it seem as if everyone agreed with the church's official stance on gender.[48] Some book club participants thought they were in a space where women could talk about matters of importance to them. But that space obliged them to put men first. It obliged them to neglect their own hardship and find religious meaning in it. Hardship that, as sociologist Jessica Calarco explains, is exacerbated by a society that forces women to stand in for the social safety net. To be the ones to take care of the kids, the elderly, and the larger society without a dime in return.[49]

## Offensive Gender Politics

Welcome handled many issues of social and political concern with tender avoidance and deflection, but it was direct about men's power over women. That is, rather than address immigration or the election of Trump openly, they relied on a theology of male headship in a heterosexual family to signal their political orientations and allegiances to the religious and political right.[50] Reasoned Defense, in particular, instructed that to be godlier, Christians must comply with patriarchy and oppose all that it stands against—movements for gender and racial justice, anti-capitalist ideas, and queer people. The group encouraged each other to take pride in being offensive about gender, and that pride aggravates social inequalities in a few ways.

First, when evangelicals get offensive about gender, they harden the walls of an ideological silo that shuts other people and ideas out of their conversation. Welcome implied, on a regular basis, that the empathetic act of trying to understand what feminists think about gender poses an existential threat to the church. It can lead to confusion, doubt, and disaffiliation. For this reason, Welcome insisted that churchgoers stick close to Christians who agree (or pretend to agree) on the "basics" of gender. Consequently, the Reasoned Defense group, no matter how extreme, was doing church correctly. That group was sticking close to like-minded people. They were steering clear of people and positions that conflicted with their take on truth. They refused to entertain or empathize with a feminist position, even for the sheer sake of debate and argumentation.

Second, when evangelicals take ownership of being offensive about gender, they fan the flames of an anti-intellectual populism that belittles critical thinking and democratic dialogue.[51] Based on the agenda that Bob set, the Reasoned Defense group was scheduled to debunk the myth that the Bible is anti-woman, a claim that he suggested skeptics (i.e., feminists) often make. Yet the group, which was verbally and numerically governed by men, quickly lost sight of that goal and instead redirected its attention to those it tacitly accused of being *anti-men*: women pastors, women who accuse men of sexual assault, feminists (predictably), and transgender and gender queer people (although never named explicitly). In making these groups out to be "anti-men," the members of Reasoned Defense positioned themselves, and by extension conservative evangelicals, as the victims of leftist suppression. As they see it, people who challenge or even question the Bible's treatment of women are enemies of the church who want to, in the words of one churchgoer, "destroy the heterosexual male." Women pastors, then, are not *real* Christians. Women pastors choose what to believe from the Bible and what they choose is in line with what right-wing populists later termed "wokeism," a phrase that was adopted into the 2022 Florida Stop Woke Act.[52] Those women, the members of Reasoned Defense said indirectly, have adapted a "woke" ideology from Black activists and feminists who seek to undo the family, the church, and the nation. Real believers, by contrast, accept and take pride in their offensive gender politics. Their so-called political incorrectness is in fact strong, basic, correct.

Third, when evangelicals insist that the Bible itself is offensive, they justify a shared religious orientation that takes the form of what sociologists Douglas Schrock and Michael Schwalbe term a "manhood act" that seeks power over others.[53] At Welcome, such justifications were achieved through selective literalism.[54] White men in the Reasoned Defense group handpicked excerpts of scripture about women's submission to read out loud. They used those scriptures to shush and interrupt the women in attendance, and to disparage and objectify women who accuse men of sexual assault. The women who were there and outnumbered by men, went along with the misogynistic interpretation of scripture. They avowed that women are unfit to lead. They attested that men must stay in charge of the church, and of women's bodies. And everyone in the group made reference to their belief in the Bible when they belittled "P. C. politics," a phrase that Republicans use to not only vilify queer people and feminists, but also the activists, academics, and organizations that mobilize for Black Lives.

Finally, when evangelicals get offensive about gender, they limit the full participation of women in their own community. There were women at Welcome, as there are in other evangelical churches, who were unsettled by the church's beliefs about gender, who were in marriages with domineering men, and who wanted to figure out how to have an authentic relationship with God without compromising their personal well-being. Some of these women came to Welcome in search of a new church home that was fairer to women than other, more traditional churches. And comparatively speaking, Welcome was better, a few told me. Church leadership gave one of these women, in particular, a warm embrace after she divorced her drug-abusing husband. They didn't excommunicate her for filing for a divorce like her old church did. They welcomed her with open arms, and she was forever grateful to Welcome for that.

There were women who wanted more from Welcome than a gentle hand of grace in adverse circumstances. These "almost feminist" women, to use Claire's term, wanted to be valued as much as men. They were, in the words of sociologist Katie Gaddini, in a "struggle to stay" evangelical.[55] They had joined a church that pledged to be good to women, but that very church preached that the Word on gender is offensive, and that the people who feel offended by it were aligned with secular culture, and not with God. Hence, in an effort to appear biblically the same as everybody else, the "almost feminist" members of the church sank into silence. That silence made it seem as if everyone in the church accepted that men are in charge of women, and that women were wrong to complain about that. That silence also deterred women from forming open and honest relationships with other women who they could be almost feminist with.

The next chapter examines how the church kept up its act of biblical sameness through another form of silence that maintains a belief in the umbrella of marital authority that Anne described.[56] It shows how the church tacitly agreed to suppress talk about LGBTQ+ people and, in the process, reinforced a pervasive yet unspoken assumption that all churchgoers have the same negative opinion of homosexuality and LGBTQ+ inclusion in the church.

# 5

# Don't Ask, Don't Tell

Darleen was sitting by herself with a Styrofoam plate of beef roast and potatoes when I took the chair beside her for Recharge, a monthly potluck for women in the church kitchen. "Hey girl! It's good to see you!" I was delighted to see her too. We had met at Welcome's catfish fry earlier in the month and hit it off, even saying goodbye with a hug. Darleen and her husband had recently moved to the area and learned about Welcome through her husband's boss. They immediately fell in love with the church. "The music was good and Bird was jumping around like he does," Darleen laughed. She and her husband decided to become official members of Welcome. They took its "Fundamentals Class," pledged to volunteer for the church, and met Bird for an interview about, as Darleen described it, "where your heart and where your mind is." At the end of the membership training, Darleen and her husband signed a covenant avowing that they are born again. "It's intimidating," she said. "Only the born again can be full members."

Small talk was not Darleen's forte. I learned this when I sat next to her at Recharge. We were two chairs down from a group of White women who were chatting about Ole Miss football and tailgating in the Grove, a ten-acre shaded plot of stunning oak, elm, and magnolia trees at the center of campus. One of those women, Cheryl, glanced at her acquaintances and then at us. "My husband is a horseback cop who patrols the downtown Square on football weekends," she announced. Nancy, who looks and dresses like Nancy Reagan, oohed and ahhed in delight about the "courageous men" and "gorgeous horses" on the police force. Cheryl's face was oozing with pride. "My son is in the ROTC," Cheryl added. "He wakes up every day at 4:30 a.m.—he has plans for the military!" Nancy and the woman next to her nodded approvingly, smiling wide. Darleen listened from our end of the stark white plastic folding table, motionless. Moments later, she shifted closer to me to talk to me alone.

As soon as Darleen learned that I did not have kids and that I have no expertise in the Bible, she lowered her voice and told me about her son. He's single, twenty-five years old, and lives out of state. "I don't think he'll ever get married," she whispered. Darleen leaned back in her chair, giving me the side eye. A thick pause ballooned between us. "Well . . . that's okay. He'll be fine," I reassured her.

Darleen grinned satisfied. "He's *really* liberal," she explained. When he comes home to visit, they have to avoid politics. Her son "*hates* Trump." Her husband, his stepfather, "*loves* Trump." Darleen's right eyelid twitched. "I'm in the middle," she groaned.

Darleen was the only one at Welcome to ever bring up Trump without my prompting, and she was also among the few to say anything about homosexuality or LGBTQ+ inclusion outside of the interview setting. Her son is gay, she told me that night over dinner, and she was worried about him. Not for his salvation. Believers go to heaven and her son is a believer, she said with certainty. Darleen worries about her son because there are no churches that will accept him. I asked Darleen if her son would be accepted at Welcome. Bird never preaches about homosexuality, I reasoned, and the church prides itself on being a place where all are welcome. Darleen slowly and deliberately shook her head no. "This is a Bible-based church," she said matter-of-factly. "They go by the Word."

Darleen's shortcut response about "the Word" stood out to me. Why didn't Darleen, a self-described "backrow Baptist" who quietly rubbed against the norm of small talk, elaborate on what going by the Word means? Aside from teaching that women and men are made by God to unify in marriage, what else was the church doing to give her, a born-again mother of a born-again gay son, the impression that LGBTQ+ people do not belong?

## That Stuff Never Comes Up

In 2015, the U.S. Supreme Court made same-sex marriage legal in all fifty states. Immediately following the decision, same-sex weddings unfolded in full public view in the South. Corey Blount and Kurt Smith, two young White Christian men who work at the university, were the first gay couple in Oxford to wed. Blount and Smith rushed to the downtown courthouse to tie the knot the day after the ruling was publicized, they said, because they knew that state governance would try to delay the issuing of same-sex marriage licenses, and they were determined to become a "normal" married couple. Blount and Smith invited friends and colleagues from work to join them that Monday morning and scouted out a circuit court judge to officiate their wedding. To their pleasant surprise, the judge was friendly, and the ceremony was "wonderfully positive," to use their friend's words, complete with a photograph of the newlyweds on the courthouse steps that headlined the local newspaper that week.[1]

Gay couples in Mississippi like Blount and Smith had a reason to suspect that the state might try to bar them from exercising their right to marry after the Court's ruling. Leaders of the Christian right were outraged by the Court's decision to legalize same-sex marriage, and made clear that they were ready to do everything in their power to stop what they called "the gay agenda" from gaining more ground.

Within less than a year after the legalization of Blount and Smith's marriage, Mississippi legislators passed the "Protecting Freedom of Conscience from Government Discrimination Act" (HB 1523), a bill that protects "sincerely held religious beliefs or moral convictions" that:

> Marriage is or should be recognized as the union of one man and one woman;
> Sexual relations are properly reserved to such a marriage; and
> Male (man) or female (woman) refer to an individual's immutable biological sex as objectively determined by anatomy and genetics at the time of birth.

The bill goes on to list the matters in which religious organizations and individuals can exercise these beliefs and convictions without legal sanction. It is a long and expansive list that covers: the provision of foster care, adoption, and childrearing; employment decisions; the refusal to solemnize a same-sex marriage; opting out of providing sex reassignment surgeries, treatments, or counseling to transgender patients; and wedding services such as photography, floral arrangements, dress making, cake or pastry artistry, catering, as well as venue rentals, hotel accommodations, limousine or other car rental services, and jewelry sales.

Basically, the law in Mississippi ensures that LGBTQ+ people can be denied what they want or need in each and every aspect of life, including a car in rural towns without public transportation or health care in places where basic medical facilities are scarce.[2] Further, if LGBTQ+ people want to exercise the one right that the federal government protects—a right to marriage—they have to do so covertly, or else risk being denied the cake, the caterer, the tuxedo, the photo, and the venue. It is a law that paved the way for other freedom of religious conscience laws. For example, in 2023 the Supreme Court ruled in the *303 Creative, LLC v. Elenis* case that Colorado's nondiscrimination law does not apply to a Christian website designer who wants to refuse to offer her website services for weddings to same-sex couples on religious grounds. The dissenting justices on the Court said that 303 Creative should be treated as a public accommodations case, not as a religious freedoms case, and that a business that is open to the public has to be open to the whole public, not only the public that it approves of. Nonetheless, the conservative majority on the Court ruled in favor of the graphic designer, effectively making it legal for her to turn people whom she considers sinful away from her business.

Project Blitz, a coalition of Christian nationalist groups that focuses on legislation, was ecstatic about the law in Mississippi. They applauded the state for launching a "missile" that enforces their cause to fuse God and country into American law.[3] I vividly recall the morning that missile dropped. Caitlyn, my cheerful undergraduate student who, in her words, "wants to be everybody's friend," was slumped over her phone on a bench outside of the class that I was teaching. "Hey, Caitlyn, how's it going today?," I asked in an upbeat tone, expecting nothing short of her usual optimism. "They passed that hateful law," she said, with red tear-soaked eyes. "I keep trying to love where I'm from, but they don't want me here." My student's defeated tone viscerally communicated what had taken place earlier that morning: it was now legal, even encouraged, for Christians to discriminate against her in innumerable ways. Later that afternoon, Ian, a sociology graduate student, barreled into my office practically panting. He rubbed his forehead, shouting, "I have got to get out of here!" I knew what he was anxious about. My heart raced. I felt helpless.[4]

The denomination to which Welcome belongs, Southern Baptist, had passed multiple resolutions that proactively connect anti-LGBTQ+

positions to the evangelical cause for religious freedom—resolutions that dress up homophobia in the rhetoric of free speech protections for straight White Christians.[5] Was Welcome, the church plant that Darleen attends, a church that supports anti-LGBTQ+ religious freedom laws? How was it handling the denomination's position that acting on same-sex desires or gender transition are not only sinful but also a violation of Christian freedom? I attended or listened to Sunday services, eagerly anticipating a sermon on homosexuality or same-sex marriage that offered insights on where the church stood on religious freedom. But I never heard that sermon, and I never heard church leadership address the issue in its workshops on gender and marriage. Apart from Reasoned Defense, everyone else avoided delving into homosexuality and LGBTQ+ welcoming when they fellowshipped or met for small group. Hence, the only way to find out what they thought about "that stuff" was in private interviews, which is why I draw heavily on interviews in this chapter.

When I asked churchgoers their opinions of LGBTQ+ people in the church, I heard a lot of loud sighs, observed many furrowed eyebrows, and sat through long pauses. Sometimes churchgoers were caught off guard by my question. Sometimes they were scared of it. They said things like: "It never comes up." "We never talk about it." "I've only talked about that with my spouse." "I'm not sure what I'm supposed to think about it or even what [Bird] thinks." "Everybody is welcomed to come to church." Or, on a few occasions, "I wish the Church would preach on it," and "The church needs to make the line clear." One interviewee clarified that, "Nobody is going to walk up to someone and tell them to their face that they are a sinner for being gay. That would not be a very nice thing to do—we're nice at Welcome."

Churchgoers were aware that gay people come, sometimes. A few told me they had noticed a man standing next to another man during service, or have run into a friend from high school, family acquaintance, or colleague from work who they know is gay or lesbian. But they never "brought that up" to anybody, as one churchgoer said, and were not in conversation with others about if or about how to welcome LGBTQ+ people to church.[6] They pretended to not see or notice "it." Pretending was easier than confronting theological inconsistencies that could put God up for debate.[7] Noticing could also make their job as a welcoming congregation complicated, just as it could make it harder to appear as if everyone fits under the umbrella that the church prescribes for gender and marriage.

Ignoring LGBTQ+ people was no small feat. The church had to actively unsee the culture wars that were brewing right in front of them in their own hometown. Shortly after the state's religious accommodations bill was passed in 2016, the university's Sarah Isom Center for Women and Gender Studies put on a Pride parade in the downtown Square, the most visible location in town.[8] LGBTQ+ community members and allies showed up dazzling in vibrant colors with a rainbow banner that read "God Loves You" and comeback signs, "No Hate in My State" and "Love is My Religion." The turnout, according to the Isom director, Jaime Harker, was bigger than anything she could have ever imagined.[9] The success of Oxford Pride inspired other first Prides across the state. Biloxi and Hattiesburg had their first Pride parades in 2017, while Starkville, home to Mississippi State University, had its first in 2018. Even Tupelo, a rural city where the American Family Association, a fundamentalist Christian organization that aggressively opposes LGBTQ+ rights, is headquartered, launched Pride in 2018 and has been going strong ever since.[10]

Small businesses and progressive congregations took a public stance on LGBTQ+ rights and religious freedom too. "Y'all means All" and "We Don't Discriminate" stickers popped up on retail windows and restaurant doors. Square Books, the iconic bookstore that sits in the center of downtown, hung cardstock "All are welcome" signs in rainbow lettering on its front doors and sold posters and heavy cotton tees of its signage. And the Unitarian Universalist Congregation of Oxford made its position on LGBTQ+ members official.[11] It enacted a "Welcoming" policy, as did the directors of the Unitarian congregation in Tupelo after organizing a series of educational workshops and sensitivity trainings on LGBTQ+ inclusivity.[12] These welcome campaigns were not entirely confined to Unitarians. The Episcopal and Presbyterian churches in Oxford were LGBTQ+ friendly, and the University Baptist Church in Starkville, a Cooperative Baptist Fellowship, was an official member of the Association for Welcoming and Affirming Baptists.[13]

Amid all of this, the Christians who lead and attend Welcome were conveniently oblivious to how their very own "all are welcome" slogan resembled that of the slant towards LGBTQ+ inclusion in religious

Figure 5.1. Pride marchers protest Mississippi's anti-LGBTQ+ religious liberty bill with "God Loves You" and "No Hate in Our State" signs. Oxford Pride, May 7, 2016. Photograph courtesy of Kevin Cozart.

communities across the nation. Lynn, who is close with church leadership, said that "this stuff" never comes up in her circle of friends. When Lynn shared this, I admitted to her that I was surprised to hear that. Oxford Pride had recently started holding its annual parade, and the placards featured in that event had spoken directly to the exclusion of LGBTQ+ Christians from the church and state. Lynn looked out the window of the coffee shop where we were sitting, located on the street where Pride takes place. Gay people show up to Welcome sometimes, she said, but she doesn't talk about that with her church friends. Talking about it could unleash tension. It could tear them apart.

Unseeing queer people, refusing to acknowledge them, and neglecting to discuss whether the church should welcome them made it difficult for Bird to decide what to do about openly gay people who came to Welcome. Sometimes it seemed like he was bringing it up to me in search of direction. During one of our informal chats, he told me about a gay couple that had emailed him to acquire his permission to visit. The email caught him off guard. Initially, he missed that the person who wrote the message was a man asking if he could bring his husband. He couldn't understand why a woman would ask if she could bring her husband. He read the email again and finally realized that it was a man, not a woman, on the other side of the message. How could he, the pastor of a church that loves everybody, say no? How could he, the pastor of a Southern Baptist church plant that preaches the Word, say yes? He decided to talk it over with Anne and concluded that he had no other choice than to tell them to come.

By the time Bird told me about the predicament he was facing, the couple had been attending the church for over a month and were, in his words, "becoming more and more brave." One member of the couple had come up to the church's makeshift altar—a plastic folding table at the front of the Recreation Center—to participate in monthly communion. Bird was stunned when the man asked for the fruit juice and cracker, and he wondered if he should have stopped him. Later that day, he talked about it with Anne, and she asked Bird questions that made him feel better about giving him communion. Was he going to deny communion to divorced people? Or to that "a-hole" who was being abusive to his wife? she asked. How could he say that one sin is greater than another? Bird came to the conclusion that it would be impossible to control who has a right to communion. Aside from preaching "hard" about heterosexual marriage, as he described it, there was little else he could do to stop gay people from coming.

Bird's doubts about how to treat the gay couple implied that his job is less complicated when gay people stay out of sight and out of mind at church. He was not the only one at Welcome who felt that way. Many churchgoers told me that they prefer to remain ignorant about someone in their circle being gay or lesbian because they were unsure of what to do with that information. In hour two of a longer-than-usual interview, Amani, whom I knew from Be the Bridge, brought up a friend she taught with at a middle school in another state. That friend was a PE coach, "wore her hair like a boy," and had pictures of her and other women on Facebook, never men. Amani continued:

> I was always worried that she was gonna tell me she was gay, so I didn't know what to say. I asked my sister [a Christian counselor], "Do I witness to her?" I don't know (laughs uncomfortably). I was kind of glad that she

> never told me, because I was like, "What do you say?" If she does tell me, is it an opportunity to share what I believe? If I share what I believe, is that offensive? Does that mean I'll never see her again?

Amani and her coach friend observed a compact of silence for years, and through that silence Amani avoided having to figure out "the Christian thing to do" if her friend were to come out as queer.[14] Eventually her friend got "shipped off someplace else," as Amani termed it, after a group of parents filed a complaint about her sexuality to school administrators. It was as if she was Black, Amani said, as "far as the level of discrimination goes." Amani, a Black teacher in a primarily White school, could relate to that feeling. But her friend never told her why she lost her job. And Amani never asked. Her friend "suffered in silence," to use Amani's words.

Amani tries to follow the church's lead. She exercises a "don't ask" method of engagement that makes her appear as if she has the same beliefs about homosexuality as other members of the church, even though in private she has doubts about what exactly those beliefs are supposed to be. When we last spoke, she was still unsure if loving queer people meant trying to change them, as it had in the past when "love the sinner but hate the sin" was in vogue, or if it meant accepting them as part of God's plan.[15] With all that uncertainty, it was simpler to just ignore "that stuff," to borrow a phrase from churchgoers. To avoid it. To unsee it. To settle on being ill-informed about how to show God's love to LGBTQ+ people.

Others in the church, however, were irritated with the don't ask, don't tell approach that dominates Welcome. Conservatives like Ray had noticed that a great deal of churches were quietly accommodating homosexuality and same-sex marriage, and he was discouraged by that. The church, to use his words, is playing a "big pretend game" and he wants it to stop.

> Many preachers keep peace in the church by not preaching regularly on issues that the congregation finds tough. . . . I think the preachers run scared that half the congregation will leave if they preach forcefully on [gay marriage, the role of women in the church, and abortion]. So they pretend. Pretend not to notice the issues, and the congregation pretends not to notice he's not preaching the issues. It's a big pretend game.

Bob from Reasoned Defense also thinks the church needs to do a better job at making "the line clear." Gay people should be welcomed to come to church, he explained, but under the condition that they be willing to become straight.[16] Bob claimed that Christians are called intolerant bigots just for sticking up for what they believe, and insisted that the church is mistaken to let its fear of those labels overshadow biblical teachings.

Cindy, who worked at the crisis pregnancy center (CPC) where I heard about Welcome, had a similar take on the conditions of LGBTQ+ inclusion that Bob laid out. Through the CPC, she says she has formed relationships with girls and young women who lost their virginity before marriage and then, through pregnancy, found the center and became born again. Sex outside of marriage, being gay, and having an abortion are sins, Cindy professed, but she appreciates that Welcome is there for people in their "darkest hour" like the pregnancy center where she works. There is, however, a line that she thinks should never be crossed: Christians should never pander to gay people who refuse to change. "You know that the Gospel can be offensive," she told me in a firm voice. "God's very clear in His Word about what he considers a sin, Amy."

Others at the church, however, felt that some gay people will never change and that the church should let them be who they want to be. When I asked Thatcher if he thinks the church should welcome gay people, he answered in one word: "Yes." When I asked him to elaborate, he said he believes in nonjudgmental Christian love:

> We were told to love one another and—we were also told not to judge others as well. That's not our job, that's God's job. It's our job to be loving and to help each other, and to get each other through this life. . . . God should be the one to judge them, not me. That's not my place.

Sarah also believes in nonjudgmental Christian love, and she thinks judging people for being gay is like judging someone for any other difference:

> You can't love everybody with stipulations. "I love you but don't be lesbian. I love you but don't be Black. Don't be Hispanic . . . don't be White with gray hair that you covered up last night with hair dye" (laughing

> awkwardly)—you know what I mean? Like "I love you BUT. . . ." That's not how the Lord works! No, He just loves you and He wants us to love one another.

For Sarah and others who consider themselves tolerant, the best thing to do was to act as if gay people were not there, even when they were. "I'm not just going to walk up to someone and call out the fact that they are a lesbian," she said. "I just don't pay any attention to it." By not paying attention to it, churchgoers like her held onto the belief that they were in an all-inclusive church, even as churchgoers like Ray and Cindy held onto theirs that gay people commit sexual sins that conflict with the church's core values.

The don't ask, don't tell approach of the church also meant that its position on LGBTQ+ membership was hard for some churchgoers to discern. Cora, who serves in a leadership capacity in children and family ministries, was unsure of where the church draws the line on membership. She had never heard the church make an explicit statement on homosexuality, and she was uninformed on how it handles gay people who want to officially join the church like she had:

> Honestly, I don't know what membership really looks like. We're members, but it was a class basically saying, "These are our values, and these are our beliefs." And the values and beliefs [taught in the class] don't mention anything about homosexuality.

Cora was apprehensive about being part of a homophobic church, she said, but realizes that she could be. She explained:

> I don't feel like I agreed to anything like that—I couldn't. I don't see how they make that call. 'Cause it's not outlined in their mission statement. Or maybe it is, and I just didn't see it. But we did the Fundamentals class, and then we did the Basics class. . . . But, I really can't say, I mean on membership. I don't know what that looks like for [Welcome] with homosexuality.

There were others in the church that had a hard time deciphering if queer people could join. Lynn said she was unfamiliar with how the church thinks about membership. After telling me that she personally thinks that a church that welcomes gay people in the doors should also permit them to become members, she said:

> I mean, I would feel really sad and upset if that were the case [that a same-sex couple were denied membership at Welcome]. "You can come to our church, but you can't join it because you're in a same-sex marriage, or same-sex relationship." I would have a problem with that. I don't feel like that's what we teach. But I'm sure somebody else would not have that same idea.

Lynn disagrees with churches that bar same-sex couples from joining but had neglected to share her opinion with others at Welcome. She knows that others feel differently about membership than she does, and she thought it best to keep her opinions to herself. Bringing that stuff up, she presumed, could cause a fight. Don't ask, don't tell was easier on everybody.

Others in the church—all of them men—were confident that Welcome restricts membership to heterosexuals. To them, there is an important difference between welcoming queer people to church and embracing them as members. When I asked Ryan what he thinks about gay people joining the church, he told me what God says about marriage:

> There are clear things about how [Welcome] feels about marriage, and how it should be, and how God says it's supposed to be. And that's coming from the scripture, and believing that it is God-breathed, and it is God saying it through the scripture. . . . It's not that they're not welcome.

For Ryan, the church's teachings on heterosexual marriage are code for what the church requires of its members: they must be or aspire to be in a heterosexual marriage. Gay people are welcome to come hear the church preach on marriage, he said. They just have to be receptive to the Word.

Benjamin, a church elder, wants the church to be "consistent" with scripture. He wants everyone to "come in and hang out and see what we're doing and find out more about it." He likes that the church welcomes "openly fat people" and people who "cuss a lot," and he thinks the church should welcome gay people too. But he has reservations about giving gay people a seat at the Welcome table. They are committing a sexual sin, which is more severe than cursing or gluttony, Benjamin explained in the most neutral tone possible. To elaborate that point, Benjamin brought up a straight couple that was cohabitating and wanted to become official members. The couple took all the required classes but were prohibited from signing the church covenant—the one that churchgoers have to sign avowing that they are born again before being granted membership. Heterosexual couples that cohabitate out of wedlock are refused membership, he implied, because they are incompliant with the Word. Benjamin had not yet witnessed a same-sex couple apply for membership or talked about that possibility with the other elders, but he was sure that they would be denied membership too.

Benjamin's comments corresponded with what Bob said about openly gay people coming to church. Being born again is a prerequisite for church membership, Bob said, and he is unable to accept that openly gay people can be true believers. "If you really want to hold a view that is contrary to the church, you are welcome to that view, but you cannot also at the same time call yourself a member." LGBTQ+ people can and should visit, he declared, but there is a big ideological difference between someone who is pridefully gay and someone who is remorsefully gay.[17] Pridefully gay people, he implied, should be deterred from church. When they show up, the church's line on gender weakens. If that line weakens, the church will abandon the umbrella of authority in marriage that God allegedly designed.

Sampson, who sometimes preaches on Sunday mornings, clarified that he prefers that gays and lesbians who are "open about it" stay away from the church. Like Bob, he thinks there is a significant difference between gay people who are ashamed of themselves, and gay people who come to church flaunting who they are. The former come to church to escape homosexuality; they deserve Christian love and compassion as they embark on that journey, he said. It's the open ones, or what some conservatives call the "militant gays," that are the problem. They have a political agenda to change the church and are defying the compact of silence and conformity that he believes God wills for their lives.

***

Welcome's don't ask, don't tell approach to LGBTQ+ people bred uncertainty, confusion, and inconsistencies about how to reach and respond to queer people. Some argued that the church should be clear that homosexuality is impermissible in the church. Several said that they welcome gay people to church in hopes that they will change. A few said that everybody should be welcomed without stipulations. And everyone tacitly acknowledged that there were all sorts of opinions about what it means to be a welcoming congregation, which is why they opted to avoid "that stuff."[18] They didn't want that stuff ripping their front of biblical sameness apart.

Reasoned Defense was the only group that addressed homosexuality and same-sex marriage directly. Once they established that women should submit to men without complaint and pronounced that feminism is intrinsically evil, its members broached the unspoken. They commented that the church had gotten too soft on gay people and avowed that the Word is and ought to be offensive to them. Darleen, the mother who desperately wanted a church to accept her gay son, was attuned to that offense. She referred to it just as the members of Reasoned Defense did when she told me in a definitive tone, "No," her son cannot join Welcome. Darleen wanted her son to find an accepting church, but she never had a chance to process what that might look like with her peers at church. The church's commitment to silence had made his exclusion incontestable, unmentionable. It had made it hard for Darleen to put her own thoughts into words. The Word on marriage excludes her son, and Welcome follows the Word, she told me. That was all she said about it. It was all she could say about it.

The next section shows how members of the Welcome community drew on the logic of don't ask, don't tell to support religious accommodations that permit Christians to refuse services to LGBTQ+ people. Unseeing queer people takes effort, and they felt that society was wrong to force them to see what they were working so hard not to see.

## Order a Plain White Cake, Not a Wedding Cake

When I tried to gauge whether churchgoers support religious accommodations like the ones in their home state, half of my interviewees were unaware of the Mississippi law or what it covers. Their ignorance surprised me. HB 1523 had made local, national, and international headlines, some of which called it "the worst" bill yet. On top of that, professors, staff, and students at the University of Mississippi had organized a town hall meeting about it, and flyers for that meeting had been scattered around a campus where members of Welcome work and attend classes.

I wanted us to start the conversation with the same information, so I provided a brief overview of religious accommodations. My script was this: "Several states, including Mississippi, have recently pushed through religious liberties bills that propose to protect the rights of religious individuals and businesses to refuse services such as counseling, bathroom accommodations, wedding services, and health care to lesbian, gay, bisexual, and transgender individuals." Following that summary, I asked whether these bills reflect their views, and if they had talked about religious freedom laws that target LGBTQ+ people with other congregants.[19]

Churchgoers seldom raised what "the Bible says" in their responses to my inquiries, and almost half had reservations about anti-LGBTQ+ religious freedom laws that authorize discrimination.[20] On several occasions, churchgoers argued that God commands Christians to love thy neighbor and not judge, and that this commandment holds true for how Christians should treat gay people. Yet later, after attesting to nonjudgmental love, these same respondents would pivot to their collective "underdog" identity as Christian, an identity that they invoked to defend Christians who are fighting to keep their "conscience clean."[21] Some complained that Christians are labeled bigots for what they believe. Some feared that the U.S. government was going to force Christians to perform same-sex weddings. And a few claimed that Christians were on the brink of losing their tax-exempt status and being jailed for preaching the Word.

The fact that gay, lesbian, and transgender people exist is fine, churchgoers maintained. The problem is that queer people have broken the compact of silence that Mississippians have long observed.[22] LGBTQ+ people have inserted themselves and their relationships into the public sphere, and from their perspective, that is unfair. One high-profile legal case that interviewees remarked on regarding such unfairness was the 2018 SCOTUS case, *Masterpiece Cakeshop v. Colorado Civil Rights*

*Commission*, when a Christian-owned cakeshop in Lakewood, Colorado, refused to bake a wedding cake for a same-sex couple.

When I asked Angie if she was familiar with religious liberties bills, she brought up the bakery in Colorado. She explained how she understood what happened: the gay couple were regulars at the bakery and when the baker refused to prepare their wedding cake, he had graciously referred the couple to other businesses who could fulfill the request, she said. Angie characterized the exchange like this:

> The bakery said, we will serve you, we're thankful for you, but this instance for a cake to celebrate your wedding, that crosses our personal conviction. I think that they handled it well. And then, of course, they went to court.

Angie went on to claim that LGBTQ+ people take Christians to court over the smallest things—their own wedding!—even when Christians try to accommodate them (i.e., recommend other businesses for a service). Her account of the incident between the evangelical cake baker and the gay customers signaled a false dichotomy that religious objectors call "conflicting rights."[23] She insisted that Christians lost the right to their personal religious convictions when LGBTQ+ people gained the right to marry.

Chancey thinks gay people are too thin-skinned. When I asked her opinion of religious freedom laws over breakfast tacos at a local eatery, she turned the question back on me, "Why does everything have to be such a big deal? Why does it have to be so personal all the time?" Christians "can't say anything anymore" without it offending somebody, she protested. When Christians take a vocal stance on the sin gay people commit, "they turn it into something political," call Christians hypocrites, or take them to court. Those behaviors, she said, infringe on religious freedom, and she was tired of it.

Brian also thinks that LGBTQ+ people are "blowing everything out of proportion." To make this point, he described a YouTube video he saw that explained a case about a florist who refused to arrange flowers for a same-sex wedding. Brian shared the background of the case that he learned from the video: how the couple were regular customers of the florist, that the florist offered to provide whatever flowers the couple wanted, and only refused to arrange them for the wedding. Brian went on:

> It got blown out of proportion. His fiancé went back and was like "She's not serving us 'cause we're gay." And she was planning on giving them the flowers, but she just wasn't going to arrange them for the purposes of a wedding. . . . I kinda feel the same way. Like, I'd sell you the flowers but I'm not going to arrange it for the wedding.

Brian concluded that the gay couple was wrong to team up with the American Civil Liberties Union (ACLU) to sue the flower shop. She could have lost her business, he said in disappointment. After watching that video, Brian decided that he does want to see more laws passed that protect religious freedom. But he wants those laws to be fair, he added. As a member of a racially marginalized group, he was apprehensive about legislation that makes it easy to discriminate against other minority groups.

When Brian reflected on the anti-LGBTQ+ religious liberty law in Mississippi, he explained that protections for business owners could evolve into a "slippery slope" of protections for those who discriminate against other groups: "I don't think it's fair because I mean . . . you're saying you can't make cakes for gay people, then what's stopping you from saying [you] can't make cake for Blacks or Latinos or Asians?" However, after speaking about the slippery slope, he went on to propose what he called a "compromise" that he believes could help both sides dodge litigation.

Brian proposed that Christians bake cakes for gay couples but should not have to, in his words, "put the topper on there" or airbrush "two dudes kissing" onto it. As Brian sees it, "It goes both ways—there's a stop where I'm violating your rights until you're violating my rights, also." Just make a cake, Brian insisted. But not wedding cakes. In other words, Christians should serve gay couples but only under the condition that gay couples agree to remain invisible. Bob said the same thing as Brian about wedding cakes: "I mean, if it was me personally and somebody asked me to bake a cake, I would probably bake them a cake and just say put on your own topper." Then Bob paused and wondered aloud why Christians are being asked to accommodate queer people in the first place. "Goodness gracious, just go to the next place."

Claire, a self-described progressive who approves of same-sex marriage and has gay friends, had inconsistent views on religious liberty laws. At first, she thought that Christians were the ones making everything into a big deal:

> From my perspective, when I first heard about that cake incident—and some incidents that happened thereafter—I just thought, I don't think that baking this cake means that you support the, that relationship. It just, it's what you do. It's not like you're donating the cake in support of it.

Then, after describing her reasons for disagreeing with Christians who refuse services, Claire admitted that she thinks same-sex couples are mistaken to request the services in the first place:

> I feel almost small-minded for saying this, but . . . like I want to say that a same-sex couple should not be refused service and that they have every right to be there. And I think that. But at the same time, I almost wish that, that if they knew that it was gonna make that baker so uncomfortable, they would almost in a respectful manner say, "Hey you bake a cake, and we'll put the topper on. You don't even have to see that, that it's same-sex, for a same-sex wedding." But then, that's belittling their relationship. And so maybe I'm just not . . . as progressively minded as I should be.

Claire wavered between two stances. She has personal religious convictions that go against laws that create what she and Brian termed a "slippery slope" that could lead to racial discrimination and segregation. But she also thinks that openly gay people should be more considerate of Christians. To resolve her internal conflict about it, she proposed that gay people order a plain white cake. When gay people "keep it to themselves," she said, both sides win. Christians retain a clear conscience, and gay people get most of the wedding services they want. From her perspective, religious liberty laws are extreme, yet she supported the notion that LGBTQ+ people being closeted about who they are and who they love is a reasonable compromise.

Ryan and Emma, a young married couple, spent several minutes pondering religious accommodations when I asked them, over afternoon coffee, their opinions of the Mississippi law. On the one hand, neither of them thought that denying services to gay people is a Christian thing to do. They believed that businesses should be legally obligated to offer their services to anyone who asks; when businesses refuse services to specific groups, they implicitly create a slippery slope of social segregation. On the other, however, both Emma and Ryan had grown tired of being shut down for their beliefs on gender and sexuality. Ryan said, "As Christians, we feel like we can't speak up or someone will think that we're judgmental, hateful, close-minded. It's like, 'I am close-minded.' Like, I think this, and no, I don't think there's another way." With a nostalgic nod to a Christian past, Emma added that younger Christians are facing unparalleled challenges. She and her peers are being confronted with "many more non-Christian laws and situations" than were previous generations. Christians who express their religious convictions, they surmised, have to prepare for backlash. "You can stick to your guns. . . . It's your right to refuse, but you have to deal with the consequences," Ryan grimaced. The LGBTQ+ community and their liberal allies, he implied, are ready to attack.

Cindy was one of a few to explicitly back religious accommodations that elevate the gender and sexual norms of conservative Christians into law. From her perspective, religious liberty became part of what she called "the political arena" to protect Christians who she claimed have been fired from their jobs and lost their livelihoods for refusing wedding services to gay people. Cindy never remarked on Kim Davis specifically, but later in the interview she indicated that she was talking about her. Davis, a former clerk in Rowan County, Kentucky, refused to issue a marriage license to a same-sex couple back in 2015, soon after the Supreme Court legalized same-sex marriage. Davis claimed that issuing marriage licenses to same-sex couples violated her religious beliefs as a member of the Apostolic Church. She was later sued, sent to jail for five days, and lost her bid for reelection as county clerk. These events cost Davis her job as a county clerk, but they also made her a celebrity in right-wing circles. When she was sent to jail, supporters showed up with signs that read "Christian hero" and "Kim Davis for President."

Cindy recognized that denying queer people services sounds harsh, but she believes, as Davis did, that Christians should care more about what God thinks than what others think. "I know that if He's saying, 'Don't do this,' I'm not gonna do it. 'Cause that's my personal conviction, okay? I believe that's my constitutionally given right to have that conviction and discernment." Cindy realizes that LGBTQ+ people might think she is being hateful, but she refused to let that change her faith. If a gay person wants to avoid a confrontation in a place of business or elsewhere, she advised, they should just say, "Thank you, anyway." Besides, she said, "gay couples should love us and show kindness just like we love them and show kindness."

Pam was adamant that Christians have a right to a clear conscience and that gay people pollute it when they are out and proud of who they are. To provide context for her position on the issue, Pam shared that she and her husband aspire to open a restaurant when they retire. It was hard for her to fathom being asked to provide wedding services to a same-sex couple. "If you are a Christian, you can't support that. If you're a baker, if you're, you know, a florist, if you're asked to do the music—I mean, you can't." She thinks they should "just go someplace else," which can be an impossible thing to do in a rural state like Mississippi that is ideologically dominated by conservative Christianity.

Darleen and Gary, both of whom have adult gay sons from previous marriages, said that they are fine with their sons being gay, and I never got the sense from them that they wanted to change them or believed they could. However, they did want LGBTQ+ individuals to stop complicating the lives of born-again Christians. When I asked them about religious accommodations that permit Christians to discriminate against their sons, they arrived at the same conclusion as everybody else at the church. They said that gay people should stop asking Christians to do things they don't want to do. For Gary, the solution was relatively straightforward: "Go to the other bakery" or order a sheet cake "without two guys on top." Darleen, the mom that I had a heart-to-heart with at Recharge, reiterated what her husband said. "Don't make it such a big deal," she remarked. Gay people get into trouble when they are up front about who or what the service is for, she added. If her son could just be discreet, he could get the service he wants without getting hurt.

"Get out of Mississippi." That was Chancey's concluding remark to my question about HB 1523. If a queer person is out and proud, they should "just move," she said firmly. Just leave Mississippi, a state that lawfully enforces Christian teachings on gender and marriage. Chancey believes her version of Christianity has a special standing in the South, and that openly gay people violate that standing. If a queer person doesn't like where they live, they can leave, she said. The ones who don't, she suggested, have to be ready for a fight, and with the understanding that they brought that fight onto themselves.

## The Politics of Silence

Conservative evangelicals have been spearheading the "culture wars" for the past several decades, and they fight that war by claiming that the moral bedrock of America is under siege.[24] LGBTQ+ people and their struggle for rights have been their principal targets in this war and are often the focus of political campaigns and interdenominational statements affirming that "God designed marriage to be a covenantal, sexual, procreative, lifelong union of one man and one woman, as husband and wife."[25]

Lately, conservative Christians have been claiming that they incur "spiritual harm" when they interact with LGBTQ+ people who, for example, request a wedding cake from a local bakery or apply for residency in an apartment complex.[26] The Southern Baptist Convention, to which Welcome belongs, has sounded an alarm about those spiritual harms and, in various ways, has charted out the anti-LGBTQ+ religious freedom platforms that galvanize the evangelical mainstream. Yet Welcome only engaged in or acknowledged the issue in indirect terms. It never addressed LGBTQ+ religious accommodations on Sunday mornings or in its Back to Basics meetings about gender, and churchgoers neglected to have conversations about these laws, the cake baker, or about how they think the church ought to treat LGBTQ+ people in the public arena. When it came to these matters, the church opted to keep the existence of gay people and the laws that discriminate against them invisible, unspoken, and therefore natural.

In *Men Like That*, historian John Howard argues that scholars need to read the silence, and that any project on queer life must refrain from privileging the spoken over the unspoken, the written over the unwritten. Silences and silencing, he writes, are as "much a part of the shaping of anxieties around homosexuality in Mississippi as expressive or repressive languages and vocabularies."[27] And according to Howard's oral histories with gay men (and men like *that*), the silence surrounding the existence of queer people—the very act of pretending to not know that someone is like that—is "not simply a cowardly denial of gay identity or a successful institutional suppression of gayness."[28] Those silences also produce unique ways of being and belonging in communities that hide gender and sexual nonconformity in plain sight.[29]

Building on Howard's research, clinical counselor John Marszalek III shows how gay and lesbian Mississippians observe a compact of silence when they enter Christian communities. One couple he interviewed, Faith and Sophie, attended church together but were not out to others there. In his interview with them, the couple describe one straight couple that sits behind them on Sundays at church and who have visited them on their farm. This couple, they explained, are "good people," but they were also conveniently unaware of Faith and Sophie's relationship, and Faith and Sophie didn't bring it up either. They were all involved in a compact of silence that privileges straight people in the church and in the wider community. That compact of silence, Marszalek points out, inhibits meaningful relationships between families and friends, and it can also tighten the door of what sociologist Bernadette Barton terms a "toxic closet" of self-hatred and shame in the Bible Belt.[30]

Welcome had its reasons for staying quiet about queer people. First, unseeing queer people reinforced the idea that the umbrella of authority in marriage is inevitable: it made it appear as if a hierarchical, heterosexual union between a cisgender man and woman is the only God-given option.[31] Second, the church didn't acknowledge queer people, or what it means to welcome them, because it didn't have to. There was not enough pressure or enough of a queer presence in the church to warrant acknowledgment of an issue that could weaken its inclusive brand. Finally, being quiet about queerness made the "pretend game" easier. Welcome was unprepared for a conversation about LGBTQ+ welcoming. It was working on nailing down the basics of gender, so it could not withstand an issue that could make some of its members look like liberals and others like right-wing bigots. As a new and growing church plant, everyone had to invest in biblical sameness, which meant avoiding LGBTQ+ people and the culture wars that surround them. Acknowledging queer people could expose different points of view or split the church, like it had other Protestant denominations.[32] It was best to practice "don't ask, don't tell." That practice maintained the facade of biblical sameness, kept queer people marginalized, and privileged the prerogatives of conservative Christians in a church that had placed the rhetoric of diversity at the heart of its identity and mission.

The next and last substantive chapter of the book picks up the subject of religious liberty again, but with attention to the religious accommodations that the church talked about and advocated for out in the open. It shows how the church banded together against what it called the "red tape" in public education, and in the process pushed forward the idea that America and Christianity must become one and the same.

6

# Take Down the Red Tape

A solid thirty seconds slid by before the school's front desk attendant looked up from her phone and forced out a smile. "What can I do for you?" she asked. "I'm here to cook lunch for the school," I replied. She glanced at the door behind me and advised me to find the big white tent out back, past the yellow school buses and air-conditioning units. I was familiar with the tent. I had been at Welcome for almost one year and had seen the church use that tent at the park for its Fun Day event, at the city pavilion for Trunk or Treat, and out in front of the Recreation Center for its annual Christmas fair.

Bird waved me over when I turned the corner of the building, thanked me for coming, and shepherded me to the back entrance of the school cafeteria. Along the way, we passed two tall White men who were stationed outside in the thick August heat underneath the glowing white canopy of the tent. They were in charge of the deep fryers. I knew their faces from church but not their names, so I remarked on the fryer baskets, Cajun seasoning, and hefty rolls of paper towels that were strewn across three six-foot folding tables underneath the tents. "This ain't no big deal," one cook chuckled. "We do 'serve the server' events all the time."

Bird dropped me off in the school's large industrial kitchen with Karen, a Southerner in her late sixties with short brown hair and carefully placed makeup. "You can bread the catfish," she directed. Hearing this, another retiree found her spot at the stainless-steel worktable and took over. My job, she told me, was to pat down wet pieces of catfish with paper towels and then pass them down to the women in charge of sifting fish through a Cajun breading mix.

Relieved to have a concrete task ahead, I introduced myself to my catfish team: Darleen, Karen, and Barb. When they learned that I was "the one doing the study," the camaraderie at the table morphed from quiet to full volume, a camaraderie that Black sociologists have been barred from when attempting to study White Christian spaces.[1] Darleen, whom

I got to know better when we spoke privately at Recharge, shared that she "just loves" how Bird delivers his sermons. She attends the earliest of two services on Sunday to "hear it fresh" from his mouth. "You never know what to expect," Karen gushed. Her old church was the "same old same old all the time. Stand up, sit down, stand up, sit down." Welcome might have a different band, or a different preacher lead the service. And Bird is exciting. "He keeps your attention," Barb added with a satisfied smile. Our conversation about church shifted steadily like our hands. Within less than an hour, we were finished with the fish and cleaning up. Karen, our unofficial boss, was proud of us. "Whoo-hoo! We're ahead of schedule!" she cheered.[2]

Once the food was fried and ready to serve, the volunteers from the church joined the school employees in the well-worn cafeteria for lunch, which the church referred to as a time for fellowship. When I entered the room, Bird introduced me to the superintendent and school principal, both of whom expressed gratitude to Bird for feeding the school staff. After our brief but informative introduction, I asked Bird about the financial logistics of renting the school for its children's ministries program. Welcome had rented the school for its vacation Bible study (VBS) program earlier that summer and, in line with what church planters advise, had determined that a gesture of gratitude was in order.[3] Welcome decided to prepare lunch for the school faculty and staff to express that gratitude.

The lines between church and school are becoming increasingly blurred. Those lines started to blur in the early twenty-first century when the U.S. Supreme Court ruled that any public school that allows civic organizations and social clubs to use its facilities must also allow religious groups.[4] It was a ruling that, in the words of the Court's dissenting voices, turned a publicly funded school system into an apparatus of religious proselytization, effectively changing what schools look like on Sundays.[5] Church plants (i.e., startup and multisite congregations) immediately took advantage of the Court's rulings.[6] They organized worship services on school grounds, baptized congregants in portable swimming pools, and established summer programs in school classrooms that make Jesus the main character of the curriculum. Why? The rent is affordable, the parking lots are large, and the buildings are centrally located. On top of those perks, churches can use the low rent to get a new church plant or ministry up and running before investing in their own building.[7]

"It's not biased," Bird assured me. Churches can only set up when school is out, and they have to pay rent when they do. Welcome was holding its annual VBS program at the school for the reasons mentioned earlier (the affordability, good parking, location, and facilities), but also because it wants to create a comfortable church experience for regular folk in the community. To him, holding VBS at a public school was like holding the Sunday worship service at the Recreation Center: it puts the unchurched at ease, he explained.

The potent smell of fried catfish, French fries, hushpuppies, peach cobbler, and vanilla ice cream had overpowered the room, prompting Bird to excuse himself from our conversation and command everyone's attention. He propped his right foot on a muted orange lunchroom table next to where the school administrators, all White and mostly male, were congregated. The cafeteria fell silent.

"We wanted to show our appreciation for you today," Bird announced to a cafeteria filled with close to forty teachers, administrators, lunchroom ladies, custodial staff, and Welcome volunteers. Bird looked over at the corner of the room where I was lunching next to Black men and women on the custodial staff. "The education system doesn't have any money," he said. "Welcome feels fortunate to help pay the rent." Then, while studying the room, he teased the teachers in a tone of sarcasm that they get "paid too much to be here," a comment that stirred a few hearty laughs. When the laughter died down, Bird mumbled awkwardly, "I'm not sure how to do this. . . ."

It was time to pray over the lunch, but it was a staff day during which school employees were required to be in the building. Compulsory prayer is prohibited at school. Bird paused for a moment and then proceeded with a quasi-prayer that inclined some people to bow their heads and a few, like me, to scan the lunchroom with eyes wide open. He thanked God, expressed gratitude to the school, and closed on a comment about the good food ahead. When it was over, he joked, "Ok, that could have been a prayer!—I'm not trying to force anything on you! If you took it as a prayer, fine." Several people chortled. A few clapped. One called out "Amen." The cafeteria resumed the noise of paper plates, plastic forks, and cheerful chitchat.

***

Welcome is located in Oxford, a college town that is, as one of my colleagues coined it, "a place of extremes." On one end of the extreme, it is a place where regular churchgoing Christians enjoy the highest level of cultural cachet and influence.[8] Where the mayor tweets prayers for students as they start the school year. Where small talk between residents involves, "Do you have a church home?" A place where LGBTQ+ people feel policed and surveilled by the watchful eye of the Bible Belt that manifests in the Christian symbols and signs that are put on display in tire shops, bakeries, and dentist offices.[9]

On the other side of the extreme, Oxford is a place where blue dots of difference shake up politically red Mississippi. Where Black activists, scholars, and students break the silence about slavery, combat racism, and protest symbols of the Confederacy.[10] Where a handful of academics, artists, and activists put on LGBTQ+ Pride parades, drag shows, and queer dance parties.[11] A place that is world-renowned for its literary scene and for having esteemed, sometimes radical, novelists and poets in residence.

Hence, the college town where Welcome sits presents the church with a unique milieu in which to do what God challenges them to do—stop the growing blue dots of difference and plant the seeds of biblical sameness in the wider community. Churchgoers accept that being in the Bible Belt makes the prospect of meeting that challenge comparatively easier than in other college towns. But they also complain that the Belt has gotten too loose and that there are too many barriers—what churchgoers deem "red tape"—that obstruct their ability to be evangelical openly and freely in their own hometown. Bird's fragmented blessing of the catfish lunch echoes how evangelicals are taking down the red tape. That quasi-prayer communicated to the school that Christians are no longer free to exercise their convictions in America anymore, and that they are fighting to move their beliefs to the center of public institutions again.

The church was particularly aggravated with the red tape in public education, a visible institution at the forefront of several landmark U.S. Supreme Court cases that enact, challenge, or modify the wall of separation between church and state.[12] For the church, "the red tape" was not limited to the administrative state or excessive bureaucracy. "The red tape" was a phrase that stands for institutions and individuals that limit the church's will to insert conservative Christianity into the hearts and minds of young people. It was a law, institution, or office of government that refuses to prioritize evangelical beliefs and values in public affairs. A "skeptic" who follows science instead of the Bible. A professor from a big coastal city. The red tape was the very existence of anyone or anything that conflicts with biblical sameness.

In this chapter, I show how churchgoers identified with one another through the repudiation of secular education and secular intellectuals (i.e., the red tape) that they believe makes it hard for them to recruit others into biblical sameness in their beloved college town. In doing so, I underscore how evangelical churchgoers come to understand themselves as victims of the red tape in America, and how they use that understanding to push for special accommodations that infringe on the rights of nonreligious, religious, and sexual minorities.

## The Red Tape at School

On a Sunday after Independence Day, Bird made his view on the wall between church and state clear. He praised church plants that meet at schools and asserted that the words "separation of church and state" do not appear in the U.S. Constitution, nor in the Declaration of Independence.[13] To an extent, Bird was right. The phrase "separation of church and state" does not appear in those founding documents. It does, however, appear in a letter that Thomas Jefferson wrote to a Baptist committee in 1802 when he referenced the Establishment Clause of the First Amendment that prohibits the U.S. government from establishing an official religion or favoring one religion over another.[14] But Bird said nothing about the Establishment Clause, or the context in which it was written or why. Instead, he focused on the exact "words," a rhetorical maneuver that let the church know that he thinks that Christians ought to be involved in the state's affairs.[15]

Bird paced at the edge of the stage, close to the congregation, and warned the church that Christian values are being quashed in America. The Ten Commandments are "the words to be feared!" Bird hollered with pride. So frightening, he scoffed, that "American government officials" have banned the Ten Commandments from the walls of schools and courthouses.[16] From what I could discern, Bird was gesturing toward recent legislation that sought to expand Christian symbolism at school. Earlier that same year, a Mississippi Democrat had introduced an amendment to the state constitution that would make the Ten Commandments an official part of public education. It would obligate schools to display a framed poster of the Decalogue of no fewer than eleven-by-fourteen inches in classrooms, auditoriums, and cafeterias, which is the same size as the "In God We Trust" mottos that have decked the walls of Mississippi schools since 2001. It would also require that the Ten Commandments be recited aloud at the beginning of each class meeting when school is in session.[17]

Bird neglected to address the legislation directly, but it was clear where he stood on the proposed law. After telling the church that the American government (i.e., the "big" secular government) stands in the way of their mission to bring the gospel to nonbelievers, he stood on the stage with his arms outstretched and warned the church in an impassioned tone that a nation that honors God will be blessed by God, and that a nation that rejects God will collapse. "That's not political, that's biblical," he added forcefully.[18]

Schools were a source of anguish for many in the church. Churchgoers were irritated with teachers who dole out too much homework, they complained to each other about standardized testing, and they openly objected to the red tape that prohibits them from sharing their faith, praying for each other, and engaging in charitable activities at school. Some even said that they "hate" that the government forbids the Bible at school. A few of the people who hated that about the government were stay-at-home moms who quit their jobs as teachers when they had children. They wanted to provide their children with a biblical education and felt equipped to teach science, math, history, social studies, and scripture on their own at home. Others at Welcome sent their kids to a private pre-K–12th grade Christian school, or supplemented their kids' public education with Bible verses and Sunday school lessons.[19]

Hannah never used "hate" to describe her feelings about the government or school, but she was annoyed with them. To use her words, she has a "heart for letting kids know that there are other choices" than sex before marriage and she was upset that the Bible could not be taught in school. She said this to me and Maura, another churchgoer, as we were cleaning up after VBS at the school where Bird prayed over the catfish lunch. Tired from cleaning but encouraged by how the church had used a public facility to teach kids about the miracles of Jesus, Hannah shared that she has an interest in youth ministry. Kids feel pressured to "do that" (have sex), Hannah said suddenly, and the church is unable to do anything about it. "Some will never attend a VBS or visit a church," she moaned hopelessly. "Some will never hear about God, or about the choices He offers them." Hannah wants to tell youth about those other choices.

The state's abstinence-only and abstinence-plus sex education curriculum is Christian friendly, but Hannah said nothing about that.[20] Instead, she lingered on the issue of Christian censorship. She relayed a vague story about "one man" who used to pick up kids and take them "somewhere" to eat and have fun afterschool. He was "fired up by the Holy Spirit" but the "red tape," to use her words, put an end to his ministry. The school eventually told him that he could no longer transport kids away from school property. The teachers were reluctant to kick the "good word out," she claimed, but they had no other choice. The red tape was making the rules.

"This school lets us be here," Hannah frowned. "But is that enough?" Hannah wants what other evangelicals across the United States want for their children: she wants her kids to share her religious beliefs and values. She wants schoolteachers to lead students in Christian prayer and to include God in the curriculum, even if no other types of prayers or religious teachings are offered.[21] For her, being Christian is an essential part of being American, and she feels that public schools are forbidding her and her kids from being either fully, and freely.

Hannah's frustration with the public school system has a long and storied history in American evangelicalism. Evangelicals' suspicion of the public school system gained traction in the 1930s during the Scopes trial and resurged again in the 1960s when the U.S. Supreme Court handed religious conservatives a series of defeats that reinforced the wall between church and state at school.[22] In *Engel v. Vitale* (1962), the Court ruled that compulsory prayer in school constituted an establishment of religion and therefore violated the First Amendment. The following year, in *Abington School District v. Schempp* (1963), the Court decided that teachers cannot read the Bible or teach scripture in school classrooms for religious purposes, as opposed to secular ones such as teaching the Bible as literature or in a historical context. Christians from a wide range of denominations were angry at the Court for these decisions and wanted to get God back in school. At the same time, the Civil Rights Movement was pushing to racially integrate schools, and White Christians in the U.S. South were worried about how the end of Jim Crow might weaken their power and prestige.[23] In response to these multilayered changes at school, White Christian parents opted for a form of Christian education that included complicity in racism.[24] They sent their children to private Baptist or Baptist-adjacent Christian academies (also known as segregation academies); homeschooled their children; and joined a conservative countermovement that regarded parents as fundamentally entitled to controlling the education of their children.[25]

Hannah and Maura stood next to each other, motionless, scanning the empty classroom. An elder from the church happened to walk by, stopped, looked down at the floor alongside them, and suggested that they leave a few church leaflets behind, scattered by the desks. If we "forget" to pick them up, he laughed, the teachers at that school aren't going to care. The school we were standing in was a public school on the outskirts of town, away from the city school. Its parents and teachers, the church elder implied, are allies in the church mission to get God back in the classroom. Forgetting a few church leaflets on the floor is a way to weaken the red tape that the parents and teachers of that school also despise.

"There are Christians at this school," Hannah added with a touch of confidence. It has a large cross on the outfield where the kids play sports and the teachers have "more freedom" to say "I love Jesus" without retribution, as another at the church described it. The school we were cleaning up was not like the city school, they said. The professors' kids attend that school, and some of them are atheists. If the church were to leave leaflets on the floor of *that* school, they might stir up trouble.

Pam, who is in her fifties, has taught at the city school for over a decade. That school, to use her words, is "very very secular." She has to be extra careful about what she says about Jesus there. There are "all kinds of kids there." Some are from liberal cities like Seattle, Washington. She has kids who "don't believe in sin" and has even had a kid "read the Satanic Bible in front of her for one whole week." But it was not always like that, she sighed. Years ago, Pam could be open about her faith. Everyone went to church, and everyone was Christian. But these days, she feels like she can barely say a word about the Bible without some liberal, some atheist, some professor's kid, turning it into a big deal:

> I have this child in my class—he's pretty strongly opposed to Christianity. He's kind of in your face about it. Mocks it. Scorns it. And that's been very gut-wrenching and very hard for me, in a school setting that . . . I don't feel like I can defend my faith at all.

"We're in *that* kind of world now," Pam exhaled loudly. It makes her mad. It makes her feel like a stranger in her own country, in her own hometown, in her own classroom.[26] The world she lives in now, according to her, does not grant her the privileges that she feels entitled to as a White churchgoing Christian in America.

The feelings Pam expressed about becoming a minority reflects what anthropologists call a place-based "worry-nostalgia."[27] She believed that her hometown was changing for the worse, and she was angry at the federal laws, college professors, and public institutions that make her feel like she is unable to do anything about it. It was that anger and nostalgia that motivated Pam and other evangelicals to vote for Trump in 2016 and again in 2024. Trump was not part of "the government" that had made her feel left behind, forgotten, and undermined by Washington, DC. Trump was different. He made her feel seen again.[28] She felt confident that Trump would nominate judges for SCOTUS who share her values, and that meant a lot to her:

> Do we have any kind of southern evangelical Supreme Court judge? No. They're Jewish. They're from the Mainline Christian churches. They're Catholic. There are no evangelical Supreme Court judges. They have a huge influence. A lot of evangelicals voted for Trump [because] he was promising to put a conservative on the Court.

Trump, and his Supreme Court justices, could make being openly Christian at school easier for Pam. With them in power, she could remove the red tape that prevents her from "calling a sin a sin" at school, to use her phrase.

Pam was adamant that evangelicals are denied special treatment even though SCOTUS, Catholic and all, had ruled in favor of American evangelicals in several recent high-profile cases. The Court had ruled that churches can convert public schools into worship spaces on off days. That high school coaches can pray for their teams on the fifty-yard line.[29] And that Christians can deny a service to someone just because they are gay. Yet for Pam, the Court had not yet gone far enough. The law still permitted women to have abortions (a law that was overturned in the 2022 *Dobson v. Jackson Women's Health Organization* decision a few years after Pam was interviewed), and compulsory prayer and Bible readings were still officially banned from public school classrooms.

***

Despite a steady rise in secularism, and in religious plurality in the United States, Christianity is still the most dominant expression of religion in public education and is in some cases actively promoted. Evangelical Protestant youth are more likely to pray or talk about their faith at school than are other groups, and 8 percent of teens nationwide report that a schoolteacher has led them in prayer and read the Bible to them. The number rises from 8 percent to 12 percent in the U.S. South, where figures of authority are more likely to read the Bible or lead students in prayer at school than in other regions of the country.[30] Further, state legislation, such as Florida's 2022 "Parental Rights in Education" (also known as "Don't Say Gay") bill, and an uptick in prayer walks on school grounds in Tennessee, Georgia, and Texas makes clear that conservative Christianity is not that far removed from school after all.[31]

Indeed, the ubiquity of Christianity at school has made Marcel's job with the Fellowship of Christian Athletes (FCA), a national organization that seeks to inject conservative Christian beliefs and values into college sports, relatively smooth.[32] Marcel had just started his job with the FCA when we met for his interview. He had spent the week traveling across Mississippi to "connect with coaches and athletes and just assist them in their walk with Christ," he said.

> The way I do it, I first go speak with the principal and just say, "Hey, I'm with the FCA, this is what FCA's about." And then if there's no

reservations from the principal, they introduce me to the coaches or a person that facilitates the FCA for that school.

Most of Marcel's work happens on the field or in the locker room, in what he calls "huddles." His job is to "just be there," as he described it, for those involved in sports. Everyone he has met has been receptive to that. The principals and coaches greet him with warm welcomes, and they leave him alone about what he does with students in his huddles.

Churchgoers like Marcel recognize that evangelicals have allies in the public school system, but they also felt that a red tape of progressive policies, people, and practices are out to destroy them and their Christian commitments. The local city school where the professors' kids go was implicated in those feelings. It was a stand-in for what leaders of the religious and political right call the radical left. But Welcome churchgoers did not call that school or the people in it leftist or liberal. Instead, they used more precise, apolitical terms—"professors" and "that school"—to connote what they believed was wrong with education.[33] If Welcome could get into that school and take down its red tape, they could protect their kids and their community from ideas, opinions, and scientific information that compromise biblical authority.

The next section focuses on how the church came up with practical ways to preserve a belief in biblical literalism in a college town where blue dots of difference were on the rise. It shows how Bob's group, Reasoned Defense, staged imaginary arguments with skeptics (i.e., feminists, liberals, atheists, and others who "believe in science") who represent the red tape and, in the process, sharpened their identity as the same kind of Bible-believing Christians.

## The Red Tape at College

Bird thinks college students are "sick" and in desperate need of God. On the Sunday morning that he said this, he told the church about a friend who was visiting from out of town. This friend, Bird explained, is a special guy. He leads mission trips all across the world. Bird leaned forward on the stage: "If you want God to mess up your life [in a good way], go on a mission trip—I'm for real, go on a mission trip and see what God does." Then, as he stood at the corner of the stage, Bird described how he and his friend spent their weekend on the downtown Square watching "thousands" of students pass by. He told the church:

> You can see their needs by looking in their faces.
> Not only can you see their needs by looking in their faces—
> You can see their needs in the clothes that they wear—
> Or, let me say, the clothes that they *don't* wear.
> My sisters in Christ, I love you!
> God has created you to be beautiful in the image of Him.
> But don't cause your brother to stumble!

Students, whom Bird characterized as young women dressed in revealing clothing, are both the promise and peril of the community. They bring energy, life, and beauty to the town, but they also make good Christian men "fall."

Watching students on the Square with his missionary friend reminded Bird of why he planted Welcome. Oxford is full of unchurched college students, he preached, and he cannot just stand by and watch his community be taken over by what social scientists call "nones"—atheists, agnostics, spiritual but not religious, or nothing in particular.[34] Bird gave the church the numbers. There are 23 million university and college students across North America, he said, but only 300,000, 1.3 percent, are involved in collegiate ministry. Bird did not specify where he got his numbers, nor did he acknowledge that UM has about twenty religious student groups on campus, and at least seven of those are evangelical Christian ministries. But I understood his point: the church has to meddle in college education, especially now that UM is growing and student enrollment soaring.

"The crowds ought to affect us," Bird exhaled in annoyance. He asked the church twice, "If our Heavenly Father had such compassion towards us, should we not show that compassion towards others?" Jesus turned his compassion into a healing power that cured the sick, Bird preached. The church has to heal the sick, be welcoming, and stop being so judgmental, he continued. It has to let young people know that they can show up to worship on Sunday morning, hungover, to accepting and loving arms. The church has to be as gratifying as a tailgate party on football weekends. "We have to have more energy, more Jesus!" Bird hollered in earnest.[35]

Before planting Welcome, Bird worked as a youth pastor and through that job developed a strong attachment to young people who inspired him to do better and be better. Some of those young people started families and followed him to Welcome. Others joined another church. A few drifted away from him and from church completely.

Bird blames college for the losses, but he also thinks churches share some of that blame. Ryan made the same point when I interviewed him and his wife Emma. He explained that college is effective at pulling young people away from the church because the church they grow up in—the church of their parents and grandparents—failed to teach them how to stick up for their faith. Those earlier generations never had to think about how to protect their faith from secularism. They didn't have to. Emma agreed. Those earlier generations, she added, seldom encourage young people to take ownership of the church, much less defend it. Consequently, Emma surmised, young people enter college unprepared for human-made scientific methods and theories that corrupt their relationship to the church and biblical truth.

When Bird brought up college during his Sunday sermons, he usually did so to tell young people that they need to be suspicious of their professors. He made this point one Sunday when he preached about a philosophy class he took in college. The professor loved asking questions but didn't like his answers, Bird explained. The professor asked the class about the tree in the woods falling—does it make a sound if no one was there to hear it? Bird told the church what he told the professor: "If no one was there to hear it, who cares!" Bird made a D in that philosophy class, he smirked, and he still cannot "understand the point of asking a question if you aren't looking for an answer." Questions about how to spread the gospel and serve the church, he preached, are good questions. Questions that are posed to explore our perception of reality are not. "You've got to own your faith!" Bird yelled. Otherwise, the philosophy, biology, or business professor might "tell you what to put your faith in."

Bob, a self-described campus minister, is also at odds with a secular college education. Like Bird, he thinks the church is "hemorrhaging" young people for one main reason: Christians are incapable of protecting what they believe from science and secular corrosion. When Bob relocated to Mississippi from California, he had a seminary degree in hand and was shopping around for a church that cares about young people. He favored Bird's expositional preaching style and felt connected to Welcome's passion for youth.

Upon learning about Welcome's small groups, Bob pitched the idea of Reasoned Defense to John, a young father with a warm smile who took charge of organizing and publicizing the small groups program. Bob had been involved in a similar apologetics group on another university campus and felt that older people in the evangelical church needed to better understand what is taught in college and what that teaching does to Christian youth. When Bob got the okay from church leadership, he had Reasoned Defense added to the list of small group options. The word got out that it was a group to learn about evangelical apologetics, prompting Pace, my graduate assistant, and seven others to sign up.

The Reasoned Defense that Bob headed up is a local extension of Ratio Christi, an evangelical apologetics organization that has over one hundred clubs on college campuses across the United States. In a video about the founding of Ratio Christi, the director and CEO, Corey Miller, explains how it began in 2008 as a small group at Appalachian State University in Boone, North Carolina. Its first participants had noticed, in his words, that there were "serious intellectual questions about Christianity being asked and nobody was answering them."[36] That group of students wanted to be better prepared for college classes that refute "absolute truth," so they decided to have regular meetings that addressed the origins of species, the differences between men and women, and God's plan for humankind. One of the original members, Brendon Helms, launched an apologetics group at the Southern Evangelical Seminary in Charlotte, North Carolina, where he attended graduate school. Soon thereafter, Helms and other founding members named what they were doing Ratio Christi (the Reason for Christ) and acquired 501(c)3 nonprofit status, a status that the organization mobilized to open chapters on secular college campuses such as Florida State University; University of California, Los Angeles; and New Brunswick Community College, to name a few.

Bob's Reasoned Defense group spent an entire semester on what Gregory Koukl, an admired evangelical apologist and leading figure in Ratio Christi, calls "tactics." In a Ratio Christi publication titled, "Is Jesus the Only Way?" Koukl writes that evangelical apologetics want to "reverse the trend of anti-intellectual Christianity" and challenge "the rampant atheism and secularism" on university and college campuses.[37]

Evangelical apologetics, he explains, organize clubs at colleges, universities, and even some high schools, because they believe that Christians need historical, scientific, and philosophical reasons for believing in God that they can use to defend their faith in college.

Bob had purchased the tactics kit at the "Are You Ready 2 Reason 4 Christ" conference when it came to Oxford in 2017, and shared those materials, free of charge, with the group. Koukl's Tactics DVD lesson was in the kit, as well as a workbook. Bob's group watched the video and followed the workbook at the church main office over the course of a fall semester, in a fluorescent-lit room next to where Bird and the church secretary have their desks.

Jim Daly, of Focus on the Family, interviewed Koukl about his book, *Tactics: A Game Plan for Discussing Your Christian Convictions*. In that interview, Koukl describes how skeptics made him doubt God.[38] He was raised in the church, but he didn't have a firm relationship with the Bible. Church was just part of his routine. At one point, somebody asked him, "Do you really believe that?" Koukl wasn't sure how to answer that question. Soon thereafter, he moved away from home to join the honors pre-law program at Michigan State University. Once there, he stopped going to church. He was secular for about six years before becoming saved again. His journey back to church after college motivated him to write *Tactics*, a book that tells Christians to have a game plan for every interaction with nonbelievers in secular settings.[39]

Koukl looks professorial in the video that Bob's group watched, pairing thick-rimmed glasses with a tweed jacket and short salt-and-pepper hair.[40] He stands upright in front of bookshelves in a darkened study. His lesson, delivered in a clear and level speaking voice, starts with a definition of tactics, which he says is different from proving that Christians have the truth. Tactics are the act of gaining control of the skeptic, of making the skeptic explain what they believe and why. Gaining control of the skeptic is akin to gaining control of red tape that limits the extent to which Christianity dominates law, society, and discourse.

The "Columbo tactic" is the tactic from Koukl's lesson plan that Bob's group spent the majority of their time on. Based off the 1970s police drama about a bumbling detective, *Columbo*, the method of this tactic is to disarm the skeptic with "innocent query." That is, to pepper skeptics with seemingly benign questions. To put them in the hot seat and be on the lookout for flaws in their logic. Different from the Socratic method, the Columbo tactic is unconcerned with open dialogue or with ensuring that different people contribute to knowledge production. The objective is to keep Christians in "the driver's seat" of an interaction, Koukl instructs, and to expose the inconsistences in the other side's beliefs.

On the evening that the group finished the Columbo tactic video lesson, Bob assigned homework. He told the group to use the Columbo tactic in the coming week and to report back on how it went. When the group reconvened a week later, they arrived eager to commiserate. Pam greeted Pace with a jovial "Hey you!" and Bob smiled as he announced that everyone except Tanner was there. Bob pulled out his phone to text Tanner, and when Tanner arrived a few minutes later, the group got started.

Pam was the first to bring up the Columbo tactic homework. She didn't do it. She thinks it's clever, but she couldn't conjure up the nerve to practice it at the city school where she works. There is too much red tape there. Plus, she added, her "militantly atheist" student gets so "emotional" every time religion comes up. "He thinks the world is bad and it's all because of Christianity." To her, his emotional response is related to Koukl's claim that the Columbo tactic will be ineffective if one or both of the parties involved are too emotional. Her student is not violent, she clarified, "he just gets so aggressive."

Pam's comment about her student agitated the group. They wanted to know if the parents are atheist, and what kind of atheist, exactly, she was dealing with. Bob launched into professor mode. He explained to Pam that the "new atheists" are "nastier" and more focused on disproving Christianity than were atheists in the past. Earlier atheists like philosopher Friedrich Nietzsche, he said, contemplated the "idea that there's nothing" and the implications of that belief. Bob transitioned to agnosticism, which he described as evolving from a person "not knowing what they believe" to whether one "can" know what they believe. Following this, Pam shared a passage in Romans that teaches that Christian morals are inherent to everyone. Her student rejects God now, but she will try to "win with the heart." She will be kind. She will bring him snacks. She will applaud his writing. She will be available. Those are her tactics for maneuvering around the red tape. "I want to be able to retire," she said in a dry, cutting tone.

The notion that the Columbo tactic is promising but impractical resurfaced again that evening. When Pam suggested that her atheist student could get her fired, Ricky leaned toward his wife and said, "That's like being the diversity director" at the university. "Basically, if you're a Christian, that's not okay," he said cynically. "You can't have a Bible on your desk," Liz, his wife, added. "You can't display your religion" there, she claimed. Bob responded with a slight smirk, "Then I just think of all the professors' doors—" "—Allies," Liz finished with a hint of irony. "They represent the other." The Columbo tactic is like "planting little seeds," she said. It gives skeptics kernels of information to think about. She takes issue with the red tape that prohibits her from sowing those seeds out in the open.

Christian persecution at UM may have felt real to the members of Reasoned Defense, but those feelings conflict with reality. It can be isolating to be anything other than Christian. My students remind me of this every time I teach sociology of religion, which I have been doing for almost ten years. Every semester, usually within the first two weeks of classes, several students will declare that they are Christian, and also announce to the class whether they go to church, where, and how often. The students who are atheist, agonistic, or questioning their faith keep that to themselves until the end of the semester, when we read books about secular humanism. And many of those students only share that information with me in private emails, letting me know that they appreciated discussing a text that undermines the myth that atheists are immoral, as sociologist Phil Zuckerman does in *Living the Secular Life*.

The campus is remarkably friendly to Christianity. It is commonplace to pass by sandwich boards throughout the week announcing worship services at Paris-Yates Chapel, a campus building topped with a Peddle Bell Tower that rings hourly and plays a hymn at 5:00 p.m. The university also has a reputation for hiring athletic coaches that appreciate the Fellowship of Christian Athletes. One of its former football coaches, Hugh Freeze, was adored by the Oxford community for his Christian-based leadership and bold statements of faith on social media. In fact, the Freedom from Religion Foundation complained that Freeze, and by extension UM, were violating the separation of church and state by allowing Freeze to tweet Bible verses and pray for his team. In short, the campus climate at UM is, as one student boasted in the *Daily Mississippian*, a place where students "feel comfortable expressing their faith" and "can rest assured that Christian symbols and practices will persist despite those, such as Freedom from Religion Foundation, who fight to remove all public displays of religion."[41] UM is by no means a place where people are losing their jobs for being Christian.

Ricky touched back on what Liz had said about LGBTQ+ allies and brought the discussion back to those he considers the red tape: liberal college professors and students who promote feminism, racial diversity, and LGBTQ+ rights. He poked fun at liberals and anyone who might claim that Jesus could love "people like that." As if mimicking the words of such people, Ricky said mockingly, "If you think about it, that's where Jesus is. . . . He's with the criminals, the prostitutes, the diversities." As Ricky finished with "diversities," he made a motion with his hands that can best be described as jazz hands, a gesture that is often used to repudiate femininity and mock homosexuality.[42] The gesture made clear that the red tape is not only emblematic of institutions that observe a separation of church and state, but also of the very existence of people who refuse to accept that White heterosexual Christian men like him should be in charge.

Realizing that their hour together was moving by fast, Bob resumed the tactics video lesson at the point where Koukl lists ways to manage conversations with skeptics. A simple question like, "What do you mean by that?" is effective, Koukl professes. It "forces the other person to be very precise about their point of view." Imagine a scenario in which a skeptic claims, "There is no God." Rather than respond emotionally or with a Bible verse, try that question, Koukl advises. It puts the skeptic on the spot and will "buy time" in the conversation, he said, a comment that underscored his complete lack of interest in creating situations for productive dialogue. Koukl shifted to an additional scenario in which someone claims that "all religions are the same" and that Christianity is no better than any other religion. He offered another Columbo prompt: "Have you studied the details of the ancient texts?"

The group wanted to practice how to defeat skeptics after the video was over, so Bob had them turn to an outdated scenario from the *Tactics* workbook in which someone is excited about California and New York issuing same-sex marriage licenses before it was legalized nationwide. Bob read the scenario out loud and waited for a participant to come up with a premeditated question that mimics the Columbo tactic. Ricky was the first to take a crack: "What does getting married mean?" He provided another: "What constitutes a marriage?" Bob asserted, "What does love have to do with a legal license?" which inspired Tanner to tell the group about a mother and son who wanted to get married because they "love each other." It was unclear if Tanner was joking or referring to something in the news, and the group carried on without asking for clarification or discussing it further. They appeared accustomed to outlandish stories like that one. Tanner's comment about the mother and son didn't even make them flinch.

The next scenario the group chose from the workbook was about abortion. The workbook had placed an apologist in an airport scene with a friend who thinks that partial-birth abortion bans are wrong. Tanner jumped at the chance to respond: "Why is this only a women's issue?" Another member proposed a follow-up to the hypothetical friend in question, "Do you even know what a partial-birth abortion is?" Bob and Tanner cautioned that the question was too aggressive. It's better to "frame it as if you're the ignorant one," another added. Others in the group supported the critique with comments like "you're an ambassador" and "be gentle" before Tanner suggested that it's okay to be offensive sometimes. "Christ is offensive," he said resolutely. Plus, he mumbled, nonbelievers can be aggressive, emotional, "flamboyant."

By the end of the meeting, the group was up to speed on the Columbo tactic, but still unconvinced that Christians are free to use it. Pam reiterated that she has to be careful with what she says at work, but that she will continue to "plant the seeds of light" in the hearts of her students. Bev and her husband Clayton attempted to console Pam, reassuring her that, as Clayton put it, "Darkness is attracted to light." That atheist student is the "darkness" and Pam's Christian heart, cookies, and guidance are the light he needs. Besides, as Koukl had argued, there has to be a season of gardening—a period of time when nonbelievers can push away from the conversation before coming back for more. Pam is the master gardener at her school; she is weeding out the red tape that blocks her students from the light. Being attentive and patient, Bev and Clayton affirmed, is proof that Pam is trimming away the red tape in every way she can.[43]

***

Despite the stated intent of evangelical apologetics, the Reasoned Defense group refused to spend their time intellectually tangling with science, doubt, or uncertainty.[44] Its members neglected to chart out a logical explanation for their faith, and side-stepped discussions that could lead to disagreements or multifaceted interpretations of the Bible. Instead, to draw on Goffman's theory on the presentation of self in everyday life, their communication was contingent on the desire to "save face" as believers in absolute truth, and by extension to prepare themselves for a battle against disbelief in the secular world.[45] The skeptic was a symbol charged with meaning and emotional energy, and the ritual repudiation of that symbol energized the group and gave it purpose.[46] Members of Reasoned Defense used the skeptic to affirm that their purpose is to oppose *them*, meaning anyone and everyone that stands on the other side of the culture wars that were sizzling at the time.

In step with Ratio Christi, Bob's Reasoned Defense group practiced how to win what I call "imaginary arguments" with skeptics. From Koukl's *Tactics* materials, they learned that the only reason to have a conversation with a skeptic is to come out on top. To walk away unscathed and unchanged. To win. To imagine their wins, Reasoned Defense practiced mock debates with what Diefendorf refers to as an "imagined secular" friend, coworker, or college professor.[47] And they had these debates for and in front of each other. Through that group practice, they hardened the idea that they were on a divine mission from God to direct what others voice, question, and contemplate in the public arena.

Reasoned Defense exaggerated its black-and-white view of the world with rhetorical force, and that view was not out of the ordinary at Welcome, nor exceptional in the evangelical tradition.[48] Other small groups at Welcome, such as the well-attended Sunday Group that met in Frank's affluent home, also viewed the world through a black-and-white lens that encouraged churchgoers to define themselves against the red tape and the people who represent it.

On the night that Frank introduced his curricula on Identity to the Sunday Group, he went up to every participant, one by one, and asked them to take a slip of paper out of a handheld basket. Most of the participants did, but with visible reluctance. "What is this?" and "I didn't do my homework," a couple giggled nervously. The slip of paper that I pulled from the basket read 1-11-09. Was it a date? A code for scripture?

I had no idea. At the close of his circuit, Frank announced that the slips of paper were meaningless. An experiment, nothing else.

Frank asked for volunteers to explain their choice to take the paper. The responses shifted from "Because you told me to" and "I trusted you," to "Peer pressure." Frank expounded on trust and ignored the remarks about authority and peer pressure. The group knows and trusts him, he declared. He turned to Anne and asked why she took the paper. Anne exclaimed, "She told me to take it!" as she playfully nudged her friend seated beside her. The main idea of the experiment had been made. "Your friend in Christ encouraged you and you listened to her," Frank smiled. Christians can trust one another and should not trust anyone else, Frank concluded.

For the second half of our lesson on Identity, Frank handed out a piece of paper with a stick man and asked the group to list the kinds of people they are in relationships with. A few members shouted out their answers: spouses, children, employers, friends. When friends came up, Frank stopped and asked if there are different kinds of friends. Hearing this, I wrote down "close friends" and "acquaintances" next to my stickman. Another stated confidently: "Believers and Nonbelievers." Frank took out a dry-erase board and set it up at the front of the room. He wrote Identity at the top in bold font. Then he drew a stickman in the center of the board before adding the proper nouns Believers and Nonbelievers next to it. He smiled warmly and reiterated that Christians put "Jesus on the throne" of their relationships. To put Jesus on the throne, they have to put Christians first. Volunteer for the church. Spend time with their Bibles. Be in community with believers.

Frank's lesson on Identity reflected what Reasoned Defense had stressed: if a believer interacts with a non-Christian, that interaction should be directed toward "planting the seed" of God into their mind. If the interaction is not oriented toward that goal, it should never materialize. Believers should cut ties with non-Christians. Don't try to understand them or build bridges. Bridges are dangerous. Bridges lead to dialogue, disbelief, and disaffiliation.

At the end of a series of lessons on Identity, Frank announced that Dave had prepared something for us about what it means to be saved. I was surprised to hear this. It was unusual to see Dave, a self-described blue-collar worker who has earned fine lines from the sun, taking the lead at Sunday Group. He was quiet during the group discussions and usually only talked to me, Frank, or his wife during the shared mealtime.

Dave smiled sheepishly, stood up from his seat on the sofa, and grabbed a piece of plain paper off the fireplace mantle. Without a word of introduction, he folded the paper into the shape of an airplane and began telling a story about two brothers: one saved, the other unsaved. "The saved brother was always trying to talk his brother into accepting the Lord, but the unsaved brother didn't go for it," Dave said. He liked drinking alcohol too much. One night they were in "conversation about it," and the saved brother tried to convince the unsaved brother again. It didn't work. Then, on their way home, the brothers got in a car accident together and died. Dave raised his voice in earnest, "Next thing you know, they were standing in line at the pearly gates—both of them." The saved brother had a ticket. It said, "Admit one." The unsaved brother didn't. He started to panic. The saved brother gave him part of his ticket, but the unsaved one was not satisfied. He asked for more. As Dave told the story, he pretended to be the saved brother and slowly tore off more paper into strips.

Dave had everyone's attention. It was unclear if the unsaved brother would have enough of the ticket to get inside the pearly gates, and Dave's solemn face provided no clues. He continued, "The unsaved brother gave St. Peter his pieces of tattered paper bit by bit." St. Peter took the pieces of paper and arranged them to spell out "H" and then "E." Dave snickered in amusement, "The brother was pleased. He thought this meant he was going to heaven!" Dave organized his strips of paper on the table out in front of us to replicate what St. Peter had spelled: HELL. The unsaved brother was banished from heaven, he clarified. Seeing this, Dave explained, the saved brother started to worry about his own fate. He nervously approached St. Peter and handed over what was left of his ticket. Dave held a crucifix up above his head and declared that St. Peter did, in fact, admit the saved brother into heaven.

"It's that simple," Dave concluded bluntly. "You got to do it on your own. You can't use my ticket," he said, as he walked back to his seat on the sofa. The group gave Dave a light round of applause. One said the story was "really neat," another called it "cool."

Dave's story was a cruder version of what the group had been hinting at, with more tact, all semester long. Nonbelievers will be brutally punished, and according to Dave, they deserve what they get. The unsaved brother had a chance to be saved, he said, and he refused that opportunity. The saved brother, then, was right to prioritize his own destiny once reaching the pearly gates. He had spent his life trying to save his brother, and that time was up.

At the close of Dave's story, Sunday Group circled back to a partial truth that drives Welcome: the red tape, by their account, was becoming stronger in the college town that they call home. A town that used to be, in Pam's words, Christian. If the church wants to survive, it has to remove the red tape. It must tell people that heaven and hell are real, that being a good person is not enough, and that not all religions are the same. It must be allowed to let people know that there is an afterlife, and that the afterlife is divided up between winners and losers in the ruthless way that Dave described.

## The Red Tape Is Coming Down

Scholars characterize Christian nationalism as a movement and ideology that promotes white supremacy, patriarchy, authoritarianism, and militarism.[49] Theologically speaking, research shows that the Americans who favor Christian nationalism are most likely to believe that the Bible is the literal word of God, that hell is a real place, and that only the born again will be saved from eternal damnation. Politically speaking, they are most likely to oppose LGBTQ+ rights, women's rights, gun control, and immigration reform, most likely to believe that Muslims do not belong in America, that Blue Lives Matter more than Black Lives, and that atheists and other non-Christian groups inflict evil on America.[50] The people who support Christian nationalism are a subset of Christians who, as historian Kristin Kobes Du Mez argues, embody a militant concept of patriarchy that prioritizes the social and political power of straight White cisgender Christian men.[51]

Christian nationalism is gaining ground at school. In fact, removing who and what the red tape represents at school (i.e., progressive ideas, public institutions, and people that counter their Christian nationalist agenda) became a primary focus of the GOP platform after Trump lost his bid for reelection in 2020. Former Republican Senator David Perdue released a "Parents' Bill of Rights" in his campaign to be elected governor of Georgia in 2022, calling on conservatives to fight for their beliefs and values at school.[52] Soon thereafter, conservatives started coming after what Trump and others have called "radical leftist indoctrination" in education. Republican government officials in various states restricted the teaching of "identity politics" and critical race theory in the public school system, state auditors and governors started to monitor and ban Diversity, Equity, and Inclusion (DEI) programs in higher education, and conservative students and administrators produced a chilling effect on educators in social contexts where MAGA Republicans are in power.[53]

Christian nationalism has been written into American law too. Over the first two decades of the twenty-first century, the Supreme Court has taken an "accommodationist" approach to religious liberty, an approach that has resulted in various rulings that privilege Christianity under the guise of equal access and free speech.[54] And, as religious historian Winnifred Fallers Sullivan points out, the Court has made these and other rulings on religious accommodations without having to specify or define what makes a belief religious or sincere.[55] The Court has even overturned *Roe v. Wade*, a landmark ruling that brings America "back to the basics" of gender[56]—basics that the evangelical church prescribes in its campaign to put men back in charge of women (chapter 4). Basics that have culminated into over thirty anti-LGBTQ+ bills, namely that target transgender people, within only one legislative session in Mississippi.[57]

In *Taking America Back for God*, sociologists Andrew Whitehead and Samuel Perry provide a robust survey study of the Christians who espouse the idea that the United States is and should be a Christian nation that puts God first. They find that the Christians who promote Christian nationalism don't necessarily come from a specific denomination or tradition; however, White Protestant evangelicals in rural parts of the U.S. South do tend to embrace and promote Christian nationalism more so than Christians in other parts of the country.

If Welcome churchgoers were asked to fill out a survey that measures the indicators of Christian nationalism, some would fall into the "favorable" or "ambassador" category. Others would not. Yet irrespective of where individual churchgoers stand on the spectrum of Christian nationalism, the church as a whole is certain that Christianity is endangered in America and that Christians must push for their rights in a secular world that rejects their belief system.

The church's most vocal members made clear that they were mad at the red tape. They blamed it for the church's loss of control, of members, of influence. To them, the red tape was anything and anyone that opposes the integration of church and state, which is why some said that they "hate the government." The government implements school policies that prohibit churches from sharing food and feeding starving children, as the moms at book club described it. The government "tricks" welfare recipients into "being comfortable," in the words of a White participant at Be the Bridge. The government "makes us poor, stupid, and sick," another in the group added. The government allows Muslims to practice Sharia Law in God's country. The government, a secular godless one, was making moral decisions about right and wrong, and those decisions had upended Christianity's influence in public institutions.

Trimming down the red tape at school, arguing with it on college campuses, and inserting conservative Christianity into law was a mainstay of the evangelical mission at Welcome. And Welcome is not alone in that mission. Its home state is a testing ground for Christian nationalist legislation that positions conservative Christians as a minority group that should be given special advantages in the public sphere.[58] In 2014, the state seal officially became "In God We Trust" as part of Mississippi's Religious Freedom Restoration Act, which vowed that the state "shall not substantially burden a person's right to the exercise of religion." Once that act was passed, teachers of every religious orientation were legally obliged to display the state seal in their classrooms. With that act in place, "In God We Trust" was also added to the state license plate, and HB 1523, an extreme anti-LGBTQ+ religious liberty bill, became law (chapter 5).[59]

In 2015, another Christian nationalist bill was signed that positioned evangelicals as an aggrieved group in need of lawful protection: House Bill 786, "The Mississippi Church Protection Act." This bill permits a church or place of worship to establish a "security program" that allows its members to carry firearms in the congregation. That bill was passed shortly after white nationalist Dylann Roof carried out his horrific anti-Black mass shooting at the Emanuel African Methodist Episcopal Church in Charleston, South Carolina. Mississippi Governor Phil

Bryant, a White conservative Christian, signed the church protection bill surrounded by other White Republicans in the month of April, the state's official Confederate Heritage month.

In a tweet about the bill, Bryant wrote that "Churches deserve protection from those who would harm worshippers," a statement that foregrounded what religious historian Anthea Butler describes as the "language of religious persecution" to dismiss the racial motivations of Roof's crime.[60] The bill's author, State Rep. Andy Gipson, a White Republican who wants to get guns into the hands of more people in more places, said that his bill was a direct response to what happened in Charleston. In Gipson's words, the bill protects churches against attack, especially small churches that "can't afford to hire security." Gipson, like other evangelical conservatives in leadership, neglected to address the racist motivations of the shooting in Charleston. Instead, he used that massacre to suggest that White Christians like him are next on a violent hit list. In doing so, he advanced a Bible Belt stereotype that secular people are fundamentally demonic and want to erase Christianity from America, a sentiment that the governor made apparent when he put his handgun in a leather belt holster and placed it on top of a well-worn Bible for a photograph that announced that the "Church Protection Act" had been signed into law.[61]

The state's most significant, seemingly progressive change to the state flag in 2020 is also part of the movement to take down the red tape. When the National Collegiate Athletic Association used its financial muscle to demand that the flag be changed, state lawmakers voted to remove the Confederate battle insignia, but under one condition.[62] The new flag had to include the state's religious freedom seal: In God We Trust. Conservative state leadership had effectively used racial strife again for their own religious gains. Gains that, to draw on Butler, support "the hegemony of white Christian men over and against the flourishing of others" in Mississippi and across the nation.[63]

Mississippi is a conservative powerhouse that has tremendous influence on what happens in the rest of America. But Mississippi is not a homogenous state devoid of change or progressive insurgence.[64] The church knows this, which is why an evangelical church in Oxford—that college town with its blue dots of difference—sees itself on a divine mission to take down the red tape. To take it down, the church practiced

Figure 6.1. Governor Phil Bryant and Mississippi legislators smile as Bryant signs The Mississippi Church Protection Act, April 15, 2016. Photograph courtesy of the Mississippi Department of Archives and History.

pushing alternative points of view out of the conversation. Practiced staying ignorant of what others think. Practiced the belief that "everybody but us," as one member of Reasoned Defense said, is on the wrong side of God.[65] They practiced doing church outside of traditional structures, which for them involved preparing catfish and peach cobbler for teachers, staff, and administrators at a public school.

Next, in the conclusion, I underscore a main argument that has driven this book: to understand the political path of American evangelicalism, we must account for how progressive perspectives are silenced at church, as well as how Christian nationalist viewpoints are exaggerated and amplified because of that silence.

# Conclusion

American evangelicalism is at war with itself, and according to investigative journalist Tim Alberta's research, much of that war is over political differences.[1] On top of that, the church is losing members and some of those losses are political. In *The Great Dechurching*, a book about the rapid decline in church membership, two evangelical pastors propose that the United States is in the middle of the "largest and fastest religious shift" in its history.[2] More churches are closing than being planted, and "dechurching" is not only happening on the Left in Mainline Protestant congregations, but also among self-identified evangelicals on the Right who feel that the church has become too soft on issues that are important to them. One of the authors is Jim Davis, the former pastor of Grace Bible Church in Oxford, a church plant that opened in a public school before Welcome. Bird brought up Davis and his book when we met to talk about the chapters of this book that I gave him and Anne to read prior to publication. Learning that people in his church had not built a strong connection was disappointing, Bird said, but as *The Great Dechurching* suggests, they have their reasons for steering clear of deep issues. The church is experiencing a record number of church dropouts, political divisiveness is intensifying in the church, and there are Christians who love being American more than God.

Prior to attending Welcome, I assumed that White evangelicals show up to church more or less the same. That assumption was rooted in research that shows that White evangelicals are invested in partisan politics and doggedly conservative.[3] But at Welcome I learned fairly quickly that evangelicals show up differently and have to work toward performing and elevating biblical sameness, and that the work they put in to achieving sameness is not solely big talk directed at outside forces, or "them."[4] That work is also directed inward at one another, as churchgoers quietly push differences aside, flee from disagreements, and ignore the controversial stuff in their everyday interactions at church. It was work that stopped the more progressive ideas and worldviews from materializing at church.

At Welcome, some churchgoers had opinions about immigration, Muslims, and race that mirror right-wing conspiracy theories. Others felt that church leaders do too little to tackle racism within their own communities. Some fully supported the church's teachings that men are biblically superior to women, while others found those interpretations of the Bible hard to digest, or even infuriating. And yet those dissimilarities rarely sprang to the surface of church. Everyone invested in incorruptible church uniformity, or what I have termed biblical sameness. That uniformity came packaged in a practice of small talk (i.e., omission, silence, avoidance, neglect) that weeds out the possibility of critical reflection and change. It is a practice that foregrounds Whiteness. A practice that includes:

- Keeping the conversation light and easy.
- Posing questions that reinforce common sentiments.
- Avoiding culture war issues in settings where differences of opinion might emerge.
- Removing terms like Black, White, Jewish, gay, and transgender from the vocabulary.
- Emphasizing the spiritual benefits of unity and togetherness.

There were, of course, moments in which churchgoers were unable to maintain a mask of sameness, such as when Black members spoke candidly about racism in the Be the Bridge group. Or when women spoke in less than flattering terms about marriage at book club. But when these disturbances bubbled up, churchgoers reestablished sameness by:

- Refraining from posing follow-up questions.
- Interrupting the speaker and moving on to someone or something else less charged.
- Calling attention to the time, and closing the conversation.
- Circling back to a subject or belief that accentuates a common denominator.
- Pointing out that God is in control.

Sticking to small talk was a strategy for building and maintaining Christian relationships, and also, at the same time, a defensive strategy for navigating the potential for religious and political rifts within the church.

Throughout my research, colleagues and friends have asked if small talk is exceptional to evangelicalism in the American South. It is not. There are plenty of other White-dominated spaces and religious groups that strategically avoid tackling subjects that might cause friction within their own communities.[5] For example, in a study of the Norwegian Church Abroad (NCA) in the United States, sociologist Lars Laird Iversen shows how everyday strategies of silence, avoidance, and small talk shape an "imagined sameness" that link Norwegian national and religious identity.[6] More specifically, he found that the staff at NCAs insisted that an unspoken contract of small talk prevailed in their community, as opposed to big talk about controversial issues, because it makes people feel welcome and reinforces the social glue—just being Norwegian—that bonds them together.[7] Likewise, in a study of converts to Catholicism who met for a weekly RCIA (Rite of Christian Initiation of Adults), sociologist Rachel Ellis found a similar dynamic at play: people in those groups silently agreed to veer away from quarrelsome culture war issues when they sensed that there were conflicting opinions in the room.[8] And both the conservative and moderately progressive Methodist churches that sociologist Dawne Moon studied refused to talk about political issues (i.e., homosexuality and same-sex marriage) because they wanted to believe that their own, personal "everyday theologies" were held by others in the church as moral, correct, and true.[9]

Small talk is a safe haven for Whiteness, just as it is for patriarchy and heterosexism, which is why it can be found anywhere and everywhere—not just in the South or at church. Small talk rushes in to protect Whiteness when a conversation becomes too personal, too political, too deep. Small talk fills in for painful truths about race and racism. Small talk pushes out frank talk about domineering men and sexual assault. Small talk makes it hard to even reflect on inequality, much less think about how to solve it. Take this book as a warning: if your community indulges in it, you might be tempted to think that things could be simpler, even better, if more of us kept our differences to ourselves. That kind of thinking can advance White Christian nationalism, a dangerous ideology and movement that seeks to control who and what counts as American.

## White Christian Nationalism Grows from Silence

In her research on public opinion, Noelle-Neumann argues that the "climate of opinion depends on who talks and who keeps quiet."[10] We are instinctively driven to minimize the prospect of rejection. We take the temperature on what others around us think before we speak up. And when we sense that we have the support of others in our social circle, or in the larger society, we feel safe, even emboldened, to proclaim our views loudly and proudly.[11] Conversely, in circumstances where we feel that our opinions are in the minority, we often spiral into silences that tank other, like-minded voices. That is, people with similar opinions stay silent together in large part because they are unaware that their opinions have company. Those silences, Noelle-Neumann argues, act back on the people who produce them, sometimes convincing seemingly silent minorities to conform to a vocal majority position.

Over and again, churchgoers heard from each other and from church leadership that they must put Christianity first in their lives. Bird encouraged the church to remember that they were on the same "team," told them to spend time with their team, cheer for their team, and fight for their team in every dimension of life. Churchgoers were hearing this "Christian first" message from evangelical leaders on the outside as well. It was the unofficial motto of the Make America Great Again campaign, and it was a motto that conservative Christian organizations and think tanks have been promoting since the inception of the religious right.[12]

The Christian first message was enacted by churchgoers in multiple ways. They stressed the importance of "doing life" with Christian family and friends when they met together for small group. They insisted on standing behind their teammates (i.e., other believers) even if they might personally disagree with how a teammate was acting on their religious beliefs, or religious liberty. They imparted that God is in control of all things, and that real believers never challenge or try to scale back His control. And the most vocal proponents of the Christian first message recurrently made clear that believers are on the "right team," and that nonbelievers are an opposing team that wants to make it hard to believe in God.

The church's emphasis on that Christian first message structured the climate of opinion at Welcome. It shaped who felt like they could speak up, and who felt like they should just stay quiet. As the second half of this book has established, the men who leaned most heavily to the Right were emboldened to speak out loud and proud about their politics in small group settings. Compared to the more moderate churchgoers, they also had a much easier time staking out their position on divisive issues during private interviews. They could safely assume that others shared their opinion since their opinion was the opinion that is shared by the Republican Party.

The most conservative churchgoers had a rhetorical toolkit at their disposal that they could draw on to defend their positions with relative ease and efficiency. They spoke clearly and confidently about their "way of life" being under attack, for example, and voiced frustration with immigrants who come to "our country" to "take our jobs." And, like their rhetorical models on the Right, these churchgoers prided themselves on being honest even if their honesty was "offensive" or "harsh."

The churchgoers who were less friendly to right-wing politics, however, were not as eager to voice their opinion with other churchgoers in the room, and often reserved their criticisms of the Republican Party for home with their spouse, a best friend, a nonreligious colleague from work, or in a side conversation or during private interviews. Unlike their staunch conservative peers, they did not have a rhetorical roadmap at their disposal. They seldom had the chance to hear other like-minded Christians express their opinions at church and this lack of experience limited their ability to communicate their thoughts in direct terms.

To this point, in the beginning stages of analytic coding, I placed some of the responses from the "almost feminist" women in the church, as well as the people who quietly supported LGBTQ+ membership, in a node titled "word salad" during my preliminary analysis of interviews in an NVivo 11 software program. At first, the word salad category was a cursory way for me to track interview responses that were confusing, inconsistent, or incomprehensible. Over time, that category shed light on what churchgoers had trouble answering with self-assurance or clarity. For example, several interviewees had a hard time squaring their purported mission of loving inclusivity with religious liberty legislation that deems homosexuality sinful. They had a hard time communicating what they thought or what they thought they should think. They rarely had the chance to speak with others openly about their views, which made articulation challenging. The interview was a space for them to practice the language of LGBTQ+ Christian inclusivity and that practice morphed into word salad.

The voice of White Christian nationalism had enforced silence, and silence eased its growth. That voice, which is public and outspoken, advocates for religious freedom laws that discriminate against LGBTQ+ people in American law and society. It deems men the God-ordained bosses of women. It argues that there is no such thing as a Black Christian, only a Christian who happens to be Black, as both Black and White members of Welcome professed. It promotes the idea that religious pluralism is bad for America, and that Christians must unite to take down "the red tape" of diversity and inclusion in public life. That voice was the one that churchgoers heard or expected to hear associated with their identity at church.

There are churches, even many churches, that want to change the association between Christian nationalism and their faith. To do so, they will have to make an intentional effort to move past small talk.[13] They will need to create spaces where members of their community can feel safe to express their grievances with political and ideological extremism. They will need to foster church spaces where individuals can learn that they have company in their silence, and can break that silence, together.

## ACKNOWLEDGMENTS

I am grateful to the members of Welcome. This book would be impossible without their cooperation. Welcome allowed me to study their church at a time of tremendous social and political division, which takes guts. They allowed me into their conversations, and that meant welcoming me into their homes with warm smiles and hot plates of food.

I thank my graduate research assistants, Heather Costa-Greger and Pace Ward, for assisting me with data collection. Both Heather and Pace were a pleasure to work with. Pace worked on this project the longest and was skilled at writing field notes. I appreciated how he reported what he observed, instead of what he was hoping to observe. Parts of chapter 4 appear in an article I published with Pace titled, "'The Tables are Turning': The Evangelical Defense of Anti-LGBTQ+ Religious Liberty," *Sociology of Religion* 84, no. 4 (2023): 406–25.

I thank the College of Liberal Arts at the University of Mississippi (UM) for providing research grants for three consecutive summers. Those grants afforded me the time needed to carry out participant observations and data analyses. I am also grateful to the Collegeville Institute for granting me the opportunity to join its "Writing Beyond the Academy" workshop and residency. My 'show, don't tell' approach to this book was spearheaded by Michael McGregor and the interdisciplinary cohort that took part in that writing residency. I thank Jennifer Mason for her astute read and suggestions when I started my writing journey, Kate Lechler for punctual edits on chapters, and Jessica Newman for her eagle eye copyedits on a near final draft. I thank the anonymous reviewers who carefully engaged with the book proposal, and the reviewer who read the full manuscript. I warmly thank Jennifer Hammer for her professionalism and assistance at every step of the publishing process. I thank Brianna Jean, Valerie Zaborski, and Jim Reilly for pushing the book forward and tidying it up.

I am thankful for my dear friend and longtime sociology comrade, Tre Wentling. Tre applauded me as if my wins were his when I was shopping the book around, and he organized a virtual writing workshop that helped me persevere while working from home with a toddler during the COVID-19 pandemic. I also thank Bek Orr, Ynesse Abdul-Malak, and Julie Torres for making that workshop an encouraging and friendly space to be.

I am thankful for Kelsy Burke. Kelsy is an extraordinary colleague. She has been there for me as I slog through an idea, a trickly methodological concern, or a piece of writing. I am grateful for Kathy Blee, who had been my dissertation advisor and mentor in my grad school days. Kathy has been an influential force in my scholarly career, and I am grateful for her perspective on the book's theoretical mark. I thank Kimberly Creasap and Jane Walsh for their scholarly energy and friendship. My sincere thanks go to Orit Avishai, Dawne Moon, Paul Lichterman, and Andrew Whitehead. Orit provided comments on my chapter about religious liberty that improved the book; Dawne shared insights on the politics of talk at the beginning stages of the project; Paul pushed me to define more precisely what is meant by sameness; and Andrew supported this book project when I was applying for fellowships and grants.

I am appreciative of and heartened by my colleagues, students, and friends in and beyond the Department of Sociology and Anthropology at UM. I thank Jodi Skipper for our powerwalks in the park (we need more of them), and for how she models what it means to be a community engaged scholar who uses research to push for racial justice outside of the academy. I am grateful to Kirsten Dellinger for being a supportive colleague who believes Mississippi can be better. I counted on Kirsten to review chapters at various points of this book journey, and her feminist perspective always felt like a breath of fresh air. I am thankful to Catarina Passidomo for the writing sessions we shared, and for the ability she has to make any room she steps into feel calmer and safer. I thank John Sonnett for acting as an informal mentor when I started my job at UM, and for reminding me that being present in the moment is hard but necessary.

I thank Willa Johnson (rest in peace) for always offering to read my work and for candidly pushing our department and the wider university to do a better job of being what it says it wants to be. I thank Kirk

Johnson for providing constructive feedback on chapter drafts and for his writing tips on how to succinctly tell a story. I thank Jeff Jackson for fact-checking my discussion of the university's history, and for offering me time off from my administrative responsibilities when I needed it. I thank James Thomas (JT) for providing feedback on the chapters that analyze the church's performance of diversity and inclusion. Brian Foster for reminding me of just how important place is. I thank Kristin Hickman for alerting me to the sources I needed in sociolinguistics. Bridget Martin for workshopping my arguments about small talk over coffee. Jaime Harker for the comments she gave me on chapters, and for her commitment to turning Oxford into a more affirming place for LGBTQ+ people. Kevin Cozart for the work he does to facilitate and document queer community in the South, and for the photograph that he contributed to this book. I thank Michael Fagans and Kerrigan Casimir for their powerful photographs, and Julie Dees for tracking down the photo of Bryant in the Mississippi Department of Archives and History. I thank Evelyn Johnson and Ms. Q for their warmheartedness and for helping me find answers, even on bad days.

I sincerely appreciate the former UM sociology MA students who I have worked closely with over the last ten years: Madeline Burdine, Danielle Buckingham, Alana Freimanis, Daniela Griffin, Brenna Paola, MJ Shappley, Pace Ward, and Ian Whalen. Their perseverance, intellect, and good vibes made my job joyful and meaningful in challenging times. I am thankful for the Center for the Study of Race and Racism at UM, particularly JT and Simone Delerme for the manuscript workshop they organized for me. That workshop, which occurred right before the manuscript went to press, was invaluable. Darren Grem urged me to clearly articulate how evangelicals selectively choose passages from the Bible to support their politics. Douglass Sullivan-González advised me to develop my ideas on the social production of homogeneity in future projects. Almas Khan shared her expertise in legal studies to underline my claims about religious liberty legislation. Jodi pushed me to consider how my own relationship to Whiteness made small talk easy for me to take part in and study. And the "three perspectives" line-by-line approach that Ryan Parsons took went above and beyond the call of duty.

Minjoo Oh and Ana Velitchkova, thank you for being my beloved friends of big hearts and big ideas. We have more holidays and celebrations to share together. Jessie Wilkerson, I cherish your sense of humor and support. I hope we end up in the same place again one day. Valerie George, you are my forever punk rock star and model of courage. You dared me to go to college and do something I love, and I did. Michelle Fried, thank you for making me laugh until my face aches. Mehr Latif and David Montero, thank you for traveling far and wide to share meals, drinks, and laughs. You two are solid gold. Wonderful Wednesday, thank you for leaning into the goofy with me, and for encouraging me to turn the beat as much as I want. Tish Kennedy and Kay Carlisle, thank you for your wisdom, for being there for us, and for always being a delight to be around. Mariana, Isabel, and Mateo Jurss, thank you for getting me and Rudy out for playtime in the fresh air. Your presence lightens our day. Thank you to our friends and family in Madrid. We can always count on your *sonrisas radiantes y brazos abiertos*.

Muma, your Southern Baptist upbringing was close to mind as I was writing this book. You remind me that we can be a different Mississippi. Thank you for being a loving mom, for always being there when I call for help, and for rubbing against the grain, softly and persistently. Didi, I miss you so much it hurts. Thank you for modeling how to create something out of Mississippi, and for always finding a way to connect to my interests and goals. I really could not have asked for a better dad. Mark, I appreciate your open mind and "I got what I need, and then some" attitude. It comforts me more than you know.

Finally, I am enormously grateful for my dream team, Alberto and Rudy. They bring sunshine to my life every single day. Alberto, this book would be impossible without you. You are always in my corner, cheering me and my ideas on, and that means the world to me. You listened to me verbally process data, you read chapters more than once, and you sat with me for hours sketching out diagrams that sharpened the arguments I present in this book. Thank you for your positivity, your enthusiasm, your gentle heart, and for taking on way more than your share of domestic duties. Rudy, my providential child, you are simply the best. Thank you for the art, the dance sessions, hugs, and kisses. You made me many colorful cards as I was finalizing this book, and those cards were bright spots in screen-filled days. Your creative mind and compassionate spirit remind me that we humans can and must do better.

# APPENDIX A

## *Doing Small Town Ethnography*

I was a witness.

Right before joining the church, I changed my hair from an asymmetric cut to a shoulder-length shag with highlights. For the first few months at Welcome, I paired my hairdo with collared shirts and slacks, but rarely ever with the boxy blazers and black garments that dominate my wardrobe. Within a few months, I came to the realization that my look might be misleading. Ethnographies are long-term projects, and I knew that when I was done with the research, I would probably still be living in Oxford. Was I going to have the same haircut forever? I eventually changed my hair back to what it was before. I cut one side shorter than the other and dyed the underside blue. My haircut became a humorous symbol of inclusion at Welcome. Bird used it to declare his love for all kinds of people. "Even people with bright blue hair," he'd joke.

Throughout this project, I tried my best to be a "witness," as Goffman describes it, who tunes into how people "react to what gets done to and around them."[1] I did my best to listen, and to pick up on their "grunts and groans," their silences, and their bodily responses.[2]

Blending in and becoming a witness was relatively easy for me, a White, mostly feminine-presenting person with a southern accent. A few at the church noticeably lightened up when they found out about my Mississippi roots. The night that I got to know Darleen, I met Nancy, a White woman in her seventies who has lived most of her life in the state. "What year are you in?" she queried from the other end of the table. Lynn, who I had met at the onset of my study, chuckled at Nancy's question. "She's not a student—she's a professor at Ole Miss! She's doing a study on the church." Nancy appeared puzzled. "Well then—where are you from?" she inquired. I told her that I had moved to Oxford from Pittsburgh, where I attended graduate school. Nancy knitted her eyebrows suspiciously, "Well, did you go to Ole Miss as an undergrad?" "Nope, no I did not." Nancy frowned. "I am from Mississippi," I added. "My whole family lives here—grandparents, cousins. Everybody." Nancy smiled, satisfied. I felt relief. My claim to Mississippi made me, the professor, less threatening.

Being a witness involved documenting what I was experiencing, feeling, or thinking as a participant of the church, and as a member of the Oxford community. The claims I present in this book about sameness are derived, to some extent, from what social scientists call "comingled" data, or observations that blur the line between researcher and researched. In an article about the prickly ethical issues that arose during her research on Bible Belt gays, Barton describes how her status as an out lesbian in Kentucky created situations in which "almost every element" of her life became data.[3] Her account of comingled data resonates. It was challenging to separate myself, my surroundings, and my job at the university from the ethnography.

Sometimes I felt like being a witness was creeping in and crowding me out. Before joining a demonstration, and when marching in Oxford Pride, I wondered if churchgoers might see a picture of me on social media or in the news and I worried about how they might react. For the most part, however, I did not let those concerns stop me from doing what I would normally do. I gave the keynote for LGBTQ+ History month at the University of Mississippi, and I stood outside the courthouse alongside Take it Down protestors demanding that the city remove its towering Confederate Monument to white supremacy from the center of town.

There was one instance, in particular, though, in which I allowed the church to control my political behavior. It involved photos that Ed Meek, one of the university's most esteemed donors and alumni from the School of Journalism and New Media, posted on Facebook. In his high-profile message, Meek posted photographs of two young Black women wearing party dresses for a night out on the town Square. Alongside their images, Meek wrote, "Enough, Oxford and Ole Miss leaders, get on top of this before it is too late." Meek warned that if local leaders fail to "protect" the standards that have made "Oxford and Ole Miss known nationally," the town's real estate values and tax revenues will plummet.

Meek's post ignited outrage. Some rushed to Meek's defense, arguing that it was ridiculous to call his message racially malicious. They charged that Oxford is becoming another New Orleans, full of drunks and prostitutes, as they put it on Facebook posts, and as they see it, Meek was reporting an ugly truth. Others, however, condemned Meek for sexual harassment and racism. The students photographed did not consent to his photographic "report," a report that depicted Black women as "lewd and lascivious" Jezebels who ruin towns and drive out White wealth.[4]

Troubled by Meek's post, I collaborated with two friends and colleagues, Jodi Skipper and Jessie Wilkerson, on an op-ed piece that scrutinized his remarks from a historical, Black feminist perspective. The night before our submission to a local paper, I attended Sunday Group and ran into Bird, who was wearing a "Hotty Toddy" T-shirt, which is both the name of an Ole Miss cheer, and the online newspaper that Meek created and developed for the School of Journalism and New Media at UM. After a few minutes of chit chat, Bird switched the subject to Ed Meek and the people who were trying to "tarnish" his name.

"He's a real good guy," Bird told me in a firm tone. There are very few Black women on the Square, I retorted hesitantly. "Why did he have to single them out?" Bird placed his hand on my shoulder and conceded that it "wasn't right or smart." But, he continued, "Why does everything have to be racial all the time?" "People," he said, make a big deal out of nothing. "You can't do anything anymore" without being attacked or ruined, he complained. Then, he looked me in the eyes and said he knows that I wouldn't do him like that. I nodded my head and silently contemplated what he meant by "that" and whether or not I was going to do it.

I called Jodi and Jessie that night and asked them to remove my name from the op-ed about Meek. I was anxious that the church would read it and become wary of me. Two days later, the piece was published in the *Daily Mississippian*.[5] I shared the piece on social media, acting as if I was also reading it for the first time. I was more a part of the church than I had allowed myself to admit. I had become a member of the Welcome community, and that membership was organizing my professional and political allegiances.

I felt it important to name Oxford.

Friends, colleagues, and reviewers questioned my choice to name Oxford. Some asked the question out of concern, others asked because naming the location of an ethnography is uncommon in sociology.

I created pseudonyms for the church, where it meets, and for the people, but I felt it was important to name the town. For starters, calling attention to real events of local concern, past and present, underscores my theory of small talk and the social production of sameness. If I were to create a pseudonym for the town and what transpires within it, the reader might think that the events I have described in this book were physically distant from the church and therefore easier to avoid. On top of that, it would be challenging to concoct a place that could stand in for Oxford, a college town that was once ground zero for white supremacy and civil rights. I could have done it. But with the permission of Welcome, I chose not to.

Further, based on what other ethnographers of small towns have written, I had come to the conclusion that creating a pseudonym for the town does little to protect research participants from harm.[6] In an instructive article about her research and writing experience for *The Stranger Next Door*, sociologist Arlene Stein describes how her research participants responded negatively to the book and the attention it received after it came out and reflects on what she would have done differently if she were to do the study again: name the small town and be more circumspect with the pen. Since I knew that I wanted to name Oxford, I was careful with the pen early on, before writing the pages of this book. My carefulness involved being a scrupulous note-taker, and then later, when I was analyzing data, that carefulness mutated into the act of empathetically accounting for how churchgoers invest in sameness.

Bird and Anne read chapters from the book when I was nearing the final stages of revision. They told me that they respected the time and attention I had put into data collection. I felt a huge weight lift off my shoulders when they said that. I expected the chapters to be hard for them to digest, and I was dreading a negative reaction. Bird said it hurt his heart, and Anne told me that she had to remind him that this was an opportunity to see what an outsider sees. They did not enjoy learning that churchgoers struggle to connect with each other but were confident in the data I presented and called it "fair."

I mostly listened.

I often found myself in a state of self-aggravated doubt about how to be a participant observer in the field. Should I remain a silent observer, or should I contribute to discussion as others did? My choice to speak up was contingent on the size of the group I was with; and the relative awkwardness of not speaking up much. For example, Sunday Group was larger (approximately twenty-four people each week) than the other small groups, and it was normal to be unobtrusive in the former. I was quiet in that group. Be the Bridge and the Women's Book Club were on the smaller side, usually ranging from seven to twelve people. It was trickier to just listen in those spaces. I participated in those groups by occasionally posing questions that were on the lips of participants, or by asking about events that the church was directly involved with (e.g., such as when I asked the women at Recharge about Shane Claiborne's visit). I was there to witness, and that meant doing away with the idea that I should encourage churchgoers to talk about things that they were not already discussing.

The act of listening was gut-wrenching sometimes. One of those times was in a private interview with Chris and Angel, a married couple in their late forties. Chris had worn my nerves down with comments he made about Muslims, who by his account, are buying up all the grocery stores and service stations so that they can take control of the essentials, and by extension, America. Later, when he brought up Mexicans who, in his words, "jump our fence, come into our country" and take jobs from "American guys," my poker face ached. At one point he asked me, "Do you think that's right?" Before I could get two sentences out of my mouth, Chris intervened to elaborate further. I listened attentively, releasing tension by tightly wringing my hands underneath the table where we were dining at a big box breakfast restaurant that stunk of burnt cheese and bagged bread.

As I listened to Chris complain about immigrants getting ahead in the line, I had the sensation of watching Hochschild's book, *Strangers in their Own Land*, lift off the page and come to life. Chris laughed about a time that he watched, in amusement, "a bunch of Mexican guys" run away from an ICE (U.S. Immigration and Customs Enforcement) van that had pulled up to a construction site where they were working. It was "hysterical" he said, "to see them take off like that." I tried to seize the opportunity to share what I think, since Chris had asked me earlier. I attempted to call attention to the global concentration of wealth and the desperate situation that working poor people find themselves in around the world. But neither Chris nor Angel expressed much interest in what I had to say, and I didn't force the issue. It was their interview. Looking back on that interview and others like it, I realized that my listening was a less troubling form of Blee's "white-knuckle research."[7] It took a toll on me. I occasionally had to take short breaks from the field, from listening.

I listened for silence too.

Silence and avoidance were social glue at Welcome, and listening out for that glue could be daunting. I had to compare what churchgoers said in private interviews with what they neglected to say in more public spaces, and I also had to be hypervigilant about documenting what was going on "outside" the church at the local and national levels. Attending to those contexts made it possible to show how the church contained talk about Trump, fled from conversations about Confederate monuments, and preached hard about heterosexual marriage, but ignored homosexuality and same-sex marriage. It also made it reasonable to ask churchgoers if they were aware of their silence and the silence of others when we touched on politically charged subjects in private interviews.[8]

I listened for how and when churchgoers gave roundabout, partial, or ambiguous answers to questions that broached potentially sensitive topics.[9] For example, when I inquired about the substance of Shane Claiborne's talk at Recharge, a churchgoer brought up his "cool" jeans. To me, the comment about his clothes had nothing to do with what I had asked. So, as described in the Introduction of this book, I probed again. And again, the substance of what Claiborne had lectured about was dodged.

Too, I listened to how churchgoers stopped follow-up questions dead in their tracks. A short conversation I had with Bonnie, a White Southerner who I stood next to at the IF: Gathering ministries conference live-streamed event, exemplifies how churchgoers fled from conversations that were unusual or uncomfortable to have in Christian settings. After learning that Bonnie came to the IF screening because she likes hearing women teach the gospel, I followed up by asking what makes a teacher different from a preacher. The Word says that women can't preach, Bonnie declared sternly. "Teachers focus on personal experience," she continued. "They don't go to seminary school." Bonnie paused for a moment. I didn't say anything. Her demeanor lightened before she added, "I'm a woman—I know it might be weird that I'm not for a woman leading, but it's just how I was grown up." Bonnie turned away from me and toward the front of the five-hundred-seat nave, where a sitting room scene for "real talk" had been staged. I got the message. She was raised Christian. End of story.

I had good help.

Two sociology graduate students assisted me with data collection when the small groups program got underway. Pace Ward collected data on Reasoned Defense, attended men's groups and a few Sunday services, and transcribed audio-recorded sermons on my behalf. Heather Costa-Greger attended the New Families group, two of the Sunday Group meetings, and volunteered at outreach events and at the hospitality table on Sunday mornings before service for one semester. Having Heather and Pace collect observation data enhanced the research process and was another way that I triangulated data collection. I prepared Heather and Pace for the field by a) guiding them through Institutional Review Board–exempt review; b) leading them through personalized semester-long qualitative research workshops; and c) holding one-on-one weekly meetings with them about their experiences and observations at the church.

Heather, who churchgoers learned was a Catholic from California, worked on the project for a little less than two semesters. Heather reports that she was seldom asked to provide her take on a piece of scripture or prompted to participate in discussions. This is likely because Heather came off to churchgoers as both unthreatening and unknowledgeable of the born-again tradition. Her field notes reveal that as a reserved, young woman in her early twenties new to the area, churchgoers approached her as someone naïve about their faith; she was not expected to have an opinion or questions. She was there to learn, and they were happy to teach her.

Pace, who churchgoers learned was a (presumably evangelical) Christian from Mississippi, worked with me longer on the project. He reports that he found it relatively easy to establish rapport with churchgoers. The

Reasoned Defense group that Pace studied encouraged him to be a full participant in their conversations and even added him to their private group chat. Pace quickly became skilled at documenting the conversational dynamics of small groups, and the data he collected proved valuable to the arguments presented in this book.

Heather and Pace remarked on what I was noticing, and I took methodological comfort in that. They both commented on how churchgoers were painfully ambiguous when they brought up current events or news, and both remarked that they felt like churchgoers tended to avoid debates and disagreements, even if they were organized to encourage the skill of argumentation, such as Reasoned Defense. When I entered the analysis stage, which I carried out through open, inductive coding in NVivo 11.4.3, Pace helped by coding the interview data. I used his assistance to cross-check my analyses.[10] Pace and I also collaborated on an article, which we published in *Sociology of Religion*, on evangelical churchgoers' support of religious accommodations that target LGBTQ+ people. Along the way, we had regular meetings in which we discussed our article and his undergraduate thesis for the Honors College, which focused on Reasoned Defense. While I did not build the concept of small talk or biblical sameness with Pace, I did locate some pieces for these concepts through our collaborative coding of triangulated data.

## APPENDIX B

# *Small Groups*

| Name | Dates and Hours | Description |
|---|---|---|
| Back to Basics | Fall 2018<br>3 hours | This short-term program covered biblical manhood and womanhood in a heterosexual marriage. It met on Sunday nights at the church office and lasted over an hour and a half. Over 100 men and women attended and were split by gender into two separate rooms and then broken up into small discussion groups. Pace attended two meetings for men. |
| Be the Bridge (BTB) | Spring 2017, Fall 2017, and Spring 2018<br>42 hours | BTB was adapted from Latasha Morrison's racial reconciliation guide and award-winning book by the same name. It met Sunday nights for three semesters in the homes of the group leaders. The first BTB group was comprised of eight women (five White, two Black, one Brown) who attended regularly. The second iteration of BTB was mixed gender and initially larger, but dropped from twelve to seven participants within the span of one semester. The meetings lasted around three hours each because of the time spent eating, discussing race, and socializing afterward. I attended fourteen meetings. |
| New Families | Fall 2017<br>16 hours | This group was for young families with small children to connect with each other over a Bible lesson or study. It met on Sunday nights for two hours in the home of the group organizer. The attendance ranged from nine to eighteen people (not counting kids); Heather attended eight meetings. |
| Reasoned Defense | Fall 2017 and Spring 2018<br>24 hours | This group focused on how to refute nonbelievers and defend truth in secular America. It met on Tuesday nights at the church office. Pace attended twelve of these meetings, which fluctuated from five to nine participants, and lasted about two hours. |
| Recharge | Fall 2017 and Spring 2018<br>10 hours | A monthly gathering for women that involved a potluck meal and short activities on Christ-centered friendships and everyday acts of ministry. The group met for about two hours on Monday nights in the kitchen at the church office. Attendance varied from ten to sixteen participants. I attended five meetings. |

(*continued*)

| Name | Dates and Hours | Description |
|---|---|---|
| The Rock | Fall 2017 and Spring 2018 10 hours | A monthly gathering on Monday nights for men that involved a hearty meal of grilled meats and lessons on leadership in the worship room at the church office. Meetings lasted over two hours and typically brought twenty-plus participants together. Sometimes the participation reached almost sixty people for the meal at the top of the gathering and then dwindled down to around twenty after the first hour. Pace attended three meetings; I attended one that was mixed gender and for married couples. |
| Sunday Group | Spring 2018 and Fall 2018 23 hours | This group focused on evangelism and putting God first. It met on Sunday nights in the home of its leader and lasted around two and a half hours. With a relatively steady attendance of twenty-four people (not counting kids), this was the largest weekly small group at the church. I attended seven meetings; Heather attended two. |
| Women's Book Club | Occasionally in 2016, 2017, and 2018 18 hours | This group met to talk about books authored by evangelical Christians. Anne or her best friend selected the books and announced the meeting dates intermittently via email to women who had signed up for notifications at the church's Recharge function. Participants took turns hosting the club in their homes and usually served a meal or hearty snacks. Seven women, on average, attended and stuck around for upward of three hours for food, discussion, and socializing. I read the books and attended six meetings. |

## APPENDIX C

# *Conferences, Outreach Events, and Sermons*

| Name | Dates and Hours | Description |
|---|---|---|
| Are you Ready 2 Reason 4 Christ? Conference | September 2017<br>3 hours | Members of Ratio Christi (a national evangelical apologetics organization) were the keynote speakers of the conference, which opened its doors on a Friday evening and ran through Saturday in the Conference Center, a 25,000-square-foot meeting space. A few locals organized the event because they wanted to give young people in Oxford a chance to learn how to defend their faith. Pace attended the conference on Saturday with a few others from Welcome. |
| IF: Gathering Conference | February 2017 and 2018<br>13 hours | The annual IF conference is live-streamed to churches and homes over the course of two days for a fee. It features a long list of celebrities in evangelical women's ministries and is considered among the most influential ministry conferences in America today. I attended IF in February 2017 on a Friday and Saturday at another church, with members of Welcome and about fifty other women. Heather watched IF in February 2018 on a Friday and Saturday with a group of five in the home of a churchgoer. |
| Outreach Events | 2017 and 2018<br>27 hours | School Catfish Lunch, Food Pantry, Egg Hunt, Spring is Here, Whole Family Day (twice), Trunk or Treat, and Welcome Christmas (twice). Outreach events occurred at the Recreation Center or at a public venue such as a park. The purpose of these events was to publicize Welcome and serve guests and members in a tangible way with food, live music, and/or a bouncy house and games for kids. Big colorful inflatable bouncy houses and welcoming signage is what attracted some nonmembers from the surrounding community to events like Egg Hunt and Whole Family Day. The outreach events that took place outdoors occurred on Sunday afternoons and attracted over two hundred people. Heather and I attended these events. |

(*continued*)

| Name | Dates and Hours | Description |
|---|---|---|
| Pro-Life Fundraising Banquet | September 2016 and 2017<br>5 hours | The banquet was a fundraiser for crisis pregnancy centers in Mississippi that brought together constituents from Protestant and Catholic congregations. It lasted about two and a half hours and was organized around a prominent figure in the pro-life movement who was brought to town to give a talk on the Christian motives behind anti-abortion activism. The banquet was held in the fellowship area of a historic Baptist church, cost $20 to attend, and included a buffet dinner. Approximately 150 attended the annual banquets that I attended in 2016 and 2017. |
| Sunday Worship | Fall 2016–Spring 2019<br>53 hours | Unless another guest speaker or associate pastor was scheduled, the Sunday sermons were led exclusively by Bird. Services were held at the Recreation Center and lasted an hour, which includes time for music/worship, prayer, and the sermon. My research team and I typically spent an additional thirty minutes to an hour at the Sunday services chitchatting with churchgoers before and after service. We attended thirty-five sermons in person; we transcribed and analyzed an additional seven sermons that I purposefully selected for transcription via an online audible streaming service that the church uses to reach listeners who were unable to join them in person. |

# APPENDIX D

## *Semi-Structured Interview Guide*

My interview guide was a living document that I modified to best match the participant and the time and context in which the interviews were conducted. Here I include the original template.

### OPENING SCRIPT

This interview will take approximately one hour of your time. I will start by asking you about your church experiences. I will also ask questions about diversity and inclusion in the church, women and men in the church, religious freedom, and your views on Christianity in America today. I want to remind you that your participation in this study is voluntary, and that you are not obliged to answer any question(s) that you don't want to. Any identifying information obtained during this study will be kept strictly confidential.

### GEOGRAPHIC BACKGROUND

How long have you lived in or around Oxford?
What do you like/dislike about living here?

### THIS CHURCH

How did you find out about this church?
What did you know about it before coming, if anything?
What was your first impression of it? Was it right?
What makes this church different from other churches you've been part of or attended?
What do you like/dislike about this church?

### MULTIRACIAL CHURCH

What do you think about the church's efforts to be multiethnic or multiracial?

How do you see it trying to accomplish that goal?
What do you think it could do better?

GENDER AND SEXUALITY

How does this church teach you to be a woman/man of God?

- Do you think this teaching is difficult for some women/men? Why?

There has been debate in recent years about what it means to welcome LGBTQ+ people into the Christian church.
What do you think about the church welcoming LGBTQ+ people?
What should that welcome look like?
Have you spoken with others in the church about welcoming LGBTQ+ congregants?
What is the church's stance on LGBTQ+ membership? What is your stance?

RELIGIOUS FREEDOM

What comes to mind when you hear the phrase "religious liberty"?
Several states, including Mississippi, have recently pushed through religious liberty bills that propose to protect the rights of religious individuals and businesses to refuse services such as counseling, bathroom accommodations, wedding services, and health care to lesbian, gay, bisexual, and transgender individuals.
What do you think about these bills? Do these bills represent your views?
Have you ever talked about these bills with others? What were those conversations like?

RELIGION AND POLITICS

Surveys show that over 80 percent of evangelicals voted for Trump.
Why do you think so many Christians support him?
What do you think about Trump?
Have you spoken to others in the church about Trump? What were those conversations like?
Some Christians feel like their religion is under attack. Do you feel that way?
If yes, what are some of the biggest threats to the Christian church today?
Have you ever felt alienated or ostracized for being Christian? Tell me about that.

CLOSING

What would you like to add or expand on before we finish up?

# NOTES

## PREFACE

1 One concern about the lack of family planning facilities in Oxford stems from the Association for American Universities' finding that sexual assault is pervasive on college campuses, especially on campuses where fraternity and hookup culture is strong. Association of American Universities, "AAU Releases 2019 Survey"; see also Wade, *American Hookup*.

2 For information about the development of crisis pregnancy centers (CPCs), see Munson, *The Making of Pro-Life Activists*; and for how evangelicals forge religious identities through their anti-abortion activism at CPCs, see Kelly, "Evangelical Underdogs."

3 McDowell, "Christian but not Religious," 73.

4 Whitehead and Perry, *Taking America Back*; see also Stewart, *The Power Worshippers*.

5 McDaniel's sentiment reflects a right-wing narrative that the "radical left" is taking over the country and turning small town communities toward moral decline. He used the phrase "low-life liberal" on Twitter when he demanded that disciplinary action be taken against James M. Thomas, a faculty member in the Department of Sociology and Anthropology at the University of Mississippi. See Flaherty, "Last-Minute Tenure Threat."

6 Pew Research Center, *Political Polarization*; for information about a multination study published in 2020 that tracks political polarization over the past forty years, see Boxell et al., "Cross-Country Trends." The study finds that affective polarization is most pronounced and growing the fastest in the United States as compared to other democratic countries.

7 Cinelli et al., "The Echo Chamber."

8 Pew Research Center, *Political Polarization*. For a historical view of how the religious right has played a major role in separating the two poles in the United States, see Balmer, *Thy Kingdom Come*.

9 Hochschild, *Strangers in Their Own Land*, see chapter 1, "Traveling to the Heart."

10 MAGA is the acronym for Donald Trump's 2016 presidential campaign slogan, "Make America Great Again."

11 See Holman, "The History of Ole Miss Mascots," for a brief history of the Confederate symbolism behind the Colonel Reb mascot, its official adaptation in the 1970s, and the controversial mascot's expulsion from the University of Mississippi in 2003. See Middleton and Ladd, "'Ole Miss' vs. 'New Miss'" for a story about

Black students and faculty who reject the moniker "Ole Miss," which was derived from Mississippi's racist plantation slavery and sharecropping system.

12 I capitalize Black, Brown, Indigenous, and White when referring to race and ethnicity. I do this in an effort to recognize that racial assignments and ascriptions, including my own as White, shapes a person's life chances, culture, and history. More specifically, by capitalizing White, I aim to draw attention to the significance of Whiteness within the context of my study and to denaturalize the idea that White people are the norm and have little investment in the maintenance of Whiteness. However, in step with other scholars who study racism and movements for white supremacy, I use lowercase font for white supremacy, white nationalism, etc. so as to avoid legitimizing white supremacist ideologies and movements. See, for example, Jones, *White Too Long*; and Blee et al., "A Constellation Approach."

13 Warner Sallman's "Head of Christ" is part of a long tradition of White Europeans creating pictures of Jesus Christ made in their own image. Regarded as the most commercialized image of Jesus in the world, the picture has been reproduced an estimated five hundred million times. See Morgan, *Icons of American Protestantism*.

14 Pensacola's punk scene, located in "L. A.," as in lower Alabama, was a standout community in the Bible Belt. See 309 Punk Project, www.309punkproject.org.

15 Colorado Springs was the home base of several influential evangelical leaders during the George W. Bush presidency. Focus on the Family, a fundamentalist Christian ministry organization centered on family values, marriage, and parenting, is based in the city, and Ted Haggard, the Bush administration's spiritual advisor, founded and pastored New Life, a ten-thousand-member megachurch there. Haggard was an outspoken opponent of same-sex marriage, and he also served as the president of the National Association of Evangelicals from 2003 to 2006. In 2006, New Life fired Haggard after a prostitute, Mike Jones, alleged that Haggard had paid him for sex on repeated occasions over the span of three years and had used crystal methamphetamine. Gorski, "Haggard Firing."

16 Bjork-James, *The Divine Institution*.

## INTRODUCTION

1 Alberta, *The Kingdom*; Bjork-James, *The Divine Institution*; Diefendorf, *The Holy Vote*.

2 Drawing on a National Congregation Study, researchers find that multiracial churches steadily increased between 1998 and 2019 and that multiracial churches will likely continue to rise. That same research team also found that evangelical churches are now just about as diverse as Catholic churches. Dougherty et al., "Racial Diversity in U.S. Congregations." However, as Korie L. Edwards shows in *The Elusive Dream*, interracial churches are often organized around the comforts and preferences of White people.

3 Bird sometimes said "multiethnic" but he usually said "multiethnical." He joked with the church that he mispronounces "big words," and multiethnic was one of those big words.

4 Zerubavel, *The Elephant in the Room*, 47; for a discussion of how denial and strategic ignorance are related, see Klintman, *Knowledge Resistance*.
5 Stewart, *The Power Worshippers*; Gorski and Perry, *The Flag and the Cross*.
6 In southern slang, "jacked up" is commonly used in place of "messed up" or "f***ed up."
7 Anthea Butler argues that evangelicalism is synonymous with racism for good reason: "The hard truth is that evangelicals are one of the most, if not the most, polarizing voting groups in America, and the racism, sexism, and patriarchal structure of their movement has embedded itself within the Republican Party." *White Evangelical Racism*, 12.
8 This is not to suggest that evangelicals are more sincere or invested in the Bible than are other groups in the Christian tradition. Instead, as Nancy Ammerman and Randall Balmer argue, "Bible believing" evangelicals commonly engage in a form of "selective literalism" that helps them stake out moral high ground on the lines they draw between right and wrong. Ammerman, *Bible Believers*; Balmer, *Thy Kingdom Come*.
9 See Balmer's functional definition of evangelicalism in *Thy Kingdom Come*.
10 Oppenheimer, "Evangelicals Find Themselves."
11 Pitt, *Church Planters*, see the chapter "Church Planting."
12 Stetzer and Bird, *Viral Churches*.
13 The quote "Love God, love each other, and love the world" is from the website for Summit Church, March 4, 2018, https://summitchurch.com. Summit is a multisite Southern Baptist church based in Durham, North Carolina, that Bird told me about and aspires to emulate.
14 Lee and Sinitiere, *Holy Mavericks*.
15 Greear, *Gaining by Losing*.
16 For an eye-opening account of how conservative evangelicals have historic ties to the business sector in the United States, see Grem, *The Blessings of Business*. The relationship between corporate and religious power that Grem documents undoubtedly shapes the religious aspirations of contemporary church planting culture.
17 Greear's emphasis on creating leaders for church planting is not unique. Church plant advocates have argued that the main job of a church is to create an army of leaders who can offer something special to as many different groups as possible. Stetzer and Putman, *Breaking the Missional Code*.
18 Small groups are central to almost every evangelical church in America today. Bielo, *Words upon the Word*.
19 Pew Research Center, *Religious Landscape Study*.
20 Data from 2019 shows that 61 percent of Mississippi lawmakers are White men, and that the largest share of the legislative body are self-proclaimed Baptists. Rozier and Skinner, "Do Your Lawmakers Look Like You?"
21 Legal scholar Joseph Ranney writes that "For most of its two hundred years of existence, the state of Mississippi has maintained a hold on the American

imagination out of all proportion to its modest size and its location far from the main centers of American power." The state's long legal history of slavery and its political pursuit of the equality among White people, writes Ranney, have been key in the historical arc of Mississippi law and in the arc of law across the nation. Ranney, *A Legal History of Mississippi*, 3.

22 Monroe, *Heritage and Hate.*

23 Smith, *American Evangelicalism.*

24 Fine, *The Fine Art of Small Talk.*

25 Tish Harrison Warren, a priest in the Anglican Church in North America, argues that ideological hostility is growing in part because Americans are not taking the time to connect with one another over mundane things like the weather. "We need quiet, daily practices that rebuild social trust. And we need seemingly pointless conversation with those around us," she writes. Warren, "How Americans Can Learn." Further, facilitators for Make America Dinner Again, a project that was started after the 2016 U.S. presidential election to facilitate dialogue across party lines, recommends that participants start by pairing off and finding common ground before moving onto more heated subjects. Luna, "I Went to a Potluck."

26 Mahajan, "My Struggle."

27 Bayles, "An Investigation into Politeness"; Coupland, *Small Talk.*

28 Coupland, *Small Talk*, 7–8.

29 Small talk, which includes gossip and chit chat, is what Wayne Brekhus terms an "unmarked" aspect of social life through which social order is realized, and therefore of sociological importance. The power of small talk to shape social norms is "politically unnoticed" because it is so taken for granted. Brekhus, "A Sociology of the Unmarked," 34.

30 Zerubavel, *The Elephant in the Room*; Klintman, *Knowledge Resistance.*

31 Lichterman, *Elusive Togetherness*, 45.

32 For example, see Dupont, *Mississippi Praying*; Moon, *God, Sex, and Politics.*

33 Eliasoph, *Avoiding Politics*, 28.

34 Moon, *God, Sex, and Politics*, 125.

35 Klintman, *Strategic Ignorance.*

36 Our conversations about okra and Mississippi may strike some as trivial, but the subfield of ethnomethodology that Harold Garfinkel introduced has pushed sociologists to reevaluate such assumptions. We build and maintain our understanding of the world, including our roles and the roles of others within it, through tacit knowledge, routinized social norms (like being polite), and ordinary, mundane conversations. See Garfinkel, "Studies of the Routine Grounds of Everyday Activities."

37 Blee, "How Field Relationships Shape Theorizing."

38 In an effort to anonymize the church, I created pseudonyms for most small groups. The only exceptions are Be the Bridge and Back to Basics. I decided to use the real names of those groups since those small group names are found in other

churches and are associated with national ministry programs across the United States.

39 Lareau, *Listening to People.*

40 Wolfinger, "On Writing Fieldnotes."

41 Blee, *Democracy in the Making.*

42 In her study of how tactical options disappear in new social movement groups, Blee traces the "intricacies of talk and interactions" as they unfold over time in meetings and events. She argues that the "rules" for what activist groups consider appropriate to raise in a meeting ultimately guide what is possible for the group to think about or debate. Blee, "How Options Disappear," 661.

43 Bean, *The Politics of Evangelical Identity.*

44 Whitehead and Perry, *Taking America Back for God.*

45 Schütz, "The Well-Informed Citizen," 468; see also Wuthnow, "Taking Talk Seriously."

46 McDowell, "Warriors and Terrorists."

47 See also Diefendorf, *The Holy Vote.* Diefendorf found the same dynamic at play in the church she studied when she tried to recruit married men for interviews.

## CHAPTER 1. THE WELCOME PLANT

1 Matt Chandler describes his Calvinist theology in a video titled, "What Is Predestination?" on The Village Church website, October 18, 2017, thevillagechurch.com. Chandler is often described by evangelical pundits and faith leaders as having close theological ties to John Piper. An influential preacher and author of *Desiring God: Meditations of a Christian Hedonist,* Piper is credited for being a leading figure in New Calvinism, and for advancing the belief that manhood and womanhood are crafted by an all-knowing God. For more on church planting practices and philosophy, see Silliman, "Wanted: Church Planters"; and Pitt, *Church Planters.*

2 For more about the Acts 29 organization that Chandler started, see the website for Acts 29, https://acts29.com. Accessed January 5, 2024.

3 Hale, *A Nation of Outsiders,* 250.

4 Elisha, *Moral Ambition,* 25.

5 O'Neill, *City of God.*

6 Pitt, *Church Planters,* 21.

7 The number of church affiliates (47,000) was taken from the Southern Baptist Convention's website on January 5, 2024, sbc.net.

8 Kennedy, "Why Is There a Growing Trend."

9 Pitt, *Church Planters,* 25.

10 According to Barna, an evangelical Christian-based research firm, church hoppers are on the rise. Nearly two out of five churchgoers attend multiple churches on a regular basis, and a growing number of people report that they want a different kind of experience than what a typical church offers. "Five Trends Defining Americans' Relationship to Churches," February 19, 2020, www.barna.com.

11 Emerson and Kim, "Multiracial Congregations"; see also Emerson and Smith, *Divided by Faith.*
12 Lakeshore and The Vine are pseudonyms that I use to protect the anonymity of Welcome.
13 I directed my undergraduate sociology of religion class to perform participant observations of religious congregations in the area, and Welcome was one of eight on the list for three consecutive semesters. Students were learning about participant observation methods and were asked to collect data on at least three services throughout the semester. Before entering the field, students were trained in research ethics and given a research template that outlined what they should document while in the research setting.
14 Marti and Ganiel, *The Deconstructed Church.*
15 For a rich description of how the style and rituals of the White-dominated Panhellenic system sustains racial segregation and oppression in the South, see Boyd, *Southern Beauty.*
16 Boyd, *Southern Beauty.*
17 Tressie McMillan Cottom argues that for beauty to function as it should (i.e., to decide who can be in the "It" crowd and who gets kicked out), it has to exclude Blackness. It has to be reserved for White women. Cottom, *Thick.*
18 Bean, *The Politics of Evangelical Identity.*
19 Burke, *The Pornography Wars.*
20 Bederman, "'The Women Have Had Charge'"; Putney, *Muscular Christianity*; Du Mez, *Jesus and John Wayne.*
21 Collins, *Interaction Ritual Chains.*
22 Goffman, *Forms of Talk*, 73.
23 Goffman, *The Presentation of Self*, 66.
24 Goffman, *The Presentation of Self*, see pages 67–86.
25 Mark verse 12:20 and on describes a woman who was married to seven different brothers throughout her life; then, in verse 23, the question is posed, "In the resurrection, when they rise again, whose wife will she be? For the seven had her as wife." In Mark 12:25, Jesus is quoted as saying, "For when they rise from the dead, they neither marry nor are given in marriage, but are like angels in heaven."
26 Smilde, *Reason to Believe.*
27 Durkheim, *The Division of Labor* and *Elementary Forms.*
28 Davis and Graham, *The Great Dechurching*; Pitt, *Church Planters.*
29 PRRI, "The 2020 PRRI Census of American Religion," 8–9.
30 Williams, "White Southern Evangelicals."
31 Williams, "White Southern Evangelicals."
32 Wollschleger, "Interaction Ritual Chains"; Durkheim, *Elementary Forms*, see the chapter "Origins of These Beliefs" to learn about collective effervescence, how it's activated, and how it creates shared morals and beliefs.
33 Bielo, *Words upon the Word*, 3.
34 Goffman, "The Interaction Order."

35 For a compelling ethnography that takes sociality in small groups seriously, see *Kincraft* by Tonde Thomas, a book that shows how Black evangelicals create their own spiritual kinship practices against the racial and political conservatism of White evangelicalism and its believe to belong mentality.

36 Goffman, *The Presentation of Self*, 49.

## CHAPTER 2. WE DON'T BUILD WALLS, WE BUILD LONGER TABLES

1 Bracey and Moore, "'Race Tests,'" 289.

2 "Church of all nations" lends credibility to the illusion that race is inevitable instead of socially created, thereby creating a basis for the oppressive structures and practices that constitute racism. Fields and Fields, *Racecraft*.

3 Yi and Graziul, "Religious Conservatives and Outsiders."

4 For research on churches as White spaces, see Bracey and Moore, "Race Tests"; and Edwards, *The Elusive Dream*. To learn about the concept of "White space" in a variety of cultural settings (such as blues music festivals) and institutions (such as law schools and police forces), see Anderson, *Black in White Space*; Combs, *Bodies Out of Place*; and Foster, *I Don't Like the Blues*.

5 Oyakawa, "Racial Reconciliation as a Suppressive Frame."

6 Thomas, *Diversity Regimes*; Lichterman, *Elusive Togetherness*.

7 Bell and Hartman, "Diversity in Everyday Discourse," 911.

8 The strategic evasion of knowledge about racism facilitates the reproduction of racism in everyday life. Mueller, "Racial Ideology or Racial Ignorance?"; Mills, *The Racial Contract*.

9 The Black/White racial binary is the primary way that race is talked about and conceived in America, and this was certainly the case at Welcome. See Rawls and Duck, *Tacit Racism*.

10 Thomas-Houston, *Stony the Road to Change*.

11 Notably, influential White Southern Baptists fueled racial aggression in the state. When the Supreme Court ruled in favor of integration, the *Jackson Daily News*, a prominent newspaper owned by the Hedermans, a powerful White family at First Baptist Church in the capital city, published a story with the headline "Greeting for Negro" on the front-page. That story spotlighted a picture of a cross that had been burned outside of Meredith's assigned student housing. Mississippi's governor, Ross Barnett, who won his election on an overtly segregationist campaign that merged Christian theology with white supremacy, attended First Baptist Church with the Hedermans—a church that was, according to Robert P. Jones, "a place where political influence and religious piety, social engineering and discipleship, white supremacy and Sunday school mixed easily." Jones, *White Too Long*, 38.

12 "The U.S. Marshals and the Integration of the University of Mississippi," U.S. Marshals Service, accessed October 15, 2024, usmarshals.gov.

13 See Doyle, *An American Insurrection*, for the full story on the conflict that erupted between federal and state authority in Oxford. Doyle shows how Meredith's

application to UM turned into a tumultuous battle between thousands of White civilians and a small troop of federal marshals. However, White aggression did not end when Meredith started his classes. There have been many egregious acts of racism since the 1960s at UM. As recently as 2014, White students hung a noose on a life-sized bronze statue of Meredith on campus (Combs et al., "The Symbolic Lynching of James Meredith"), and in 2019 three students were suspended from Kappa Alpha fraternity after a disturbing photo of them surfaced on social media. In the photo, the White students are posed with firearms next to a historical marker memorializing Emmett Till, a fourteen-year-old Black kid who in 1955 was violently murdered in Money, Mississippi. Racial microaggressions are also pervasive at UM and in the surrounding Oxford community. A 2014–2015 race diary report shows that within the span of a year, undergraduate study participants had witnessed, experienced, or been a part of over 1,300 incidents of microaggressions, which the authors classify as racist, sexist, and homophobic insults that find expression verbally, nonverbally, and environmentally in private, semi-private, and public spaces on and near campus. Johnson et al., "Mapping Microaggressions."

14 See "Forethought" and the chapter "Of the Sons of Master and Man," in Du Bois, *The Souls of Black Folk.*

15 Thomas, *Diversity Regimes*, 168.

16 Southern Baptist Theological Seminary, "Report on Slavery and Racism." See Jones, *White Too Long*, for a critical account of how Southern Baptist leadership apologized for the findings presented in this report, promised to reconcile race relations, and then failed to meet that promise.

17 Dupont, *Mississippi Praying*; Tisby, *The Color of Compromise.*

18 Matthew's take on segregation is characteristic of the sociological theory of homophily, or the tendency of individuals to flock toward people with similar experiences and backgrounds. This expression downplays how the "flocks" are built from white supremacy and the social production of race and racial hierarchies.

19 Rev. Dr. Martin Luther King, Jr., bemoaned the fact that church is the most racially segregated hour of the week, and raised that point to cast light on the blatant hypocrisy of the White church and its disinterest in upending Jim Crow segregation in the U.S. South. Unlike Matthew, Dr. King was not condoning or naturalizing the segregation of church.

20 Morrison, *Be the Bridge.*

21 Rawls and Duck, *Tacit Racism.*

22 Mueller, "Racial Ideology or Racial Ignorance?"

23 See the chapter "Staging Difference, Performing Diversity," in Thomas, *Diversity Regimes.* See also Sara Ahmed, *On Being Included*, for how institutions of higher education fail the people who embody diversity when they focus almost exclusively on making symbolic commitments to inclusivity.

24 See, for example, Oliver and Shapiro, *Black Wealth/White Wealth.*

25 Burke and McDowell, "White Women Who Lead," 91–92.

26 Burke and McDowell, "White Women Who Lead."
27 Burke and McDowell, "White Women Who Lead."
28 In *Church Planters*, Pitt shows that church planters, whom he considers entrepreneurs, take the risk of church planting because they feel called to do it, or because they find that the spiritual rewards are worth the risk.
29 Jones, "Racism Among White Christians."
30 Jones, "Racism Among White Christians."
31 Emerson and Smith, *Divided by Faith*.
32 Ray, "A Theory of Racialized Organizations"; Butler, *White Evangelical Racism*.
33 Mueller, "Racial Ideology or Racial Ignorance?," 148; see also Mills, "White Ignorance."
34 Hill, *The Everyday Language of White Racism*.
35 Glass, "Fool's Gold."
36 Edwards, *The Elusive Dream*. In this groundbreaking study of churches that try to fulfill Dr. King's dream of racial integration, Edwards finds that in order for an interracial church to retain its White members, it has to put their needs first, which, in the end, reproduces the racist structures that the church was started to oppose.

## CHAPTER 3. AMERICA IS DIVIDED (BUT THE CHURCH CANNOT BE)

1 For a discussion of anti-Muslim racism in the Trump years, see McDowell, "Muslim Punk in an Alt-Right Era"; for data on far-right mobilization at the time, see Miller and Graves, "When the 'Alt-Right' Hit the Streets."
2 Aziz, *The Racial Muslim*; see also Selod and Embrick, "Racialization and Muslims."
3 Knocking religious outsiders is a common practice of distinction that structures the beliefs, values, and political identities of evangelicals. See Bean, *The Politics of Evangelical Identity*; and Guhin, *Agents of God*. It was not out of the ordinary for Welcome churchgoers to deride religious outsiders, particularly Muslims and atheist professors, without concern for being perceived as bigoted or "too political." More specifically, they treated Muslims like "a suspect race," and that treatment strengthened the belief that one must be White and/or Christian to truly be American (Aziz, *The Racial Muslim*, 26).
4 Aziz, *The Racial Muslim*.
5 See Dupont, *Mississippi Praying*.
6 Interviewees claimed that evangelicals went to the polls for Trump not because he himself is an upright man of faith, but because of what he does *for* them; see Marti, *American Blindspot*.
7 Bonilla-Silva, *Racism without Racists*; Burke, "Colorblind Racism."
8 Munson, *Abortion Politics*.
9 Bean (*The Politics of Evangelical Identity*) finds that evangelicals use subtle partisan cues to signal their political allegiances. She argues that political signaling shapes the political identities and orientation of the entire religious body.
10 Zerubavel, *The Elephant in the Room*, 3.

11 Aziz, *The Racial Muslim.*
12 Over 80 percent of White evangelicals voted for Trump in the 2016 election. For more on the election and evangelical politics, see Djupe and Claassen, *The Evangelical Crackup?*
13 For a theoretically informative discussion of how cultural and institutional contexts shape compliance with religious norms, see Avishai, "'Doing Religion' in a Secular World." Avishai argues that conservative religious women create their own religious subjectivities by complying to norms that draw distinct boundaries between themselves and secular Others. Different from Avishai's focus on the symbolic boundaries that conservative women draw between religious subjectivities and nonreligious ones, I underscore how the evangelical project of "doing" church entails silence and denial that safeguards a belief that everyone at the church is the same.
14 Klintman, *Knowledge Resistance*, see the discussions of strategic ignorance that start on pages 118 and 144; see also Zerubavel, *The Elephant in the Room.*
15 See Crespino, *In Search of Another Country*, for a lucid account of how White church leaders fanned conspiracy theories in Mississippi during the 1960s Black church burnings by the Ku Klux Klan. See also Berman, "How a 'False Flag' Cry."
16 The neo-Confederates that marched in Oxford share ideas, emotions, and practices with other extremist white supremacy groups—"a general opposition towards racial, gender, and sexual equality, political expressions of fear and anger, and antidemocratic practices." Blee et al., "A Constellation Approach," 436.
17 There were many events that transpired within a week's time on the University of Mississippi campus in February of 2019, including eight UM basketball players taking a knee during the national anthem in protest at a game that took place on the same Saturday that the neo-Confederates held their rally in town. For an illustrative overview of student demonstrations that week and the university's response to them, see the article by Campbell, "A Week in the Life of Ole Miss."
18 Between 2016 and 2018 there was a "major upswing in street mobilization by far-Right groups, making it one of the most active periods of on-the-ground extremist activity in decades." Miller and Graves, "When the 'Alt-Right' Hit the Streets."
19 Garza, *The Purpose of Power.*
20 Dupont, *Mississippi Praying.*
21 For a research-driven analysis of the core set of practices, beliefs, and emotions that explain the persistence of white supremacist extremist groups and organizations, see Blee et al., "A Constellation Approach."
22 Tisby, *The Color of Compromise.*
23 Alberta, *The Kingdom.*
24 Graham, "The Pastors Being Driven Out by Trumpism."
25 Schade, *Preaching in the Purple Zone*, 2.
26 Buggs et al., "Systemic Anti-Black Racism Must Be Dismantled."
27 A small group of Black and White Southern Baptist pastors signed a statement calling for racial reconciliation and racial justice. Chandler, "Diverse Group of Pastors Sign Deep South Racial Justice Statement."

28 hooks, *All About Love.*

29 Rawls and Duck, *Tacit Racism*; see also Agha, "Registers of Language"; Eliasoph, *Avoiding Politics*; Lichterman, *Elusive Togetherness.*

30 Black pastors, authors, and influencers in the evangelical tradition have pointed out that talk about structural racism and white supremacy are too often ignored in the evangelical church, and these leaders are challenging the church to take on those conversations. See Tisby, *How to Fight Racism.*

31 Skipper, *Behind the Big House*, 139.

32 My definition of speaking into the void is inspired by Kimberlé Crenshaw's argument that Black women speak into a void between gender and race when they try to call attention to the unique, intersecting injustices they face. Crenshaw, "Demarginalizing the Intersection of Race and Sex."

33 Cooper, *Eloquent Rage*, see the chapter "White-Girl Tears."

34 In a private interview on a later date, I learned that Charise was disappointed that hardly anyone in the BTB group reached out to her on the day that Castile's killer was acquitted.

35 For a theoretical discussion of "barriers to asking," see Gibson, "Enduring Illusions," 296.

36 Southern Poverty Law Center, "SPLC Reports."

37 Tisby, *The Color of Compromise.* For an explanation of the term "staging diversity," see Thomas, *Diversity Regimes*; and for an account of how the rhetoric and performance of "inclusivity" gets in the way of actual change, see Ahmed, *On Being Included.*

38 Jones, *White Too Long*, 235.

39 Oyakawa, "Racial Reconciliation as a Suppressive Frame."

40 For details on the SBC fallout, see Green, "A Resolution Condemning White Supremacy."

41 For a rich discussion of how White, heterosexual, masculine domination underpins evangelical Christianity, see Du Mez, *Jesus and John Wayne.*

42 Goffman, *Stigma.*

## CHAPTER 4. BACK TO BASICS

1 In her opening remarks, Blasey Ford stated, "I am here today not because I want to be. I am terrified. I am here because I believe it is my civic duty to tell you what happened to me while Brett Kavanaugh and I were in high school." See Kavanaugh Hearing Transcript.

2 Deborah Ramirez and Julie Swetnick also accused Brett Kavanaugh of sexual misconduct.

3 Welcome made paperback copies of The Economy Edition of the *English Standard Version* available to churchgoers free of charge at a high-top table near the entrance of the building where services were held.

4 Gothard's umbrella has been widely used in Christian ministries since its inception to detail a theological understanding of a hierarchical order that puts men

over women and men and women over children; for similar related imagery in evangelical ministries, see Bjork-James, *The Divine Institution*, 34–35.

5 Lavin, *Wild Faith*.

6 Gallagher, "The Marginalization of Evangelical Feminism"; Griffith, *God's Daughters*.

7 The Promise Keepers was a massive evangelical Christian ministries campaign that championed racial reconciliation, family headship, and service. The organization preached that men have a moral obligation to lead their wives spiritually, socially, and politically and asked men to abandon an aggressive leadership style in favor of a "tender" approach that balances firmness with compassion, care with strength of will. Bartkowski, *The Promise Keepers*; Heath, "Soft-Boiled Masculinity."

8 See Harding, *The Book of Jerry Falwell*, for an ethnographic account of how Falwell, a leading Southern Baptist figure and conservative activist, positioned himself as an anti-feminist authority figure who was determined to keep White Christian men in charge. For more contemporary portrayals of the relationship between male supremacy and the evangelical faith, see *The Divine Institution* by Bjork-James; and *Jesus and John Wayne* by Du Mez.

9 Weber, *The Protestant Ethic*.

10 McGregor, "Chick-fil-A CEO."

11 Pascoe, *Dude, You're a Fag*.

12 Flynt's program, which was explicitly religious, was backed by the Families Resource Center, a statewide initiative to provide support services to parents, youth, and children in the state. Vassallo, "Families First's Johnny Flynt," and "Family Resource Center Touches Lives."

13 Diefendorf terms the rhetorical move that Ray made the "imagined secular," *The Holy Vote*, 5.

14 Lavin, *Wild Faith*; Levings, *A Well-Trained Wife*.

15 Jerkins, "Trad Wives Are Thriving."

16 West and Zimmerman, "Doing Gender."

17 Noelle-Neumann, *The Spiral of Silence*.

18 The emphasis on masculine responsibility is not unique to the evangelical church. In "Gender and Cultivating the Moral Self in Islam," Aliya Hamid Rao finds that Muslim men practice what she calls "responsible masculinity," a mode of masculinity that sharply distinguishes how women and men "do gender" and by extension "do religion," 414.

19 See Flood, "'Toxic Masculinity,'" and Harrington, "What Is 'Toxic Masculinity'?" for a discussion of the term's meaning, misuse, and mischaracterization, and its popularity in social media.

20 Wayne's use of the term "fake news" to dismiss information that conflicts with his worldview has a long history in the racial politics of Mississippi. When the Ku Klux Klan made the national headlines for bombing Black churches in the 1960s, white Mississippians charged that racial violence in the state was "the work

of agent provocateurs trying to draw media attention" to make Mississippi look bad. Crespino, *In Search of Another Country*. Further, a 2019 Pew study found that a solid majority of Republican and Republican-leaning independents think that made-up news is a very big problem, and conservative talk radio hosts and media outlets such as Breitbart and Fox News promote their brands in direct contrast to what they call the "left-wing fake news" of mainstream media. Further, top Republican officials, including Trump, use the phrase "fake news" to describe any and all news that interferes with their agenda, including news about the 2020 election results that declared Joe Biden president. See Mitchell et al., "Many Americans Say Made-Up News Is a Critical Problem"; and Peters, "Wielding Claims of 'Fake News.'" For a scholarly analysis of how alternative facts, like the ones that Wayne shared, spread and threaten U.S. democracy, see O'Connor and Weatherall, *The Misinformation Age*.

21 Looking back, I should have expected to hear the church address gender more explicitly than other social issues. The White men who lead the evangelical church can use gender to signal their positions on other social matters and without the risk of legal sanction or intra-congregation backlash. Bjork-James, *The Divine Institution*; Balmer, *Thy Kingdom Come*.

22 Diefendorf, *The Holy Vote*, 3.

23 For a succinct account of how political correctness was turned into a pejorative by right-wing leaders and commentators, see Clive Hamilton, "Political Correctness: Its Origins and the Backlash Against It," *The Conversation*, August 30, 2015. For how racism and sexism intersect to remove Black women's labor from African American families, see Collins, *Black Feminist Thought*, 72–78.

24 The 2017 Women's March and its sister marches gathered nearly a hundredfold more participants than an average U.S. protest. See Beyerlein et al., "The 2017 Women's March." And, as Beyerlein and Ryan show in their study of faith-based support for the Women's March, progressive religious groups or congregations such as the Unitarian Universalist Association, Episcopal Church, and Reformed Judaism also participated in the demonstration to resist Trump. A sizable majority of White evangelical Protestants, on the other hand, supported Trump and did not appreciate the Women's March. Beyerlein and Ryan, "Religious Resistance to Trump."

25 I tried to find news sources about a Baptist church in Chicago, a big city that votes Democrat, that was fighting to have a woman pastor around that time, but I couldn't. There was, however, a Baptist church in a small town outside of Knoxville, Tennessee, that had made the news at that time for hiring Rev. Ellen Di Giosia to pastor its congregation. When Rev. Di Giosia's seat went up for vote at the Tennessee Baptist Convention in November 2017, the representatives, or "messengers," as they are called in the Convention, refused to grant Rev. Giosia the status of messenger. After a more than 140-year relationship, First Baptist in Jefferson City was expunged from the state's Convention for violating the "Baptist Faith and Message," which was amended in 2000 to bar women from the office of pastor. See Meyer, "Congregation, Tennessee Baptist Convention." The members

of Reasoned Defense may have been referring to that church in Tennessee or to news about an American Baptist church, which has a history of women in leadership roles and had expressed support for women who were expelled from the Southern Baptist Convention for serving as pastors.

26 For a historical overview of evangelical antipornography efforts, see Burke, *The Pornography Wars*; for an account of why and how Protestant men are more likely than any other group to consider themselves addicts of pornography even when their pornography use is lower than most, see Perry, *Addicted to Lust*.

27 Burke and Haltom, "Created by God and Wired to Porn"; see also Seidman, *The Social Construction of Sexuality*; and Fausto-Sterling, *Sexing the Body*, for robust theoretical arguments about the political and scientific construction of a sex/gender/sexuality system that has tried to erase the existence of intersex, transgender, and queer people.

28 At the meeting, Bob did not elaborate on the Free the Nipple movement or his understanding of what it seeks to accomplish. The phrase "Free the Nipple" soared on social media in 2015, exceeding other gender-related terms such as "equal pay" and "gender equality," after a group of women exercised their lawful right to be in Times Square topless. Acosta, "Free the Nipple?"

29 Burke, *Unbound*.

30 Wade, *American Hookup*.

31 For PRRI data on sexual assault and harassment claims, see Davis et al., "Young People Set."

32 Vandermaas-Peeler et al., "Partisanship Trumps Gender."

33 Beth Moore eventually left the SBC in 2021. After she criticized Trump's abusive behavior toward women and advocated for victims of sexual abuse, the organization had turned her—a once beloved icon of women's ministries—into a pariah. She was labeled "liberal" and "woke" and was renounced for taking the lead during a Sunday morning church service. Moore still considers herself a Baptist but not a Southern Baptist. See Smietana, "Beth Moore Says She's No Longer Southern Baptist."

34 Ward, *The Tragedy of Heterosexuality*, 27.

35 Dias and Graham, "Southern Baptists Vote."

36 On the Michigan pastor quoted in an *LGBTQ Nation* article about the SBC's decision to ban women pastors, see Russell, "Southern Baptists Vote."

37 Wells, *Crusade for Justice*.

38 Damaging and animalistic stereotypes of Black men and women's sexuality have historically been used to legitimate white supremacy and anti-Black violence; see Collins, *Black Sexual Politics*.

39 Wolf and Wolf, *Hope Heals*; Rivers, *Redeeming Love*.

40 *Falling Free* encourages women to create what is called a "table of welcome" in evangelical communities. Or more specifically, to welcome strangers into one's home and church community and make an effort to understand, more directly, what they are going through.

41 Martin, *Falling Free*, 69. Martin was drawing on the "angry black man" stereotype in her description of Robert, a stereotype that Black feminist scholars account for in their research on gendered racism. See Wingfield, "The Modern Mammy and the Angry Black Man"; and Collins, *Black Sexual Politics* for insightful discussions of how race and gender intersect in the stereotypes of "wild" and "angry" Black men and how those stereotypes are used to justify white supremacy and heterosexist patriarchy.

42 Martin, *Falling Free*, 85.

43 Martin, *Falling Free*, 72.

44 Martin argues that freedom in service of God is the opposite of the "*Say no! Stay home!*" message that bombards women in American popular culture, and effectively warns women that self-care is toxic to their faith. Martin, *Falling Free*, 79.

45 For more on this trend in evangelical ministries media by and for women, see Burke and McDowell, "White Women Who Lead."

46 Ward, *The Tragedy of Heterosexuality.*

47 hooks, *Feminism Is for Everybody*, see the chapter "Consciousness-Raising: A Constant Change of Heart."

48 Noelle-Neumann, *The Spiral of Silence.*

49 Calarco, *Holding It Together*; see also Moreton, "Why Is There So Much Sex."

50 Like the churches that Bjork-James studied in Colorado Springs, Colorado—a city coined the "Evangelical Vatican"—Welcome sought to normalize patriarchy and heterosexuality through seemingly nonpartisan cues that resonate with Republican politics. Bjork-James, *The Divine Institution*; Bean, *The Politics of Evangelical Identity.*

51 Jouet, *Exceptional America.* Jouet argues that beliefs in biblical inerrancy and born-again salvation are anti-intellectual and that anti-intellectualism lays the groundwork of authoritarian populism—a social and political system in which members generally distrust democratic principles of inquiry and skepticism.

52 Harriot, "War on Wokeness."

53 Schrock and Schwalbe, "Men, Masculinity, and Manhood Acts."

54 Balmer, *Thy Kingdom Come.*

55 Gaddini, *The Struggle to Stay.*

56 Bjork-James, *The Divine Institution* (see the chapter "Same Sex Attraction and the Limits of God's Love"); also Carter, *The Heart of Whiteness.*

## CHAPTER 5. DON'T ASK, DON'T TELL

1 Kirkland, "Lafayette County Issues."

2 Mississippi is known as a "medical desert." Recent reports on the health care crisis in Mississippi predict that nearly half of the state's hospitals could close due to rising health care costs in poor rural communities that are unable to access private health insurance. See Goldberg, "Over Half of Mississippi's Rural Hospitals." Critics of these closures point out that Republican leadership help the medical desert grow when they forgo federal funding that could provide Medicaid coverage for

Mississippians. See LaFraniere, "'We're Going Away.'"; and Hawkins, "'Stupidity of Politics,'" to learn about the state's Medicaid refusal and hospital closures.

3 Stewart, *The Power Worshippers*, 163.

4 Ian did end up leaving the state for a PhD program in sociology at U.C. Boulder, but his affinity for the people that the missile had set out to destroy moved with him. Ian carried out PhD research on queer resilience in rural contexts, and with a keen eye towards the way that fear structures LGBTQ+ subjectivities, religiosities, and communities in Mississippi.

5 See, for example, "the Defense of Marriage," "Biblical Sexuality," and "Exercising Religious Freedom and Free Speech" resolutions on the Southern Baptist Convention's website (sbc.net).

6 I used the acronym LGBTQ+ when I asked churchgoers about queer inclusion; however, churchgoers never used that acronym themselves. Instead, they used "gay" and "lesbian" synonymously with LGBTQ+, which is reflected in how I present their perspectives in this chapter.

7 In *God, Sex, and Politics*, Moon drew similar conclusions about congregants' reluctance to address or debate homosexuality out in the open with each other in church spaces.

8 The 2016 parade is commonly regarded as the first Pride event to take place in Oxford, but one also took place there in 1992 when the National Organization for Women organized a march for members of Mississippi's LGBTQ+ community. See Kraus, "Mapping In/Exclusion," to learn about the march in 1992 and in 2016 from the perspective of Pat Miller, a trailblazing Mississippian, who participated in both marches.

9 Queer Mississippi Oral Histories Project interview with Jaime Harker.

10 See Campbell, "Seeing Queer Joy in Mississippi," to learn about LGBTQ+ mobilization for Pride in Oxford, Starkville, and Tupelo.

11 Unitarian Universalism (UU) promotes principles of wisdom and spirituality that are "grounded in the humanistic principles of the world's religions." As one minister of UU explains, "The Principles are not dogma or doctrine, but rather a guide for those of us who choose to join and participate in Unitarian Universalist religious communities." For a list of those principles, visit www.uua.org, and for a historical overview of UU's beginnings and its relationship to social justice movements and progressive faith traditions, see Harris, *Historical Dictionary of Unitarian Universalism.*

12 Under the leadership of Ronda McDowell (my mom) and Bob Spencer, the UU of Tupelo took part in the Unitarian Universalist Association's required "Welcoming Congregations Program," which was designed to prepare congregations for the inclusion of bisexual, gay, lesbian, and transgender people. Unitarian Universalist Association, uua.org.

13 The Coalition of Welcoming Congregations (CWC) is one such organization that brings together religious leaders and LGBTQ+ people and their allies from different denominations to form a supportive network of communities that affirm

and advocate for LGBTQ+ people of faith (www.clgs.psr.edu). The Association of Welcoming and Affirming Baptists (AWAB) coalition requires a religious congregation or organization to petition for membership. In order to become a member of AWAB, a church has to welcome and affirm LGBTQ+ individuals in their congregational materials, perform marriages among members of the LGBTQ+ community, and implement nondiscriminatory employment practices (www.awab.org). University Baptist Church is the only AWAB church listed for Mississippi, and that church is located near Mississippi State University, the only other R1 (Research 1) institution in the state.

14 LGBTQ+ people can use silence to remain in good standing with religious traditions and communities that are vital to them, and research has shown that gay Christians, in particular, may be attracted to churches that are theologically conservative on sexuality but, at the same time, do not openly condemn homosexuality. See, for example, Yi et al., "Gay Seouls."

15 Moon and Tobin, "Sunsets and Solidarity."

16 For illustrative ethnographic accounts of ex-gay conversion therapies and ministries that attempt to turn gay people straight, see Gerber, *Seeking the Straight and Narrow*; Wolkomir, *Be Not Deceived.*

17 Conservatives like Bob are part of a larger Christian community that wants LGBTQ+ people who attend their churches to engage in constant displays of shame that prove that they want to change something that most LGBTQ+ people cannot change. Moon and Tobin, "Sunsets and Solidarity."

18 Unseeing queerness was pervasive at Welcome, but is not unique to it, to Mississippians, or to the U.S. South. Diefendorf finds a similar phenomenon at play in a megachurch in a Pacific Northwest suburban city. The church she studied replaced a "love the sinner, hate the sin" approach to homosexuality with lessons on the importance of being and staying in a heterosexual marriage. *The Holy Vote.*

19 For an elaborate version of these findings on the evangelical support for religious liberty, see McDowell and Ward, "The Tables Are Turning."

20 For what Mississippians think the Bible says about homosexuality, see Rogers, *Conditionally Accepted.*

21 Kelly, "Evangelical Underdogs."

22 Howard, *Men Like That.*

23 Ebin and Price, "The Great American Rights Bake Off," 589.

24 Griffith, *Moral Combat*; Fetner, *How the Religious Right.*

25 The quoted statement about heterosexual marriage is an excerpt from the "Nashville Statement," which was authored and signed by an interdenominational coalition of evangelicals called The Council on Biblical Manhood and Womanhood, https://cbmw.org. The anti-LGBTQ+ politics of evangelicalism are pronounced in the United States but not unique to it. Journalists report that the Christian right's fight against the gay agenda has also been exported overseas to a global web of political figures and religious leaders that share its agenda to stop

LGBTQ+ people from obtaining jobs, homes, families, marriage, and health care. See Perkins, "U.S. Religious Right at Center of Anti-LGBTQ+ Message."

26 Ebin and Price, "The Great American Rights Bake Off," 589.

27 Howard, *Men Like That*, 30.

28 Howard, *Men Like That*, 31.

29 Whalen, "Governing Silence."

30 Barton, *Pray the Gay Away*, 88. See also Moon and Tobin, "Sunsets and Solidarity," for a discussion of how conservative churches push LGBTQ+ Christians into "sacramental shame" that maintains heterosexuals' sense of righteous superiority in the church.

31 Sumerau et al., "Contemporary Religion and the Cisgendering of Reality."

32 For how United Methodist Church (UMC) clergy from different political standpoints tackled the fallout that occurred in 2019 when the UMC decided to preserve their prohibition against same-sex marriage and LGBTQ+ ordination, see Krull and Gilliland, "'You Know, the Church Has Never Agreed.'" They find that clergy used various strategies to address the issue, including what they call a "constrained prophetic voice" in support of LGBTQ+ people, 324.

## CHAPTER 6. TAKE DOWN THE RED TAPE

1 Bracey and Moore, "Race Tests."

2 For how religious community and belonging gets created out of the preparation and sharing of food, see Pérez, *In the Kitchen*.

3 In a list of tips about how to church plant in a school, Doug Foltz, a self-described expert, advises planters to make a personal connection with decision makers and, if possible, serve the school in some tangible way ("Thinking about Planting a Church in a School?").

4 A few Supreme Court of the United States (SCOTUS) rulings created an opportunity for churches to take advantage of schools. In the *Lamb's Chapel v. Center Moriches Union Free School District* (1993) case, the Court ruled in favor of an evangelical church that wanted to use the school space after hours to show a film series on Christian family values. At the time, the local school board was allowing various community groups to use its facilities but not churches or religious groups, out of concern that doing so violates the First Amendment's Establishment Clause (i.e., the separation of church and state). The Court, however, disagreed with the school board and ruled that religious groups must be given "equal access" to public facilities. In *Good News Club v. Milford Central School* (2001), the Court extended its "equal access" principle to public grade schools. The Good News Club, a Christian organization, had requested to use the cafeteria of an elementary school for its weekly after-school meetings consisting of adult-led prayers, religious songs, and Bible lessons. The school superintendent denied Good News access, arguing that its purpose conflicted with the principled separation of church and state. Good News appealed, arguing that its right to free speech had been violated. SCOTUS sided with Good News; it held that a religious

group had a right to meet at the school under the free speech clause of the First Amendment since other groups were able to meet at the school. Witte et al., *Religion and the American Constitutional Experiment.*

5 The law on a church's use of a school for Sunday services, however, is not yet resolved. In step with the Second Circuit Court of Appeal's 2011 ruling in *Bronx Household of Faith v. Board of Educ. New York*, 650 F.3d 30 (2nd Cir. 2011), SCOTUS affirmed that a public school can constitutionally bar a church from holding its worship services on school grounds, even if schools are obligated to allow religious groups to meet in their buildings like other civic organizations and social clubs. Freedom from Religion Foundation, "Churches Meeting at Public Schools."

6 As early as 2011, a *USA Today* report found that ten of the largest and fastest growing school districts in the United States rent their facilities to religious congregations, and that Acts 29, the church planting organization discussed in chapter 1, had started plants in public school buildings. Gordon, "'Instant Churches.'"

7 Pitt, *Church Planters.*

8 Thomas-Houston, *Stony the Road to Change.*

9 Barton, *Pray the Gay Away.*

10 Jodi Skipper has been working to break the silence about slavery and tell the truth about the big plantation houses in Mississippi since starting her job at the University of Mississippi. Her book *Behind the Big House* gives readers an honest, up-close look at what it takes to interpret and communicate the terrifying history of slavery in the U.S. South, and describes her long-standing collaboration with the community-driven program, Behind the Big House, in Holy Springs, Mississippi. In her book, she also sketches out the professional risks she took to carry out her work in an academic department and institution that focuses on publications for tenure and promotion. Black students have also taken tremendous risks to their physical and emotional safety at UM. In 2015, Dominque Scott, a sociology student and member of the NAACP, said that she felt "terrified" when she rallied to have the state flag with the Confederate battle emblem removed from campus. She and others were scared of the pro-Confederate groups that had come to campus that day with signs that read "Black Lives Don't Matter." Kirkland, "UM NAACP Rally."

11 For evidence of this claim about LGBTQ+ spaces and expression in Mississippi, see the Queer Mississippi Oral Histories and related projects, which are archived on eGrove, the University of Mississippi's digital repository.

12 Legal scholars point out that the public school is one of the most obvious extensions of the state in any community, and that the SCOTUS rulings of the mid-twentieth century that removed religious teachings and prayers from school were rooted in the principle that the purpose of school is to "stand as a model of constitutional democracy in the local community and to provide a vehicle for the communication and demonstration of democratic values and abilities to its students." In those historic landmark cases, the Supreme Court argued that there

can be no relaxation between a wall of separation between church and state and ruled that religious instruction and prayer could not be allowed in school. By the turn of the twenty-first century, however, the Supreme Court changed course and started to take an "equal access" approach that sought to protect the free speech of religious groups and people. Witte et al., *Religion and the American Constitutional Experiment*, 233.

13 The Supreme Court popularized Jefferson's phrase "wall of separation between church and state" in its 1879 decision in *Reynolds v. United States*, and in 1947 in *Everson v. Board of Education of Ewing*.

14 After various levels of the U.S. government had debated and proposed different versions of a religious liberty provision clause, a joint House–Senate committee authored what became the final language of the First Amendment in the Bill of Rights: "Congress shall make no Law respecting an establishment of Religion, or prohibiting the free exercise thereof." Witte, *Religion and the American Constitutional Experiment*, 109.

15 For a broad overview of what Americans think about the separation of church and state and the roots of the U.S. Constitution, see Pew Research Center, *In U.S., Far More Support than Oppose Separation of Church and State*. Pew shows that White evangelicals are more likely than other groups to believe that the Constitution was inspired by God and reflects God's vision for America, and by extension, also support the intermingling of church and state in public property and institutions.

16 The U.S. Supreme Court struck down the displays of the Ten Commandments at school in *Stone v. Graham* (1980), noting that the display of the Decalogue in a public school served a religious purpose and therefore violated the Establishment Clause in the U.S. Constitution that forbids the state from promoting a particular religion or religious values. Witte et al., *Religion and the American Constitutional Experiment*, 237.

17 The bill to make the Ten Commandments part of the classroom and early morning recitations did not pass in Mississippi. It has, however, inspired other state representatives to take up similar legislation. In a 2024 fight to display the Decalogue in school, Republican Rep. Dodie Horton of Louisiana made explicit that she did not care if Muslims, atheists, or other religious groups do not see themselves or their moral compass reflected in the Ten Commandments. She wants the Ten Commandments in the classroom because she, to use her words, is "concerned with our own children seeing what God's law is." Larose, "Ten Commandments in Classroom Bill."

18 The idea that a preacher is biblical and not political has a long history in the evangelical church. The White church not only used that idea to shirk responsibility for Jim Crow segregation and racial discrimination in the 1950s and '60s (Dupont, *Mississippi Praying*) but also to dismiss the fact that evangelicals, like other faith traditions, have a biased view of God that maintains "the color line," among other social inequalities. Du Bois, *A Reader*.

19 Not everyone at Welcome could afford to send their kids to private schools or homeschool their children. Their options for an alternative, Christian-based education were contingent on class status and income.

20 The state's sex education curriculum follows an "opt-in" policy that requires written permission from parents and guardians before a student can participate in an abstinence-only or abstinence-plus course, and both courses emphasize that the only appropriate relationship for sexual intercourse is a monogamous heterosexual marriage. Sex Education Collaborative, "Mississippi," www.sexeducationcollaborative.org.

21 Kramer, "70% of White evangelicals"; further, almost half of White American evangelicals (41 percent) want public school teachers to be allowed to lead students in Christian prayer, even if no other types of religious prayers are offered. Horowitz, "Parents Differ Sharply by Party."

22 The Scopes trial, also known as the Scopes Monkey Trial, was an American legal case brought by the state of Tennessee against a high school teacher, about the teaching of human evolution in school. Witte et al., *Religion and the American Constitutional Experiment.*

23 Bolton, *The Hardest Deal of All.*

24 Tisby, *The Color of Compromise*, 16.

25 Balmer, *Thy Kingdom Come*; Crespino, *In Search of Another Country.*

26 Hochschild, *Strangers in Their Own Land.*

27 Trainer et al., "Worry-Nostalgia."

28 Hochschild, *Stolen Pride*; Wuthnow, *The Left Behind.*

29 *Kennedy v. Bremerton School District* (2022).

30 Pew Research Center, *For a Lot of American Teens* and *Religion in the Public Schools.*

31 See Freedom from Religion Foundation, "School 'Prayer Walks.'"

32 FCA is a long-standing organization that seeks to inject conservative Christian beliefs and values into sports. Fellowship of Christian Athletes, *God's Game Plan.*

33 Notably, the church signaled its negative view of *that* school (the public city school) like it did *that stuff* (i.e., LGBTQ+ people and issues) without having to address *them* on *that* side of the political spectrum in direct terms. By just saying "that," churchgoers were able to maintain the line that "politics" do not belong in church while also effectively conveying that they do, in fact, support the political right. Bean documents a similar dynamic in her study on the evangelical support of Republican politics. While the evangelicals she studied did not make explicit statements of support for Republicans or openly dehumanize liberals or Democrats, they did use subtle partisan cues to communicate where they stand, and should stand, on the political spectrum. *The Politics of Evangelical Identity.*

34 For a robust study of religious "nones" and what they believe, see Baker and Smith, *American Secularism.* In 2021, Pew reported that 28 percent of U.S. adults fall into the "nones" category, and in 2024 Pew found that most of those nones believe in God or a higher power, but not in a biblical God. Pew Research Center, *About Three-in-Ten U.S. Adults Are Now Religiously Unaffiliated* and *Religious Nones.*

35 It is not unusual for evangelical pastors to have misgivings about a college education. They are aware that moving away from home for college alone is enough to pull young people away from church, and that college-educated adults are also less likely to be socially conservative Christians than adults who never attend college. Baker and Smith, *American Secularism.*

36 Miller, "The Story of Ratio Christi."

37 Koukl, "Is Jesus the Only Way?"

38 Focus on the Family, "Share Your Faith"; see also Koukl, *Tactics.*

39 To make the game apparent, the book jacket is a black and white chessboard, and a pawn replaces the letter "i" in the title *Tactics.*

40 Koukl, "Tactics Video Study, Session 1."

41 Moses, "UM Promotes Religious Freedom."

42 Pascoe, *Dude, You're a Fag.*

43 Pat's comment about being "the light" for her students in darkness reflected what the evangelical Christian punks I got to know from various parts of the United States said about their ministry in underground music. McDowell, "'Christian but not Religious.'"

44 Through campus ministries, online trainings, and national conferences, Ratio Christi promises to give students thought-out reasons for following Jesus, equip professors to share their faith on campus, and prepare believers for reasoned and open debate with skeptics about "absolute Truth." www.ratiochristi.org.

45 See Goffman, *The Presentation of Self,* for a robust theoretical discussion of how people build and save face in social interactions. Goffman argued that individuals have to work cooperatively to maintain their own self-image and the self-image of others; the self does not come naturally or effortlessly.

46 Geertz, *The Interpretation of Cultures*; Durkheim, *Elementary Forms*; Collins, *Interaction Ritual Chains.*

47 Diefendorf, *The Holy Vote.*

48 Smith, *American Evangelicalism.*

49 Stewart, *The Power Worshippers*; Perry and Gorski, *The Flag and the Cross.*

50 Whitehead and Perry, *Taking America Back.*

51 Du Mez, *Jesus and John Wayne.*

52 Joyce, "'Parental Rights' Started on the Fringe."

53 For an investigative report on the anti-DEI campaign, see Confessore, "'America Is Under Attack.'"

54 For a broad overview of how SCOTUS is ruling in favor of conservative Christianity, see Greenhouse, "Should Courts Assess?"; and Joshi, *White Christian Privilege,* for a historical account of how White Christians have enjoyed unmatched privileges and power in and beyond U.S. law.

55 Sullivan, *The Impossibility.*

56 An abortion restriction law in Mississippi set the overturning of *Roe v. Wade* in motion. The Mississippi law that restricted abortion to the first fifteen weeks of pregnancy had been authored to provoke a legal battle that would reach the

Supreme Court, and it did. The Jackson Women's Health Organization, which was the only abortion provider in the state, sued Thomas E. Dobbs, the state health officer with the Mississippi State Department of Health. Citing the SCOTUS decisions of the past, the Jackson clinic argued that women have a constitutional right to choose abortion at a later stage of pregnancy, and that Mississippi's law was violating that right. The Jackson Clinic lost the case. The outlook of Justice Samuel Alito, and the Christian nationalist ideology that he represents, had been on a winning streak and had won again. Talbot, "Justice Alito's Crusade."

57 Minta, "'This is a complete attack.'"

58 Stewart, *The Power Worshippers* (see the chapter, "The Blitz: Turning the States into Laboratories of Theocracy").

59 The law mobilized the American Atheists to join the Mississippi Humanist Association and three Mississippi residents in a lawsuit against the state for its efforts to impose Christianity on its citizenry. And it inspired other states to take up similar Christian nationalist legislation that places God in the classroom again; see for example Balingit, "Does 'In God We Trust' Belong in Schools?"

60 Butler, *White Evangelical Racism*, 134.

61 Black churches were violently attacked by White extremists during Freedom Summer in the 1960s. The Ku Klux Klan targeted Black churches because of the significant role the church played in the Black community and in civil rights organizing. However, most White Mississippians denounced church bombings as an attack on Christian brotherhood and used their opposition to Black church bombings to distinguish themselves from the "true racists" who "brought unwanted outside attention" to the state, attention that was making Jim Crow segregation harder to maintain. White moderate church leaders even took up donations to rebuild Black churches and adopted resolutions that called on their members to work toward racial harmony. But when they did, they emphasized their mission to act in the spirit of Christ, and not about the church's complicity in a social, political, and legal system that promoted racial segregation and by extension racist acts of violence. Crespino, *In Search of Another Country*, 145.

62 Blinder, "How College Sports."

63 See Butler's chapter "How Firm a Foundation" in *White Evangelical Racism*, especially page 135, for a direct account of how White evangelical Christians weaponize movements for racial justice for their own strategic ends, and in the process practice a "willful blindness" to racism in America.

64 Harker, *The Lesbian South.*

65 Ward, "Everybody But Us."

## CONCLUSION

1 Alberta, *The Kingdom.*

2 Davis and Graham, *The Great Dechurching*, xxii. Davis and Graham define a dechurched person as "someone who used to go to church at least once per month but now goes less than once a year."

3 Bean, *The Politics of Evangelical Identity*; Crespino, *In Another Country*.

4 Davis and Graham, authors of *The Great Dechurching*, also point out that congregations once united are now divided over their seemingly irreconcilable views on racism, climate change, reproductive rights, and gun control.

5 Eliasoph, *Avoiding Politics*; Klintman, *Knowledge Resistance*.

6 Iversen, "Silence and Sameness," 544.

7 Iversen, "Silence and Sameness."

8 Ellis, "Silent Disagreement."

9 Moon, *God, Sex, and Politics*, 62.

10 Noelle-Neumann, *The Spiral of Silence*, 4.

11 Noelle-Neumann, *The Spiral of Silence*. The "train test" featured in Noelle-Neumann's book is an illustrative example of the spiral. She and her research team found that smokers are more willing to participate in a conversation about smoking on the train if they feel supported by an aggressively vocal person with similar views on smoking. However, in instances in which there was no support of a fellow outspoken passenger, smokers withdrew from conversations about smoking and kept their opinions to themselves on the train.

12 Balmer, *Thy Kingdom Come*.

13 For recent research on political polarization in the church, see Alberta, *The Kingdom*; and Davis and Graham, *The Great Dechurching*. Both of these books suggest that evangelical leaders and churchgoers are concerned, if not disturbed, by the extreme right and are trying to figure out what to do about it.

APPENDIX A

1 Goffman, "On Fieldwork," 126.

2 Goffman, "On Fieldwork," 125.

3 Barton, "My Auto/Ethnographic Dilemma," 432.

4 For a critical discussion of the jezebel stereotype, see the chapter "Mammies, Matriarchs, and Other Controlling Images" in Collins, *Black Feminist Thought*. My colleagues and friends Jodi Skipper and Jessica Wilkerson published a critique of Meek's post in a letter to the editor titled "Why We Must Center Black Women's Experiences."

5 Skipper and Wilkerson, "Why We Must."

6 Stein, "Sex, Truths, and Audiotape"; Scheper-Hughes, "Ire in Ireland."

7 Blee, "White-Knuckle Research."

8 Schweiger and Tomiak, "Researching Silence."

9 Clayman, "Answers and Evasions."

10 Taylor and Bogdan, *Introduction to Qualitative Research*.

# BIBLIOGRAPHY

### NEWSPAPERS AND MAGAZINES

*Activist History Review*
*Atlantic*
*Baptist News Global*
*Christianity Today*
*Daily Mississippian*
*Denver Post*
*Guardian*
*Hotty Toddy News*
*Inside Higher Ed*
*LGBTQ Nation*
*Mississippi Free Press*
*Mississippi Today*
*Mother Jones*
*New York Times*
*Religion News*
*Salon*
*Tennessean*
*Washington Post*
*Word & Way*

### BOOKS, JOURNAL ARTICLES, AND REPORTS

Acosta, Deborah. "Free the Nipple?" *New York Times*, January 26, 2016. http://nytimes.com.

Agha, Asif. "Registers of Language." In *A Companion to Linguistic Anthropology*, edited by Alessandro Duranti. Blackwell, 2004.

Ahmed, Sara. *On Being Included: Racism and Diversity in Institutional Life*. Duke University Press, 2012.

Alberta, Tim. *The Kingdom, The Power, and The Glory*. Harper Collins, 2023.

Ammerman, Nancy T. *Bible Believers: Fundamentalists in the Modern World*. Rutgers University Press, 1987.

Anderson, Elijah. *Black in White Space: The Enduring Impact of Color in Everyday Life*. University of Chicago Press, 2021.

Association of American Universities. "AAU Releases 2019 Survey on Sexual Assault and Misconduct." October 15, 2019. http://aau.edu.

Avishai, Orit. "'Doing Religion' in a Secular World: Women in Conservative Religions and the Question of Agency." *Gender and Society* 22, no. 4 (2008): 409–33.

Aziz, Sahar. *The Racial Muslim: When Racism Quashes Religious Freedom*. University of California Press, 2021.

Baker, Joseph O., and Buster G. Smith. *American Secularism: Cultural Contours of Nonreligious Belief Systems*. New York University Press, 2015.

Balingit, Moriah. "Does 'In God We Trust' Belong in Schools? More and More States Say Yes." *Washington Post*, December 1, 2018. http://washingtonpost.com.

Balmer, Randall. *Thy Kingdom Come: How the Religious Right Distorts Faith and Threatens America*. Basic Books, 2007.

Barna Group. "Five Trends Defining Americans' Relationship to Churches." February 19, 2020. http://barna.com.

Bartkowski, John. *The Promise Keepers: Servants, Soldiers, and Godly Men*. Rutgers University Press, 2004.

Barton, Bernadette. "My Auto/Ethnographic Dilemma: Who Owns the Story?" *Qualitative Sociology* 31, no. 2 (2008): 431–45.

Barton, Bernadette. *Pray the Gay Away: The Extraordinary Lives of Bible Belt Gays*. New York University Press, 2014.

Bayles, Rebecca. "An Investigation into Politeness, Small Talk and Gender." *Innervate* 1 (2008-2009): 10–17.

Bean, Lydia. *The Politics of Evangelical Identity: Local Churches and Partisan Divides in the United States and Canada*. Princeton University Press, 2014.

Bederman, Gail. "'The Women Have Had Charge of the Church Work Long Enough': Men and the Religion Forward Movement of 1911–1912 and the Masculinization of Middle-Class Protestantism." *American Quarterly* 41, no. 3 (1989): 432–65.

Bell, Joyce M., and Douglas Hartman. "Diversity in Everyday Discourse: The Cultural Ambiguities and Consequences of 'Happy Talk.'" *American Sociological Review* 72, no. 6 (2007): 895–914.

Berman, Russell. "How a 'False Flag' Cry has Divided Republicans in Oregon." *Atlantic*, February 10, 2021. http://theatlantic.com.

Beyerlein, Kraig, and Peter Ryan. "Religious Resistance to Trump: Progressive Faith and the Women's March on Chicago." *Sociology of Religion* 79, no. 2 (2018): 196–219.

Beyerlein, Kraig, Peter Ryan, Aliyah Abu-Hazeem, and Amity Pauley. "The 2017 Women's March: A National Study of Solidarity Events." *Mobilization* 23, no. 4 (2018): 425–49.

Bielo, James S. *Words upon the Word: An Ethnography of Evangelical Group Bible Study*. New York University Press, 2009.

Bjork-James, Sophie. *The Divine Institution: White Evangelicalism's Politics of the Family*. Rutgers University Press, 2021.

Blee, Kathleen. "White-Knuckle Research: Emotional Dynamics in Fieldwork with Racist Activists." *Qualitative Sociology* 21, no. 4 (1998): 381–99.

Blee, Kathleen. *Democracy in the Making: How Activist Groups Form*. Oxford University Press, 2012.

Blee, Kathleen. "How Options Disappear: Causality and Emergence in Grassroots Activist Groups." *American Journal of Sociology* 119, no. 3 (2013): 655–81.

Blee, Kathleen. "How Field Relationships Shape Theorizing." *Sociological Methods & Research* 48, no. 4 (2017): 739–62.

Blee, Kathleen, Robert Futrell, and Pete Simi. "A Constellation Approach to Understanding Extremist White Supremacy." *Mobilization: An International Quarterly* 28, no. 4 (2023): 435–44.

Blinder, Alan. "How College Sports Spurred Mississippi to Seriously Reconsider Its State Flag." *New York Times*, June 27, 2020. http://nytimes.com.

Bolton, Charles C. *The Hardest Deal of All: The Battle Over School Integration in Mississippi, 1870–1980*. University Press of Mississippi, 2007.

Bonilla-Silva, Eduardo. *Racism without Racists: Color-Blind Racism and the Persistence of Racial Inequality in America*. Rowman and Littlefield, 2010.

Boxell, Levi, Matthew Gentzkow, and Jesse M. Shapiro. "Cross-Country Trends in Affective Polarization." *Review of Economics and Statistics* 106, no. 2 (2024): 557–65.

Boyd, Elizabeth Bronwyn. *Southern Beauty: Race, Ritual, and Memory in the Modern South*. University of Georgia Press, 2022.

Bracey, Glenn, and Wendy Leo Moore. "'Race Tests': Racial Boundary Maintenance in White Evangelical Churches." *Sociological Inquiry* 87, no. 2 (2017): 282–302.

Brekhus, Wayne. "A Sociology of the Unmarked: Redirecting Our Focus." *Sociological Theory* 16, no. 1 (1998): 34–51.

Buggs, S. G., C. Pittman Claytor, S. J. García, O. Imoagene, V. Keith, H. Khoshneviss, C. Lee, S. Mayorga-Gallo, V. E. Ray, and W. D. Roth. "Systemic Anti-Black Racism Must Be Dismantled: Statement by the American Sociological Association Section on Racial and Ethnic Minorities." *Sociology of Race and Ethnicity* 6, no. 3 (2020): 289–91.

Burke, Kelsy. *The Pornography Wars: The Past, Present, and Future of America's Obscene Obsession*. Bloomsbury Press, 2023.

Burke, Kelsy, and Trenton M. Haltom. "Created by God and Wired to Porn: Redemptive Masculinity and Gender Beliefs in Narratives of Religious Men's Pornography Addiction Recovery." *Gender & Society* 34, no. 2 (2020): 233–58.

Burke, Kelsy, and Amy McDowell. "White Women Who Lead: God, Girlfriends, and Diversity Projects in a National Evangelical Ministry." *Sociology of Race and Ethnicity* 7, no. 1 (2021): 86–100.

Burke, Meghan A. "Colorblind Racism: Identities, Ideologies, and Shifting Subjectivities." *Sociological Perspectives* 60, no. 5 (2017): 857–65.

Burke, Tarana. *Unbound: My Story of Liberation and the Birth of the Me Too Movement*. Flatiron Books, 2021.

Butler, Anthea. *White Evangelical Racism: The Politics of Morality in America*. University of North Carolina Press, 2021.

Calarco, Jessica. *Holding It Together: How Women Became America's Safety Net*. Penguin, 2024.

Campbell, Ellie. "A Week in the Life of Ole Miss: February 2019 and the Fight to Take Down the Confederate Statue." *Activist History Review*, December 16, 2019. http://activisthistory.com.

Campbell, Ellie. "Seeing Queer Joy in Mississippi: Pride Parades in Tupelo, Starkville, and Oxford." Master's thesis, University of Mississippi, 2022.

Carter, Julian. *The Heart of Whiteness: Normal Sexuality and Race in America: 1880–1940*. Duke University Press, 2007.

Chandler, Diana. "Diverse Group of Pastors Sign Deep South Racial Justice Statement." *Word & Way*, October 28, 2020. http://wordandway.org.

Cinelli, Matteo, Gianmarco De Francisci Morales, Alessandro Galeazzi, and Michele Starnini. "The Echo Chamber Effect on Social Media." *PNAS* 118, no. 9 (2021): 1–8.

Clayman, Steven E. "Answers and Evasions." *Language in Society* 30 (2001): 403–42.

Collins, Patricia Hill. *Black Feminist Thought: Knowledge, Consciousness, and the Politics of Empowerment*. Routledge, 1990.

Collins, Patricia Hill. *Black Sexual Politics: African Americans, Gender, and the New Racism*. Routledge, 2004.

Collins, Randall. *Interaction Ritual Chains*. Princeton University Press, 2004.

Combs, Barbara H. *Bodies Out of Place: Theorizing Anti-Blackness in U.S. Society*. University of Georgia Press, 2022.

Combs, B. H., K. Dellinger, J. T. Jackson, K. A. Johnson, W. M. Johnson, J. Skipper, J. Sonnett, and J. M. Thomas. "The Symbolic Lynching of James Meredith: A Visual Analysis and Collective Counter Narrative to Racial Domination." *Sociology of Race and Ethnicity* 2, no. 3 (2016): 338–53.

Confessore, Nicholas. "'America Is Under Attack': Inside the Anti-DEI Crusade." *New York Times*, January 20, 2024. http://nytimes.com.

Cooper, Brittney. *Eloquent Rage: A Black Feminist Discovers Her Superpower*. St. Martin's Press, 2018.

Cottom, Tressie McMillan. *Thick and Other Essays*. The New Press, 2019.

Coupland, Justine. *Small Talk*. Routledge, 2014.

Crenshaw, Kimberlé. "Demarginalizing the Intersection of Race and Sex: A Black Feminist Critique of Antidiscrimination Doctrine, Feminist Theory and Antiracist Politics," *University of Chicago Legal Forum* 1, no. 8 (1989): 139–67.

Crespino, Joseph. *In Search of Another Country: Mississippi and the Conservative Counterrevolution*. Princeton University Press, 2007.

Davis, Carolyn J., Daniel Cox, Rob Griffin, and Robert P. Jones. "Young People Set to Impact the Debate on Women's Health Issues." Public Religion Research Institute (PRRI), April 17, 2018. http://prri.org.

Davis, Jim, and Michael Graham (with Ryan Burge). *The Great Dechurching: Who's Leaving, Why Are They Going, and What Will It Take to Bring Them Back?* Zondervan, 2023.

DiAngelo, Robin. *White Fragility: Why It's So Hard for White People to Talk about Racism*. Beacon Press, 2018.

Dias, Elizabeth, and Ruth Graham. "Southern Baptists Vote to Further Expand Restrictions on Women as Leaders." *New York Times*, June 14, 2023. http://nytimes.com.

Diefendorf, Sarah. *The Holy Vote: Inequality and Anxiety among White Evangelicals.* University of California Press, 2023.

Djupe, Paul A., and Ryan L. Claassen, eds. *The Evangelical Crackup?: The Future of the Evangelical-Republican Coalition*. Temple University Press, 2018.

Doane, Ashley. "Beyond Color-blindness: (Re) Theorizing Racial Ideology." *Sociological Perspectives* 60, no. 5 (2017): 975–91.

Dougherty, Kevin D., Mark Chaves, and Michael O. Emerson. "Racial Diversity in U.S. Congregations, 1998–2019." *Journal for the Scientific Study of Religion* 59, no. 4 (2020): 651–62.

Doyle, William. *An American Insurrection: The Battle of Oxford, Mississippi, 1962.* Anchor Books, 2003.

Du Bois, W. E. B. *A Reader*, edited by Meyer Weinberg. Harper and Row, 1970.

Du Bois, W. E. B. *The Souls of Black Folk* (1903). Bedford Books, 1997.

Du Mez, Kristin Kobes. *Jesus and John Wayne: How White Evangelicals Corrupted a Faith and Fractured a Nation*. W. W. Norton & Company, 2020.

Dupont, Carolyn. *Mississippi Praying: Southern White Evangelicals and the Civil Rights Movement, 1945–1975*. New York University Press, 2013.

Durkheim, Emile. *The Division of Labor in Society* (1893). Free Press, 1984.

Durkheim, Emile. *The Elementary Forms of Religious Life* (1912). Oxford University Press, 2008.

Ebin, Chelsea, and J. Ricky Price. "The Great American Rights Bake Off: Freedom of Religion v. Freedom from Discrimination." *New Political Science* 41, no. 4 (2019): 588–603.

Edwards, Korie Little. *The Elusive Dream: The Power of Race in Interracial Churches.* Oxford University Press, 2008.

Eliasoph, Nina. *Avoiding Politics: How Americans Produce Apathy in Everyday Life.* Cambridge University Press, 1998.

Elisha, Omri. *Moral Ambition: Mobilization and Social Outreach in Evangelical Megachurches*. University of California Press, 2011.

Ellis, Rachel. "Silent Disagreement: Microinteractional Solutions to Moral Dissent among Catholic Converts." *Journal for the Scientific Study of Religion* 56, no. 2 (2017): 383–97.

Emerson, Michael O., and Karen Chai Kim. "Multiracial Congregations: An Analysis of Their Development and a Typology." *Journal for the Scientific Study of Religion* 42, no. 2 (2003): 217–27.

Emerson, Michael O., and Christian Smith. *Divided by Faith: Evangelical Religion and the Problem of Race in America*. Oxford University Press, 2006.

Fausto-Sterling, Anne. *Sexing the Body: Gender Politics and the Construction of Sexuality*. Basic Books, 2000.

Fellowship of Christian Athletes. *God's Game Plan: The Athlete's Bible*. Baker Publishing, 2014.

Fetner, Tina. *How the Religious Right Shaped Lesbian and Gay Activism*. University of Minnesota Press, 2008.

Fields, Karen E., and Barbara J. Fields. *Racecraft: The Soul of Inequality in American Life*. Verso, 2012.

Fine, Debra. *The Fine Art of Small Talk: How to Start a Conversation, Keep it Going, Build Networking Skills—and Leave a Positive Impression!* Hachette Books, 2005.

Flaherty, Colleen. "Last-Minute Tenure Threat." *Inside Higher Education*, May 16, 2019. http://insidehighered.com.

Flood, Michael. "'Toxic masculinity': what does it mean, where did it come from – and is the term useful or harmful?" *The Conversation*, September 21, 2022. http://theconversation.com.

Focus on the Family with Jim Daly. "Share Your Faith with Grace and Purpose—Greg Koukl." YouTube, July 14, 2021. https://www.youtube.com/watch?v=20DCuVj9_xg.

Foltz, Doug. "Thinking about Planting a Church in a School? Read This First." ChurchPlants, January 1, 2014. http://churchplants.com.

Foster, B. Brian. *I Don't Like the Blues: Race, Place, and the Backbeat of Black Life*. University of North Carolina Press, 2020.

Freedom from Religion Foundation. "Churches Meeting at Public Schools." January 2012. http://ffrf.org.

Freedom from Religion Foundation. "School 'Prayer Walks' Walk all over Constitution." August 10, 2021. http://ffrf.org.

Friedman, Jonathan, and Nadine Farid Johnson. *Banned in the USA: The Growing Movement to Censor Books in Schools*. Pen America: The Freedom to Write, September 19, 2022. http://pen.org.

Gaddini, Katie. *The Struggle to Stay: Why Single Evangelical Women are Leaving the Church*. Columbia University Press, 2022.

Gallagher, Sally. "The Marginalization of Evangelical Feminism." *Sociology of Religion* 65, no. 3 (2004): 215–37.

Garfinkel, Harold. "Studies of the Routine Grounds of Everyday Activities." *Social Problems* 11, no. 3 (1964): 225–50.

Garza, Alicia. *The Purpose of Power: How to Build Movements for the 21st Century*. Penguin Random House, 2021.

Geertz, Clifford. *The Interpretation of Cultures: Selected Essays*. Basic Books, 1973.

Gerber, Lynne. *Seeking the Straight and Narrow: Weight Loss and Sexual Reorientation in Evangelical America*. University of Chicago Press, 2011.

Gerson, Kathleen, and Sarah Damaske. *The Science and Art of Interviewing*. Oxford University Press, 2020.

Gibson, David R. "Enduring Illusions: The Social Organization of Secrecy and Deception." *Sociological Theory* 32, no. 4 (2014): 283–306.

Glass, Leah E. "Fool's Gold: DEI and the Performance of Race-Consciousness." *Contexts* 22, no. 2 (2023): 36–41.

Goffman, Erving. *The Presentation of Self in Everyday Life*. Anchor Books, 1959.

Goffman, Erving. *Forms of Talk*. University of Pennsylvania Press, 1981.

Goffman, Erving. "The Interaction Order: American Sociological Association, 1982 Presidential Address." *American Sociological Review* 48, no. 1 (1983): 1–17.

Goffman, Erving. *Stigma: Notes on the Management of Spoiled Identity*. Simon & Schuster, 1986.

Goffman, Erving. "On Fieldwork." Transcribed and edited by Lyn H. Lofland. *Journal of Contemporary Ethnography* 18, no 2 (1989): 123–32.

Goldberg, Michael. "Over Half of Mississippi's Rural Hospitals Are at Risk of Closing." *PBS News Hour*, November 22, 2022. http://pbs.org.

Gordon, Tracy. "'Instant Churches' Convert Public Schools to Worship Spaces." *Religion News*, July 26, 2011. http://religionnews.com.

Gorski, Eric. "Haggard Firing, Gay Question Separate." *Denver Post*, November 6, 2006. http://denverpost.com.

Gorski, Phillip S., and Samuel Perry. *The Flag and the Cross: White Christian Nationalism and the Threat to American Democracy*. Oxford University Press, 2022.

Graham, Ruth. "The Pastors Being Driven Out by Trumpism: Why Some Evangelical Pastors in the U.S. Are Quitting in Large Numbers," *The Daily*, September 23, 2022. http://nytimes.com.

Greear, J. D. *Gaining by Losing: Why the Future Belongs to Churches that Send*. Zondervan, 2016.

Green, Emma. "A Resolution Condemning White Supremacy Causes Chaos at the Southern Baptist Convention." *Atlantic*, June 14, 2017. http://theatlantic.com.

Greenhouse, Linda. "Should Courts Assess the Sincerity of Religious Beliefs?" *Atlantic*, May 5, 2022. http://theatlantic.com.

Grem, Darren. *The Blessings of Business: How Corporations Shaped Conservative Christianity*. Oxford University Press, 2016.

Griffith, Marie R. *God's Daughters: Evangelical Women and the Power of Submission*. University of California Press, 1997.

Griffith, Marie R. *Moral Combat: How Sex Divided American Christians & Fractured American Politics*. Basic Books, 2017.

Guhin, Jeffrey. *Agents of God: Boundaries and Authority in Muslim and Christian Schools*. Oxford University Press, 2021.

Hale, Grace Elizabeth. *A Nation of Outsiders: How the White Middle Class Fell in Love with Rebellion in Postwar America*. Oxford University Press, 2011.

Harding, Susan F. *The Book of Jerry Falwell: Fundamentalist Language and Politics*. Princeton University Press, 2001.

Harker, Jaime. *The Lesbian South: Southern Feminists, the Women in Print Movement, and the Queer Literary Canon*. University of North Carolina Press, 2018.

Harrington, Carol. "What Is 'Toxic Masculinity' and Why Does It Matter?" *Men and Masculinities* 24, no. 2 (2021): 345–52.

Harriot, Michael. "War on Wokeness: The Year the Right Rallied around a Made-Up Menace." *Guardian*, December 21, 2022. http://thegaurdian.com.

Harris, Mark W. *Historical Dictionary of Unitarian Universalism*. 2nd ed. Rowman & Littlefield, 2018.

Hawkins, Drew. "'Stupidity of Politics': Medicaid Expansion Effort Dies in Mississippi." *Mississippi Public Broadcasting*, May 7, 2024. http://mpbonline.org.

Heath, Melanie. "Soft-Boiled Masculinity: Renegotiating Gender and Racial Ideologies in the Promise Keepers Movement." *Gender & Society* 17, no. 3 (2003): 423–44.

Hill, Jane H. *The Everyday Language of White Racism*. Wiley-Blackwell, 2008.

Hochschild, Arlie Russell. *Strangers in Their Own Land: Anger and Mourning on the American Right*. The New Press, 2016.

Hochschild, Arlie Russell. *Stolen Pride: Loss, Shame, and the Rise of the Right*. The New Press, 2024.

Holman, Jordan. "The History of Ole Miss Mascots: A Look Back at the University's Mascots," *Daily Mississippian*, August 31, 2018. http://thedmonline.com.

*The Holy Bible: English Standard Version*. Crossway, 2001.

hooks, bell. *Feminism Is for Everybody: Passionate Politics*. South End Press, 2000.

hooks, bell. *All About Love: New Visions*. William Morrow Paperbacks, 2018.

Horowitz, Juliana M. "Parents Differ Sharply by Party Over What Their K–12 Children Should Learn at School." Pew Research Center, October 26, 2022. http://pewresearch.org.

Howard, John. *Men Like That: A Southern Queer History*. University of Chicago Press, 1999.

Iversen, Lars Laird. "Silence and Sameness in the Norwegian Church Abroad." *Journal for the Scientific Study of Religion* 60, no. 3 (2021): 540–54.

Jerkins, Morgan. "Trad Wives Are Thriving in the Post-Dobbs Era." *Mother Jones*, July–August 2024.

Johnson, Kirk A., Willa M. Johnson, James M. Thomas, and John J. Green. "Mapping Microaggressions on a Southern University Campus: Where Are the Safe Spaces for Vulnerable Students?" *Social Problems* 68, no. 1 (2021): 1–18.

Jones, Robert P. *White Too Long: The Legacy of White Supremacy in American Christianity*. Simon & Schuster, 2020.

Jones, Robert P. "Racism Among White Christians Is Higher Than Among the Nonreligious. That's No Coincidence." *NBC News*, July 27, 2020. http://nbcnews.com.

Joshi, Khyati Y. *White Christian Privilege: The Illusion of Religious Equality in America*. New York University Press, 2020.

Jouet, Mugambi. *Exceptional America: What Divides Americans from the World and from Each Other*. University of California Press, 2017.

Joyce, Kathryn. "'Parental Rights' Started on the Fringe—Now It's the GOP's Winning Issue." *Salon*, January 12, 2022. http://salon.com.

Kavanaugh Hearing Transcript. *Washington Post*, September 27, 2018. http://washingtonpost.com.

Kelly, Kimberly. "Evangelical Underdogs: Intrinsic Success, Organizational Solidarity, and Marginalized Identities as Religious Movement Resources." *Journal of Contemporary Ethnography* 43, no. 4 (2014): 419–55.

Kennedy, Rodney. "Why Is There a Growing Trend toward Elder Governance in Southern Baptist Churches?" *Baptist News Global*, April 18, 2024. http://baptistnews.com.

Kirkland, Logan. "Lafayette County Issues First Same-Sex Marriage." *Daily Mississippian*, June 29, 2015. http://thedmonline.com.

Kirkland, Logan. "UM NAACP Rally Met with Confederate Opposition." *Daily Mississippian*, October 16, 2015. http://thedmonline.com.

Klintman, Mikael. *Knowledge Resistance: How We Avoid Insight from Others*. Manchester University Press, 2019.

Koukl, Greg. *Tactics: A Game Plan for Discussing Your Christian Convictions*. Zondervan, 2009.

Koukl, Greg. "Tactics Video Study, Session 1: The Columbo Tactic, by Gregory Koukl." YouTube, May 25, 2017. https://www.youtube.com/watch?v=csrSA3nPP7I.

Koukl, Greg. "Is Jesus the Only Way?" Rutgers University Ratio Christi. Accessed April 20, 2024. www.rutgersratiochristi.com.

Kramer, Stephanie. "70% of White Evangelicals Report that It Is Very Important that Their Kids Have Similar Religious Beliefs and Values." Pew Research Center, February 6, 2023. http://pewresearch.org.

Kraus, Julia. "Mapping In/Exclusion: Queer Identity in Oxford, Mississippi." Master's thesis, University of Mississippi, 2024, egrove.olemiss.edu.

Krull, Laura M., and Claire Chipman Gilliland. "'You Know, the Church has Never Agreed on Everything': Analyzing the Prophetic and Pragmatic Voice in Clergy Sermons." *Sociology of Religion* 84, no. 3 (2023): 324–48.

LaFraniere, Sharon. "'We're Going Away': A State's Choice to Forgo Medicaid Funds Is Killing Hospitals." *New York Times*, March 28, 2023. http://nytimes.com.

Lareau, Annette. *Listening to People: A Practical Guide to Interviewing, Participant Observation, Data Analysis, and Writing It All Up*. University of Chicago Press, 2021.

Larose, Greg. "Ten Commandments in Classroom Bill Advances in Louisiana; Legal Challenge Likely." *Louisiana Illuminator*, April 10, 2024. http://lailluminator.com.

Lavin, Talia. *Wild Faith: How the Christian Right Is Taking Over America*. Legacy Lit, 2024.

Lee, Shayne, and Phillip Sinitiere. *Holy Mavericks: Evangelical Innovators and the Spiritual Marketplace*. New York University Press, 2009.

Levings, Tia. *A Well-Trained Wife: My Escape from Christian Patriarchy*. St. Martin's Press, 2024.

Lichterman, Paul. *Elusive Togetherness: Church Groups Trying to Bridge America's Divisions*. Princeton University Press, 2005.

Loewen, James W. "Sundown Towns and Counties: Racial Exclusion in the South." *Southern Cultures* 15, no.1 (2009): 22–47.

Luna, Jenny. "I Went to a Potluck that Embraced Awkward Political Conversations." *Mother Jones*, November 22, 2017. http://motherjones.com.

Mahajan, Karan. "My Struggle with American Small Talk." *New Yorker*, June 4, 2016. http://newyorker.com.

Marsh, Charles. *God's Long Summer: Stories of Faith and Civil Rights*. Princeton University Press, 1997.

Marszalek III, John F. *Coming Out of the Magnolia Closet: Same-Sex Couples in Mississippi*. University Press of Mississippi, 2020.

Marti, Gerardo. *American Blindspot: Race, Class, Religion, and the Trump Presidency*. Rowman and Littlefield, 2020.

Marti, Gerardo, and Gladys Ganiel. *The Deconstructed Church: Understanding Emerging Christianity*. Oxford University Press, 2014.

Martin, Shannan. *Falling Free: Rescued from the Life I Always Wanted*. Nelson Books, 2016.

McDowell, Amy. "Warriors and Terrorists: Antagonism as Strategy in Christian Hardcore and Muslim 'Taqwacore' Punk Rock." *Qualitative Sociology* 37, no. 3 (2014): 255–76.

McDowell, Amy. "Muslim Punk in an Alt-Right Era." *Contexts* 16, no. 3 (2017): 63–5.

McDowell, Amy. "Christian but not Religious: Being Church as Christian Hardcore Punk." *Sociology of Religion* 79, no. 1 (2018): 55–77.

McDowell, Amy, and Pace Ward. "'The Tables Are Turning': The Evangelical Defense of Anti-LGBTQ+ Religious Liberty." *Sociology of Religion* 84, no. 4 (2023): 406–25.

McGregor, Jena. "Chick-fil-A CEO Dan Cathy Steps into Gay-Marriage Debate." *Washington Post*, July 19, 2012. http://washingtonpost.com.

Meyer, Holly. "Congregation, Tennessee Baptist Convention Split over Church's First Female Pastor." *Tennessean*, November 14, 2017. http://tennessean.com.

Middleton, Christian, and Donna Ladd. "'Ole Miss' vs. 'New Miss': Black Students, Faculty on How to Reject Racism, Step Forward Together." *Mississippi Free Press*, August 15, 2020. http://mississippifreepress.org.

Miller, Cassie, and Howard Graves. "When the 'Alt-Right' Hit the Streets: Far-Right Political Rallies in the Trump Era." Southern Poverty Law Center, August 10, 2020. http://splcenter.org.

Miller, Corey. "The Story of Ratio Christi." YouTube, accessed April 20, 2024. https://ratiochristi.org/about/.

Mills, Charles W. *The Racial Contract*. Cornell University Press, 1997.

Mills, Charles W. "White Ignorance." In *Race and Epistemologies of Ignorance*, edited by S. Sullivan and N. Tuana. State University of New York Press, 2007.

Minta, Molly. "'This is a complete attack': At least 31 anti-LGBTQ+ bills introduced this session in Mississippi." *Mississippi Today*, January 31, 2023. http://mississippitoday.org.

Mitchell, Amy, Jeffrey Gottfried, Galen Stocking, Mason Walker, and Sophia Fedeli. "Many Americans Say Made-Up News Is a Critical Problem that Needs to be Fixed." Pew Research Center, June 5, 2019. http://pewresearch.org.

Monroe, Stephen. *Heritage and Hate: Old South Rhetoric at Southern Universities*. University of Alabama Press, 2021.

Moon, Dawne. *God, Sex, and Politics: Homosexuality and Everyday Theologies*. University of Chicago Press, 2004.

Moon, Dawne, and Theresa W. Tobin. "Sunsets and Solidarity: Overcoming Sacramental Shame in Conservative Christian Churches to Forge a Queer Vision of Love and Justice." *Hypatia: A Journal of Feminist Philosophy* 33, no. 3 (2018): 451–68.

Moreton, Bethany. "Why Is There So Much Sex in Christian Conservatism and Why Do So Few Historians Care Anything About It?" *The Journal of Southern History* 75, no. 3 (2009): 717–38.

Morgan, David. *Icons of American Protestantism: The Art of Warner Sallman*. Yale University Press, 1996.

Morrison, Latasha. *Be the Bridge: Pursuing God's Heart for Racial Reconciliation*. WaterBrook, 2019.

Moses, Lauren. "UM Promotes Religious Freedom Through Its Campus Culture." *Daily Mississippian*, March 3, 2020. http://thedmonline.com.

Mueller, Jennifer C. "Racial Ideology or Racial Ignorance? An Alternative Theory of Racial Cognition." *Sociological Theory* 38, no. 2 (2020): 142–69.

Munson, Ziad. *The Making of Pro-Life Activists*. University of Chicago Press, 2009.

Munson, Ziad. *Abortion Politics*. Polity Press, 2018.

Noelle-Neumann, Elisabeth. *The Spiral of Silence: Public Opinion—Our Social Skin*. University of Chicago Press, 1993.

O'Connor, Cailin, and James Owen Weatherall. *The Misinformation Age: How False Beliefs Spread*. Yale University Press, 2020.

O'Neill, Kevin Lewis. *City of God: Christian Citizenship in Postwar Guatemala*. University of California Press, 2010.

Oliver, Melvin, and Thomas M. Shapiro. *Black Wealth/White Wealth: A New Perspective on Racial Inequality*. Routledge, 2006.

Oppenheimer, Mark. "Evangelicals Find Themselves in the Midst of a Calvinist Revival." *New York Times*, January 3, 2014. http://nytimes.com

Oyakawa, Michelle. "Racial Reconciliation as a Suppressive Frame in Evangelical Multiracial Churches." *Sociology of Religion* 80, no. 4 (2019): 496–517.

Pascoe, C. J. *Dude, You're a Fag: Masculinity and Sexuality in High School*. University of California Press, 2007.

Pérez, Elizabeth. *In the Kitchen: Cooking, Talking, and the Making of Black Atlantic Traditions*. New York University Press, 2016.

Perkins, Tom. "U.S. Religious Right at Center of Anti-LGBTQ+ Message Pushed Around the World." *Guardian*, July 9, 2023. http://theguardian.com.

Perry, Samuel L. *Addicted to Lust: Pornography in the Lives of Conservative Protestants*. Oxford University Press, 2019.

Peters, Jeremy W. "Wielding Claims of 'Fake News,' Conservatives Take Aim at Mainstream Media." *New York Times*, December 25, 2016. http://nytimes.com.

Pew Research Center. *Religious Landscape Study*. Pew Research Center, 2014. http://pewresearch.org.

Pew Research Center. *Political Polarization in the American Public*. Pew Research Center, June 12, 2014. http://pewresearch.org.

Pew Research Center. *For a Lot of American Teens, Religion is a Regular Part of the Public School Day*. Pew Research Center, October 3, 2019. http://pewresearch.org.

Pew Research Center. *Religion in the Public Schools*. Pew Research Center, October 3, 2019. http://pewresearch.org.

Pew Research Center. *In U.S., Far More Support than Oppose Separation of Church and State*. Pew Research Center, October 28, 2021. http://pewresearch.org.

Pew Research Center. *About Three-in-Ten U.S. Adults Are Now Religiously Unaffiliated*. Pew Research Center, December 14, 2021. http://pewresearch.org.

Pew Research Center. *Religious Nones in America, Who They Are and What They Believe*. Pew Research Center, January 24, 2024. http://pewresearch.org.

Pitt, Richard N. *Church Planters: Inside the World of Religion Entrepreneurs*. Oxford University Press, 2022.

Public Religion Research Institute. "The 2020 PRRI Census of American Religion." Accessed June 5, 2025. https://prri.org/wp-content/uploads/2021/07/PRRI-Jul-2021-Religion.pdf.

Putney, Clifford. *Muscular Christianity: Manhood and Sports in Protestant America, 1880–1920*. Harvard University Press, 2001.

Queer Mississippi Oral Histories Project, University of Mississippi. http://egrove.olemiss.edu/queer.ms.

Ranney, Joseph. *A Legal History of Mississippi: Race, Class, and the Struggle for Opportunity*. University Press of Mississippi, 2019.

Rao, Aliya Hamid. "Gender and Cultivating the Moral Self in Islam: Muslim Converts in an American Mosque." *Sociology of Religion* 76, no. 4 (2015): 413–35.

Rawls, Anne Warfield, and Waverly Duck. *Tacit Racism*. University of Chicago Press, 2020.

Ray, Victor. "A Theory of Racialized Organizations." *American Sociological Review* 84, no. 1 (2019): 26–53.

Rivers, Francine. *Redeeming Love*. Multnomah Books, 1997.

Rogers, Baker A. *Conditionally Accepted: Christians' Perspectives on Sexuality and Gay and Lesbian Civil Rights*. Rutgers University Press, 2019.

Rozier, Alex, and Kayleigh Skinner. "Do Your Lawmakers Look Like You?" *Mississippi Today*, February 6, 2019. http://mississippitoday.org.

Russell, John. "Southern Baptists Vote to Ban Women Pastors because They'll Lead to Support for Same-Sex Marriage." *LGBTQ Nation*, June 15, 2023. http://lgbtqnation.com.

Schade, Leah D. *Preaching in the Purple Zone: Ministry in the Red-Blue Divide*. Rowman and Littlefield, 2019.

Scheper-Hughes, Nancy. "Ire in Ireland." *Ethnography* 1, no. 1 (2000): 117–40.

Schrock, Douglas, and Michael Schwalbe. "Men, Masculinity, and Manhood Acts." *Annual Review of Sociology* 35 (2009): 277–95.

Schütz, Alfred. "The Well-Informed Citizen: An Essay on the Distribution of Knowledge." *Social Research* 13, no. 4 (1946): 463–78.

Schweiger, Elisabeth, and Kerstin Tomiak. "Researching Silence: A Methodological Inquiry." *Millennium: Journal of International Studies* 50, no. 3 (2023): 623–46.

Seidman, Steven. *The Social Construction of Sexuality*. W. W. Norton & Company, 2014.

Selod, Saher, and David G. Embrick. "Racialization and Muslims: Situating the Muslim Experience in Race Scholarship." *Sociology Compass* 7, no. 8 (2013): 644–55.

Silliman, Daniel. "Wanted: Church Planters. Reward: $50,000." *Christianity Today*, January 11, 2022. http://christianitytoday.com.

Skipper, Jodi. *Behind the Big House: Reconciling Slavery, Race, and Heritage in the U.S. South*. University of Iowa Press, 2022.

Skipper, Jodi, and Jessica Wilkerson. "Why We Must Center Black Women's Experiences." *Daily Mississippian*, September 25, 2018. http://thedmonline.com.

Smietana, Bob. "Beth Moore Says She's No Longer Southern Baptist." *Christianity Today*, March 9, 2021. http://christianitytoday.com.

Smilde, David. *Reason to Believe: Cultural Agency in Latin American Evangelicalism*. University of California Press, 2007.

Smith, Christian. *American Evangelicalism: Embattled and Thriving*. University of Chicago Press, 1998.

Southern Baptist Theological Seminary. "Report on Slavery and Racism in the History of the Southern Baptist Theological Seminary." December 12, 2018. http://sbts.edu.

Southern Poverty Law Center. "SPLC Reports Over 160 Confederate Symbols Removed in 2020." February 23, 2021. http://splcenter.org.

Stein, Arlene. "Sex, Truths, and Audiotape: Anonymity and the Ethics of Exposure in Public Ethnography." *Journal of Contemporary Ethnography* 39, no. 5 (2010): 554–68.

Stetzer, Ed, and Warren Bird. *Viral Churches: Helping Church Planters Become Movement Makers*. Jossey-Bass, 2010.

Stetzer, Ed, and David Putman. *Breaking the Missional Code: Your Church Can Become a Missionary in Your Community*. Broadman & Holman, 2006.

Stewart, Katherine. *The Power Worshippers: Inside the Dangerous Rise of Christian Nationalism*. Bloomsbury Publishing, 2020.

Sullivan, Winnifred Fallers. *The Impossibility of Religious Freedom*. Princeton University Press, 2005.

Sumerau, J. E., Ryan T. Cragun, and Lain A. B. Mathers. "Contemporary Religion and the Cisgendering of Reality." *Social Currents* 3, no. 3 (2016): 293–311.

Talbot, Margaret. "Justice Alito's Crusade against a Secular America Isn't Over." *New Yorker*, August 28, 2022. http://newyorker.com.

Taylor, Steven J., and Robert Bogdan. *Introduction to Qualitative Research Methods: A Guidebook and Resource*. 3rd ed. John Wiley & Sons, Inc., 1998.

Thomas, James M. *Diversity Regimes: Why Talk Is Not Enough to Fix Racial Inequality at Universities*. Rutgers University Press, 2020.

Thomas, Tonde. *Kincraft: The Making of Black Evangelical Sociality*. Duke University Press, 2021.

Thomas-Houston, Marilyn. *Stony the Road to Change: Black Mississippians and the Culture of Social Relations*. Cambridge University Press, 2004.

Tisby, Jemar. *The Color of Compromise: The Truth about the American Church's Complicity in Racism*. Zondervan, 2019.

Tisby, Jemar. *How to Fight Racism: Courageous Christianity and the Journey toward Racial Justice*. Zondervan, 2021.

Trainer, Sarah, Jessica Hardin, Cindi SturtzSreetharan, and Alexandra Brewis, "Worry-Nostalgia: Anxieties around the Fading of Local Cuisines and Foodways." *Gastronomica* 20, no. 2 (2020): 67–78.

Vandermaas-Peeler, Alex, Daniel Cox, Maxine Najle, Molly Fisch-Friedman, Rob Griffin, and Robert P. Jones. "Partisanship Trumps Gender: Sexual Harassment, Woman Candidates, Access to Contraception, and Key Issues in 2018 Midterms." Public Religion Research Institute (PRRI), October 3, 2018. http://pewresearch.org.

Vassallo, Steve. "Family Resource Center Touches Lives in Meaningful Ways." *Hotty Toddy News*, February 13, 2018. http://hottytoddy.com.

Vassallo, Steve. "Families First's Johnny Flynt Delivers Inspirational Messages about Fatherhood." *Hotty Toddy News*, March 26, 2018. http://hottytoddy.com.

Wade, Lisa. *American Hookup: The New Culture of Sex on Campus*. W. W. Norton & Company, 2017.

Ward, Jane. *The Tragedy of Heterosexuality*. New York University Press, 2020.

Ward, Pace. "Everybody But Us: Constructing Evangelical Identities by Defining the Skeptic." Honors College thesis, University of Mississippi, 2019.

Warren, Tish Harrison. "How Americans Can Learn to Live Together Again." *New York Times*, October 24, 2021. http://nytimes.com.

Weber, Max. *The Protestant Ethic and the Spirit of Capitalism* (1930). Routledge, 2001.

Wells, Ida B. *Crusade for Justice: The Autobiography of Ida B. Wells*, edited by Alfreda M. Duster. University of Chicago Press, 2020.

West, Candace, and Don H. Zimmerman. "Doing Gender." *Gender and Society* 1, no. 2 (1987): 125–51.

Whalen, Ian M. "Governing Silence: Contextualizing the Emergence of Queer Subjectivity in the Rural South." PhD diss., Department of Sociology, University of Colorado Boulder, 2024.

Whitehead, Andrew L., and Samuel L. Perry. *Taking America Back for God: Christian Nationalism in the United States*. Oxford University Press, 2020.

Williams, Daniel K. "White Southern Evangelicals Are Leaving the Church," *Christianity Today*, August 2, 2022. http://christianitytoday.com.

Wingfield, Adia Harvey. "The Modern Mammy and the Angry Black Man: African American Professionals' Experiences with Gendered Racism in the Workplace." *Race, Gender & Class* 14, no. 1/2 (2007), 196–212.

Witte Jr., John, Joel A. Nichols, and Richard W. Garnett. *Religion and the American Constitutional Experiment*. Oxford University Press, 2022.

Wolf, Katherine, and Jay Wolf. *Hope Heals: A True Story of Overwhelming Loss and an Overcoming Love*. Zondervan, 2016.

Wolfinger, Nicholas H. "On Writing Fieldnotes: Collection Strategies and Background Expectancies." *Qualitative Research* 2, no. 1 (2002): 85–93.

Wolkomir, Michelle. *Be Not Deceived: The Sacred and Sexual Struggles of Gay and Ex-Gay Christian Men*. Rutgers University Press, 2006.

Wollschleger, Jason. "Interaction Ritual Chains and Religious Participation." *Sociological Forum* 27, no. 4 (2012): 896–912.

Wuthnow, Robert. "Taking Talk Seriously: Religious Discourse as Social Practice." *Journal for the Scientific Study of Religion* 50, no. 1 (2011): 1–21.

Wuthnow, Robert. *The Left Behind: Decline and Rage in Rural America.* Princeton University Press, 2018.

Yi, Joseph, and Christopher Graziul. "Religious Conservatives and Outsiders: Determinants of Cross-Racial Ties among White Christians." *Review of Religious Research* 59, no. 2 (2017): 231–50.

Yi, Joseph, Gowoon Jung, Sual Serna Segura, Joe Phillips, and Jerry Z. Park. "Gay Seouls: Expanding Religious Spaces for Non-Heterosexuals in South Korea." *Journal of Homosexuality* 65, no. 11 (2018): 1457–83.

Zerubavel, Eviatar. *The Elephant in the Room: Silence and Denial in Everyday Life.* Oxford University Press, 2006.

Zuckerman, Phil. *Living the Secular Life: New Answers to Old Questions.* Penguin, 2015.

# INDEX

Page numbers in *italics* indicate Figures, Photos, and Tables

## ABOUT THE AUTHOR

Amy D. McDowell is Associate Professor of Sociology at the University of Mississippi. Her research on how religion and secularism collide in American culture has been published in leading sociology journals on race, religion, and gender.